Scott Foresman

ELL Teaching Guide

Editorial Offices: Glenview, Illinois • Parsippany, New Jersey • New York, New York
Sales Offices: Needham, Massachusetts • Duluth, Georgia • Glenview, Illinois
Coppell, Texas • Sacramento, California • Mesa, Arizona

ISBN: 0-328-14600-5

2 3 4 5 6 7 8 9 10 V004 14 13 12 11 10 09 08 07 06 05

Contents

Unit 4: Our Changing World

Unit 5: Responsibility

Unit 6: Traditions

Scott Foresman Reading Street

Overview of Weekly Support for English Language Learners

The ELL Teaching Guide provides weekly lesson materials to support English language learners with scaffolded comprehension instruction and vocabulary development. It builds on the Student Edition and on literacy instruction in the Teacher's Edition. Support for English language learners and teachers is based on the Three Pillars, developed by Dr. Jim Cummins:

Activate Prior Knowledge/Build Background
Access Content
Extend Language

Scott Foresman Reading Street provides these resources:

- **Student Edition** that builds every student's reading and language skills
- **Decodable Readers** for practicing emergent literacy skills (grades K–3)
- **Leveled Readers** for differentiated instruction
- **Teacher's Edition** with ELL instructional strategies built into the lesson plans
- **ELL Readers** that develop English language learners' vocabulary and comprehension skills
- **ELL Posters** with high-quality illustrations and five days of activities supporting key vocabulary and concepts
- **Ten Important Sentences** to focus on comprehension while expanding English
- **ELL and Transition Handbook** that supports teachers' professional development and students' transition to advanced levels of English proficiency
- **ELL Teaching Guide** see below

ELL Teaching Guide Features

"Week at a Glance" Lesson Planners offer a quick reference to the ELL support materials for each lesson of the year.

"Picture It!" Comprehension Lessons provide teaching strategies for each comprehension skill. A reproducible "Picture It!" student practice page helps students learn the key comprehension skill through illustrations, graphic organizers, sheltered text, and ELL-friendly activities.

Vocabulary Activities and Word Cards stimulate language production and reinforce target vocabulary. Small-group and partner activities use reproducible Word Cards to practice listening, speaking, reading, and writing. Home-language activities allow students to connect their prior knowledge to key vocabulary and concepts in English.

Multilingual Summaries of each main reading selection provide a brief, accessible summary in English and translations of the summary in the next most common five languages among the U.S. school population: Spanish, Chinese, Vietnamese, Korean, and Hmong. Students and parents can use the summaries to prepare for reading, build comprehension, support retellings, and strengthen school-home connections.

ELL Reader Lessons and Study Guides support every ELL Reader with scaffolded instruction to help students understand and respond to literature. The reproducible Study Guides support students' comprehension and provide writing and take-home activities for learners at various English proficiency levels.

Multilingual Lesson Vocabulary provides translations of the target vocabulary in Spanish, Chinese, Vietnamese, Korean, and Hmong.

Iris and Walter

Student Edition pages 16–35

Week at a Glance	Customize instruction every day for your English Language Learners.				
	Day 1	Day 2	Day 3	Day 4	Day 5
Teacher's Edition	Use the ELL Notes that appear throughout each day of the lesson to support instruction and reading.				
ELL Poster 1	• Assess Prior Knowledge • Develop Concepts and Vocabulary	• Preteach High-Frequency Words	• Review Character and Setting	• Neighborhood Riddles	• Monitor Progress
ELL Teaching Guide	• Picture It! Lesson, pp. 1–2 • Multilingual Summaries, pp. 5–7	• ELL Reader Lesson, pp. 212–213	• Vocabulary Activities and Word Cards, pp. 3–4 • Multilingual Summaries, pp. 5–7		
ELL Readers		• Teach *Off to School We Go!*	• Reread *Off to School We Go!* and other texts to build fluency		
ELL and Transition Handbook	Use the following as needed to support this week's instruction and to conduct alternative assessments: • Phonics Transition Lessons • Grammar Transition Lessons • Assessment				

Picture It! Comprehension Lesson

Character and Setting

Use this lesson to supplement or replace the skill lesson on pages 13a–13b of the Teacher's Edition.

Teach

Distribute copies of the Picture It! blackline master on page 2.

- Ask children to look at the picture story and describe what happens.
- Read the sentences aloud. Ask: *Who is the story about?*
- Share the Skill Points (at right) with children.
- Have children give you examples from the pictures that helped them determine the setting of the story.

Practice

Read aloud the directions on page 2. Have children answer the questions about character and setting in the story.

Answers for page 2: 1. Julie **2.** friendly **3.** (Guide children to talk about where the story happens.) in front of Julie's new home

Skill Points

✓ **Characters** are the people or animals in a story.

✓ The author tells you what characters are like, what they think, and what they say and do.

✓ The **setting** is where and when a story happens.

✓ The setting can be a real place or an imaginary one.

Name ______________________________

Look at the pictures. **Read** the story.

A New Home

Julie is sad. She and her parents have a new home. She misses her old home.

Julie meets a new friend. Her name is Nina, and she is very nice.

The two girls ride bikes. They have fun!

Answer the questions below.

1. Who is the story about?
O two men O Julie's mom and dad O Julie

2. What is Nina like?
O not nice O friendly O sad

3. Talk about the setting of the story. Where does the story happen?

Vocabulary Activities and Word Cards

Copy the Word Cards on page 4 as needed for the following activities.
Use the blank cards for additional words that you want to teach.
Also see suggestions for teaching vocabulary in the ELL and Transition Handbook.

Everyday Game	What's the Word?	Fishing Game
• Give each child a set of Word Cards in alphabetical order. • Read the words aloud as a group. Then have each child tell what two of the words mean. • As a group, discuss how children might use these words every day. Ask volunteers to give example sentences: *The flower is beautiful. She is my friend. We went in the front door.*	• Give each child a set of Word Cards to look at during the activity. Keep another set at the front of the room. • Ask a volunteer to come to the front of the room and choose a Word Card without showing it to the group. • Have the child write the word on the board, leaving out two or three letters. The child should write an underscore for any missing letters, for example: c o _ _ t r _ (*country*). • Ask the other children to write down the word and fill in the missing letters. Have a volunteer use the word in a sentence. • Continue until each child has had at least one turn at the front of the room and all the Word Cards have been used.	• Use one or more sets of Word Cards. Attach a metal paper clip to each card, and put the words in a bucket. Tie a string to a short stick and fasten a magnet to the loose end of the string. • Have children take turns "fishing" for words. • When a child "catches" a word, he or she reads it and tells what it means. If the word is defined correctly, the child keeps the card. If not, the child returns the card to the bucket. • The child with the most "fish" when the bucket is empty wins the game.

beautiful	country
friend	front
someone	somewhere

Multilingual Summaries

English

Iris and Walter

Iris and Grandpa took a walk. Iris told Grandpa that she did not like the country. She had no one to play with. Then, they saw a ladder. It hung from a tree. Iris climbed the ladder. She saw a tree house. It was Walter's. Iris and Walter became friends.

Iris and Walter played together every day. Walter let Iris ride his pony. Iris taught Walter how to roller-skate. She told him about the city. Sometimes she dreamed about it. Iris was happy to have a new friend in the country.

Spanish

Iris y Walter

Iris y su abuelo salieron a dar un paseo. Iris le dijo a su abuelo que a ella no le gustaba el campo. Ella no tenía con quien jugar. Luego, vieron una escalera. Estaba colgada de un árbol. Iris subió por la escalera. Vio una casa en el árbol. La casa era de Walter. Iris y Walter se hicieron amigos.

Iris y Walter jugaban todos los días. Walter dejaba que Iris montara su pony. Iris le enseñó a Walter a patinar. Le habló de la ciudad. Iris soñaba a veces con ella. Iris estaba muy feliz de tener un amigo nuevo en el campo.

Multilingual Summaries

Chinese

艾瑞絲與華特

艾瑞絲陪祖父散步，她跟祖父說她不喜歡鄉下，因為沒人可以陪她玩。走著走著，他們突然看到一條梯子，從樹上垂掛下來。艾瑞絲爬上梯子後，看到一間樹屋，那是華特的樹屋。艾瑞絲和華特因此成了好朋友。

艾瑞絲和華特每天都玩在一起，華特讓艾瑞絲騎他的小馬，艾瑞絲教華特滑溜冰鞋，還跟他說城市裡的事情，因為有時候艾瑞絲會夢到。艾瑞絲很高興，可以在鄉下交到新朋友。

Vietnamese

Iris và Walter

Iris và Ông của cô bé cùng đi dạo. Iris nói với Ông rằng cô không thích vùng quê. Cô không có ai để chơi. Vào lúc đó, hai người thấy một cái thang leo. Thang treo trên cây. Iris leo lên thang này. Cô bé thấy một ngôi nhà bé trên cây. Nhà này là của Walter. Iris và Walter trở thành đôi bạn.

Iris và Walter chơi với nhau mỗi ngày. Walter cho Iris cưỡi con lừa của mình. Iris chỉ cho Walter biết cách đi giày có bánh xe trượt. Cô kể cho bạn nghe về thành phố. Có đôi lúc cô bé mơ về thành phố. Iris vui mừng có một bạn mới ở vùng quê.

Multilingual Summaries

Korean

아이리스와 월터

아이리스는 할아버지와 산책을 하다가 할아버지에게 시골을 좋아하지 않는다고 말한다. 함께 놀 친구가 없기 때문이다. 그때 이들은 나무에 매달려 있는 사다리를 하나 발견한다. 아이리스는 사다리를 타고 올라가 나무에 있는 집을 보게 되는데 그것은 월터의 집이었다. 아이리스와 월터는 친구가 된다.

이 둘은 매일 함께 논다. 월터는 아이리스에게 자기 조랑말을 태워주고, 아이리스는 월터에게 롤러스케이트 타는 법을 알려준다. 아이리스는 월터에게 도시에 대해 이야기 해주며 가끔씩 도시 꿈을 꾸기도 한다. 아이리스는 시골에서 새로운 친구를 만나 기뻐한다.

Hmong

Iris thiab Walter

Iris thiab nws yawg nkawd mus taug kev. Iris qhia rau nws yawg tias nws tsis nyiam nyob lub tebchaws no. Tsis muaj leejtwg nrog nws ua si li. Ces nkawd txawm pom ib tug ntaiv. Tus ntaiv ntawd dai rau ib tsob ntoo. Iris mus nce tus ntaiv. Nws txawm pom ib lub tsev nyob rau saum tsob ntoo. Lub tsev ntawd yog Walter lub. Iris thiab Walter nkawd tau los ua phoojywg.

Iris thiab Walter ua si ua ke txhua txhua hnub. Walter cia Iris caij nws tus nees. Iris qhia Walter kom nws paub caij khau dov. Nws tau qhia Walter txog lub nroog. Muaj tej lub caij nws ua npau suav txog. Iris zoo siab nws muaj ib tug phoojywg tshiab nyob rau lub tebchaws no.

Exploring Space Student Edition pages 46–59

Week at a Glance	Customize instruction every day for your English Language Learners.				
	Day 1	**Day 2**	**Day 3**	**Day 4**	**Day 5**
Teacher's Edition	Use the ELL Notes that appear throughout each day of the lesson to support instruction and reading.				
ELL Poster 2	• Assess Prior Knowledge • Develop Concepts and Vocabulary	• Preteach High-Frequency Words	• Review Main Ideas and Details	• Interview with an Astronaut	• Monitor Progress
ELL Teaching Guide	• Picture It! Lesson, pp. 8–9 • Multilingual Summaries, pp. 12–14	• ELL Reader Lesson, pp. 214–215	• Vocabulary Activities and Word Cards, pp. 10–11 • Multilingual Summaries, pp. 12–14		
ELL Readers	• Reread *Off to School We Go!*	• Teach *The First Trip to the Moon*	• Reread *The First Trip to the Moon* and other texts to build fluency		
ELL and Transition Handbook	Use the following as needed to support this week's instruction and to conduct alternative assessments: • Phonics Transition Lessons • Grammar Transition Lessons • Assessment				

Picture It! Comprehension Lesson

Main Idea and Details

Use this lesson to supplement or replace the skill lesson on pages 43a–43b of the Teacher's Edition.

Teach

Distribute copies of the Picture It! blackline master on page 9.

- Ask children to look at the picture and describe what they see.
- Read the paragraph aloud. Ask: *What is this paragraph about?* (Astronauts)
- Share the Skill Points (at right) with children.
- Have children tell you which sentence contains the main idea. Then ask them to find the details.

Practice

Read aloud the directions on page 9. Have children write the main idea and the details in the web.

Answers for page 9: *Main Idea:* Astronauts are people who go into space. *Details:* wear special clothes; use special tools; live in space for months; on a space shuttle

Skill Points

✓ The topic is what a selection is about. The **main idea** is the most important idea about the topic.

✓ Small pieces of information tell more about the main idea. These small pieces are called **details.**

Name ______________________________

Look at the picture. **Read** the paragraph.

- What are the sentences and picture mostly about? **Write** the main idea in the middle oval.
- What are some smaller pieces of information? **Write** details in the other ovals.

Astronauts

Astronauts are people who go into space. Sometimes they live in space for many months. They wear special clothes and use special tools. These astronauts are on a space shuttle. Each of them has an important job to do.

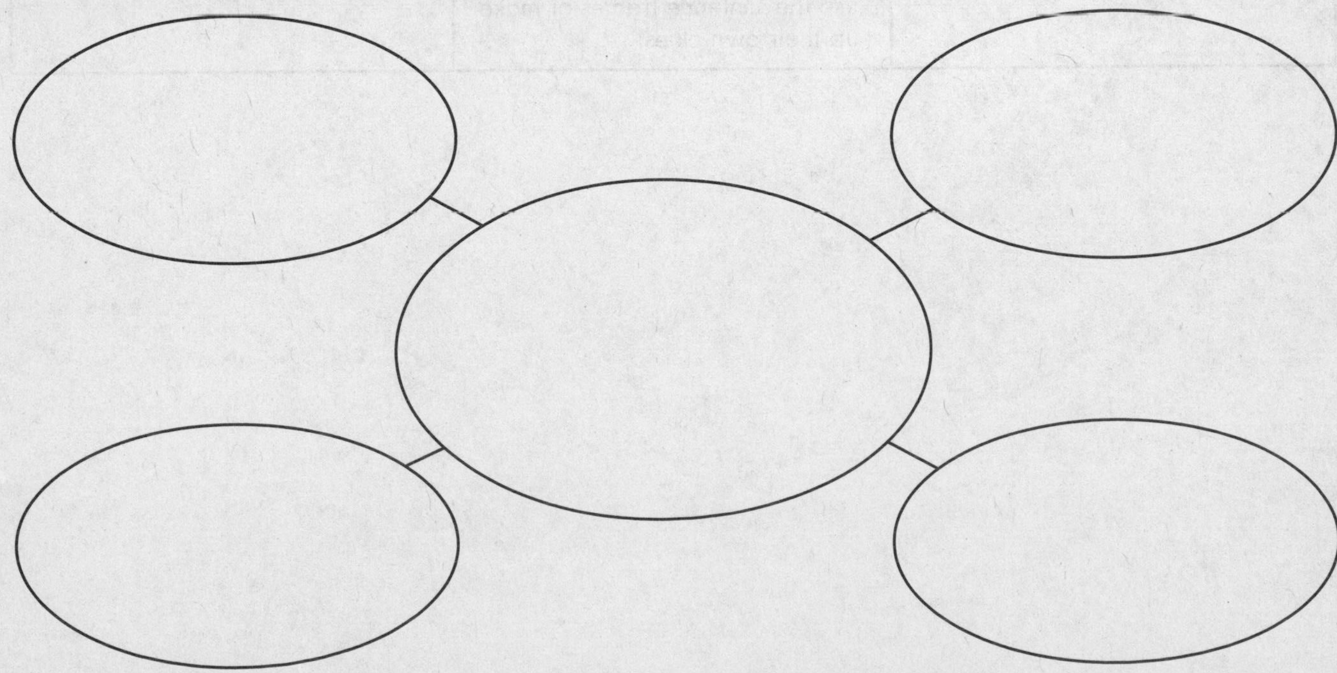

Vocabulary Activities and Word Cards

Copy the Word Cards on page 11 as needed for the following activities.
Use the blank card for an additional word that you want to teach.
Also see suggestions for teaching vocabulary in the ELL and Transition Handbook.

Exploration Concentration	Mind Reader	Exploring Space Is Fun!
• Give two sets of Word Cards to each group of two or three children. Have each group mix the cards together and spread them out face down. • One child at a time picks up a card, reads it aloud, and tries to find its matching card. • When a child has a match, he or she says a phrase or sentence using that word. • The game ends when all the cards have been matched.	• Give each child a set of Word Cards. Have children spread out their cards face up so they can see them. • Write these sentence frames on the board: *This word starts with the letter _____. This word means _____. This word ends with the letter _____.* • Pick up a Word Card and give children clues about the word by reading and completing the sentence frames. • Children hold up the correct Word Card when they believe they have the answer. • The child who correctly guesses the word may choose another card and provide the group with the next riddle. Allow children to use the sentence frames or make up their own clues.	• Give one set of Word Cards to each child. Have children place the cards face up so they can see them during the activity. • Make sure the ELL Poster for Unit 1, Week 2 is visible. • Ask children to say an original sentence that uses one of the words and describes an aspect of the Poster. • Continue until each child has had the opportunity to make up a sentence.

everywhere	live
machines	move
woman	work
world	

Multilingual Summaries

English

Exploring Space with an Astronaut

Astronauts fly shuttles into space. A shuttle is like a rocket. Eileen Collins was the shuttle's first woman pilot. She worked on a team with other astronauts. In space, astronauts float inside the shuttle. Their sleeping bags are tied to the wall. Astronauts exercise to stay strong.

Astronauts do experiments. They fix problems in the shuttle. They have many tools. Eileen's crew tested telescopes. They also took X-ray photographs of stars. The astronauts studied plants.

If you want to be an astronaut, you should study math and science. You should enjoy going to new places. You should also enjoy working with people on a team.

Spanish

Explorar el espacio con un astronauta

Los astronautas vuelan al espacio en transbordadores. Un transbordador es como un cohete. Eileen Collins fue la primera mujer piloto de un transbordador. Ella trabajaba en un equipo con otros astronautas. En el espacio, los astronautas flotan dentro del transbordador. Los sacos de dormir están amarrados a la pared. Los astronautas hacen ejercicios para mantenerse fuertes.

Los astronautas hacen experimentos. Arreglan problemas en el transbordador. Tienen muchas herramientas. La tripulación de Eileen probaba telescopios. También les hacía fotografías de rayos X a las estrellas. Los astronautas estudiaban las plantas.

Si quieres ser astronauta, debes estudiar matemáticas y ciencias. Te debe gustar ir a lugares nuevos. También te debe gustar trabajar en equipo con otras personas.

Multilingual Summaries

Chinese

跟太空人一起探索太空

太空人乘坐太空梭進入太空，太空梭的樣子有點像火箭。愛林・柯林斯是太空梭上的第一名女船長，她和其他太空人在同一個小組裡面工作。在太空中，太空艙裡的太空人是飄浮著的，因此睡袋必須固定在牆上。太空人還要運動，以維持強壯的體格。

太空人要做實驗，太空梭故障時也要負責修理，他們有很多工具。愛林的組員會測試望遠鏡，也會幫星星拍 X 光照片，以及研究植物。

假如你想當太空人，必須要唸數學和科學、喜歡到新的地方探險，還要喜歡團隊工作。

Vietnamese

Thám Hiểm Không Gian Với Một Phi Hành Gia

Các phi hành gia bay những chiếc phi thuyền con thoi vào không gian. Phi thuyền con thoi giống như một hỏa tiễn. Eileen Collins là nữ phi công đầu tiên của phi thuyền con thoi. Cô cùng làm việc với các phi hành gia khác trong nhóm. Trong không gian, các phi hành gia lơ lửng bên trong phi thuyền. Túi ngủ của họ được cột vào tường. Các phi hành gia tập thể dục để giữ cho khỏe mạnh.

Phi hành gia thi hành các cuộc thí nghiệm. Họ sửa chữa những hư hỏng trong phi thuyền. Họ có nhiều dụng cụ. Phi hành đoàn của Eileen thử nghiệm các kính viễn vọng. Họ cũng chụp ảnh của các vì sao bằng tia X. Phi hành gia nghiên cứu thực vật.

Nếu em muốn trở thành một phi hành gia, em nên học toán và khoa học. Em phải thích đi đến những nơi mới lạ. Em cũng phải thích làm việc với những người khác trong một nhóm.

Multilingual Summaries

Korean

우주 비행사와 우주 탐사를

우주 비행사들은 로켓 같은 우주 왕복선을 타고 우주를 비행한다. 에일린 콜린스는 우주 왕복선을 타는 첫 번째 여성으로 다른 우주 비행사들과 한 팀이 되어 일을 한다. 우주에서 비행사들은 왕복선 안을 떠다니기 때문에 이들의 침낭은 벽에 묶여 있다. 이들은 건강을 유지하기 위해 운동을 한다.

우주 비행사들은 실험도 하고 우주 왕복선 안의 고장난 부분도 수리한다. 이들은 기구들도 많이 가지고 있다. 에일린의 팀은 망원경을 시험해 보고 별의 X선 사진을 찍으며 식물에 대한 공부도 한다.

우주 비행사가 되고 싶으면 수학과 과학을 공부해야 하며 새로운 곳에 가는 것, 그리고 사람들과 팀을 이뤄 일하는 것을 좋아해야 한다.

Hmong

Mus Xyuas Nruab Ntug Nrog Ib Tug Tibneeg Kawm Txog Nruab Ntug

Cov tibneeg kawm txog nruab ntug caij dav hlau mus rau saum nruab ntug. Lub dav hlau no zoo li lub hoob pob tawg rhe. Thawj thawj tug pojniam uas tsav yam dav hlau no yog Eileen Collins. Nws ua haujlwm nrog ib pab kawm txog nruab ntug. Thaum nyob saum nruab ntug, cov tibneeg no ya sab hauv lub dav hlau. Lawv muab cov hnab pw khi rau ntawm phab ntsa. Cov tibneeg kawm txog nruab ntug siv zog ua haujlwm kom lawv muaj zog ntxiv.

Cov tibneeg kawm txog nruab ntug xyaum kawg txog tej txujci. Lawv kho tej teebmeem hauv lub dav hlau. Lawv muaj ntau yam cuabyeej siv. Cov ua haujlwm nrog Eileen lawv kawm txog lub looj qhovmuag tsom saum nruab ntug. Lawv muab cov hnub qub los yees dua xoo faim faj. Cov tibneeg kawm txog nruab ntug kuj kawm txog tej xyoob tej ntoo.

Yog koj xav ua ib tug tibneeg kawm txog nruab ntug, koj yuav tau kawm txog lej thiab tej txujci. Koj nyiam thiab txaus siab mus xyuas tej qhov chaw tshiab. Koj nyiam ua haujlwm nrog lwm cov tibneeg ua ib pab ib pawg.

Henry and Mudge and the Starry Night

Student Edition pages 72–87

Week at a Glance	Customize instruction every day for your English Language Learners.				
	Day 1	**Day 2**	**Day 3**	**Day 4**	**Day 5**
Teacher's Edition	Use the ELL Notes that appear throughout each day of the lesson to support instruction and reading.				
ELL Poster 3	• Assess Prior Knowledge • Develop Concepts and Vocabulary	• Preteach High-Frequency Words	• Nature Show	• Nature Story	• Monitor Progress
ELL Teaching Guide	• Picture It! Lesson, pp. 15–16 • Multilingual Summaries, pp. 19–21	• ELL Reader Lesson, pp. 216–217	• Vocabulary Activities and Word Cards, pp. 17–18 • Multilingual Summaries, pp. 19–21		
ELL Readers	• Reread *The First Trip to the Moon*	• Teach *I Spy Fun*	• Reread *I Spy Fun* and other texts to build fluency		
ELL and Transition Handbook	Use the following as needed to support this week's instruction and to conduct alternative assessments: • Phonics Transition Lessons • Grammar Transition Lessons • Assessment				

Picture It! Comprehension Lesson

Character and Setting

Use this lesson to supplement or replace the skill lesson on pages 69a–69b of the Teacher's Edition.

Teach

Distribute copies of the Picture It! blackline master on page 16.

- Ask children to look at the picture story and tell what is happening.
- Read the sentences aloud. Ask: *Who is the story about?* (Ana, Pedro, and their Dad)
- Share the Skill Points (at right) with children.
- Have children look at the pictures and sentences to find clues about the characters and setting.

Practice

Read aloud the directions on page 16. Have children answer the questions about the characters and setting of the story.

Answers for page 16: 1. by a lake **2.** summer **3.** (Guide children to talk about how Ana and Pedro feel.) Sample response: They like to camp. I can tell because they are smiling and Ana says it was a great day.

Skill Points

✓ **Characters** are the people or animals in a story.

✓ Authors tell what the characters look like, how they act, and how they think and feel.

✓ The **setting** is where and when the story takes place.

Name ______________________________

Look at the pictures. **Read** the story.

A Camping Trip

Ana and Pedro hike with their dad. It is a beautiful summer day.

They find a good place to camp. Dad and Pedro put up the tent. Ana makes a place for the fire.

"What a great day," says Ana. Pedro smiles and nods.

Answer the questions below.

1. Where are Ana, Pedro, and their father?
O in the city O at their house O by a lake

2. What time of year is it?
O summer O fall O winter

3. Talk about how Ana and Pedro feel about camping. Tell how you know.

Vocabulary Activities and Word Cards

Copy the Word Cards on page 18 as needed for the following activities.
Use the blank card for an additional word that you want to teach.
Also see suggestions for teaching vocabulary in the ELL and Transition Handbook.

Puzzle Pieces	Go Fish	Tell a Story
• Give pairs of children sets of Word Cards. • Have the children cut each card into two puzzle pieces of different shapes. • Ask children to mix up the puzzle pieces, lay them face up, and take turns putting words back together. As they do so, children should read the words aloud. • Ask the children to write or say a sentence using each word.	• Have groups of three or four children play Go Fish. Give each group four sets of Word Cards. • Have one child mix up the Word Cards and pass out five cards to each child. The remaining cards should be placed face down in a pile. • Before play begins, children look at their cards and lay down any matching pairs, saying the words aloud. • Children take turns asking other players if they have certain words, the object being to find a match. For example, if a child has the word *bear*, he or she should ask a player: *Do you have the word* bear? • If the other player has the card, he or she must give it up, and the first player puts down the pair, saying the word aloud and defining it. If not, the other player says *Go Fish,* and the first player picks a card from the pile. • Play continues until all pairs have been made.	• Give two Word Cards to each child, and arrange the children in a circle. • Start a story with a sentence that uses one of the words. For example: *My mother did something funny.* • The next child continues the story, finding a way to use one of his or her words in a sentence. Children can help each other make sentences. • Children take turns until all the Word Cards have been used and the group decides that the story is complete.

bear	**build**
couldn't	**father**
love	**mother**
straight	

Multilingual Summaries

English

Henry and Mudge

Henry's family was going camping. They took Henry's big dog, Mudge, with them. Henry's mother knew how to camp. Henry thought about animals that they might see. He was excited.

The family drove to the lake. They went hiking. Henry saw a fish jump. He saw deer. Mudge smelled many things. The family set up the tent. Mudge ate some of the food. Henry's father played the guitar.

At night, the family lay on a blanket. They looked at the stars. Mudge chewed a log. The family sang songs. They got in the tent. They went to sleep. Everything was quiet.

Spanish

Henry y Mudge

La familia de Henry se preparaba para ir de campamento. Llevaban con ellos al perro grande de Henry, Mudge. La mamá de Henry sabía acampar. Henry pensaba en los animales que verían. Estaba emocionado.

La familia condujo hasta el lago. Salieron a hacer una caminata. Henry vio saltar un pez. Vio un oso. Mudge olía muchas cosas. La familia armó la carpa. Mudge comió un poco. El papá de Henry tocó la guitarra.

Por la noche, la familia se acostó sobre una manta a mirar las estrellas. Mudge mordisqueaba un tronco. La familia cantaba canciones. Después, se metieron en la carpa para dormir. Todo quedó muy silencioso.

Multilingual Summaries

Chinese

星空下的亨利與馬奇

亨利一家人去露營，他們把亨利的大狗「馬奇」也一起帶去玩。亨利的媽媽知道怎樣露營，亨利在想他們可能會看到哪些動物，越想越興奮。

他們一家人開車到了湖邊，然後開始步行。亨利看到一條魚跳出湖面，還看到野鹿，馬奇也聞到很多東西的氣味。他們把帳篷搭起來，馬奇吃了一些食物，亨利的爸爸在彈吉他。

到了晚上，一家人躺在毯子上看星星，馬奇在一旁啃樹枝，大家唱著歌。後來累了，所以進帳篷睡覺。四周很安靜。

Vietnamese

Henry và Mudge

Gia đình của Henry đi cắm trại. Họ đem con chó to của Henry, Mudge, với họ. Mẹ của Henry biết cách cắm trại. Henry đang nghĩ về những con thú họ có thể thấy. Cậu ta nôn nao.

Gia đình lái xe đến một hồ. Họ đi bộ. Henry thấy một con cá nhảy. Cậu thấy một con nai. Mudge đánh mùi được nhiều thứ. Gia đình dựng lều. Mudge ăn một số thức ăn. Ba của Henry chơi đàn ghi-ta.

Đêm đến, gia đình trải chăn ra. Họ ngắm sao trời. Mudge gặm một khúc gỗ. Gia đình ca hát. Họ vào lều. Họ đi ngủ. Mọi vật yên tĩnh.

Multilingual Summaries

Korean

헨리와 머지, 그리고 별이 빛나는 밤

헨리의 가족은 큰 개 머지를 데리고 캠핑을 간다. 헨리의 엄마는 야영하는 방법을 안다. 헨리는 동물들을 보게 된다는 생각에 들떠 있다.

헨리 가족은 차를 타고 강가로 가서 하이킹을 한다. 헨리는 물고기가 뛰어오르는 것도 보고 사슴도 본다. 머지는 주변의 냄새를 맡는다. 헨리 가족은 텐트를 치고 머지는 음식을 먹는다. 헨리의 아버지는 기타를 친다.

밤이 되자 헨리 가족은 담요 위에 누워 별을 바라보고 머지는 통나무를 씹는다. 가족은 노래를 부르고 텐트 안으로 들어가 잠을 잔다. 세상이 온통 고요하다.

Hmong

Henry thiab Mudge

Henry tsevneeg mus pw pem havzoov. Lawv coj nws tus dev loj, Mudge, nrog lawv mus. Henry niam paub kev mus pem havzoov yuav zoo li cas. Henry xav txog tej yam tsiaj uas lawv yuav mus pom. Nws zoo siab heev.

Lawv tsevneeg tsav lub tsheb mus txog nram ib lub pas dej. Lawv mus nce roob. Henry pom ib tug ntses dhia. Nws pom ib tug mos lwj. Mudge hnov ntau yam ntxhiab. Lawv tsevneeg tsa lawv lub tsev ntaub. Mudge noj lawv ib co zaum mov. Henry txiv ntaus lub kis ta.

Thaum ntsaus ntuj, lawv tsevneeg muab ib daim pam coj los pua pw. Lawv saib cov hnub qub. Mudge noj ib ya ntoo. Lawv tsevneeg hu nkauj. Ces lawv mus rau hauv lub tsev ntaub. Lawv mus pw tsaug zog. Txhua yam nyob ntsiag twb to.

A Walk in the Desert Student Edition pages 100–119

Week at a Glance	Customize instruction every day for your English Language Learners.				
	Day 1	**Day 2**	**Day 3**	**Day 4**	**Day 5**
Teacher's Edition	Use the ELL Notes that appear throughout each day of the lesson to support instruction and reading.				
ELL Poster 4	• Assess Prior Knowledge • Develop Concepts and Vocabulary	• Preteach High-Frequency Words	• Review Main Ideas and Details	• Interview with a Desert Animal	• Monitor Progress
ELL Teaching Guide	• Picture It! Lesson, pp. 22–23 • Multilingual Summaries, pp. 26–28	• ELL Reader Lesson, pp. 218–219	• Vocabulary Activities and Word Cards, pp. 24–25 • Multilingual Summaries, pp. 26–28		
ELL Readers	• Reread *I Spy Fun*	• Teach *The Saguaro Cactus*	• Reread *The Saguaro Cactus* and other texts to build fluency		
ELL and Transition Handbook	Use the following as needed to support this week's instruction and to conduct alternative assessments: • Phonics Transition Lessons • Grammar Transition Lessons • Assessment				

Picture It! Comprehension Lesson

Main Idea and Details

Use this lesson to supplement or replace the skill lesson on pages 97a–97b of the Teacher's Edition.

Teach

Distribute copies of the Picture It! blackline master on page 23.

- Ask children to look at the picture and describe what they see.
- Read the paragraph aloud. Ask: *What is the paragraph mainly about?* (living in the desert)
- Share the Skill Points (at right) with children.
- Have children look at the picture and words to understand the main idea and details.

Skill Points

✓ The **main idea** is the most important idea in a story.

✓ Small pieces of information tell more about the main idea. These small pieces are called **details.**

Practice

Read aloud the directions on page 23. Have children write the main idea and the details in the graphic organizer.

Answers for page 23: *Main Idea*: Only a few plants and animals can live in the hot, dry desert. *Details*: Cactus keeps water in stem; Tortoise has hard shell that protects it; Lizards use the Sun's heat.

Name ___________________________

Look at the picture. **Read** the paragraph.

- What is the most important idea? **Write** that idea in the Main Idea box below.
- What information supports the main idea? **Write** it in the Detail boxes.

Living in the Desert

Only a few plants and animals can live in the hot, dry desert. A cactus keeps water in its stem. A desert tortoise has a hard shell. The shell protects it from the Sun. Lizards use the Sun's heat to warm their bodies.

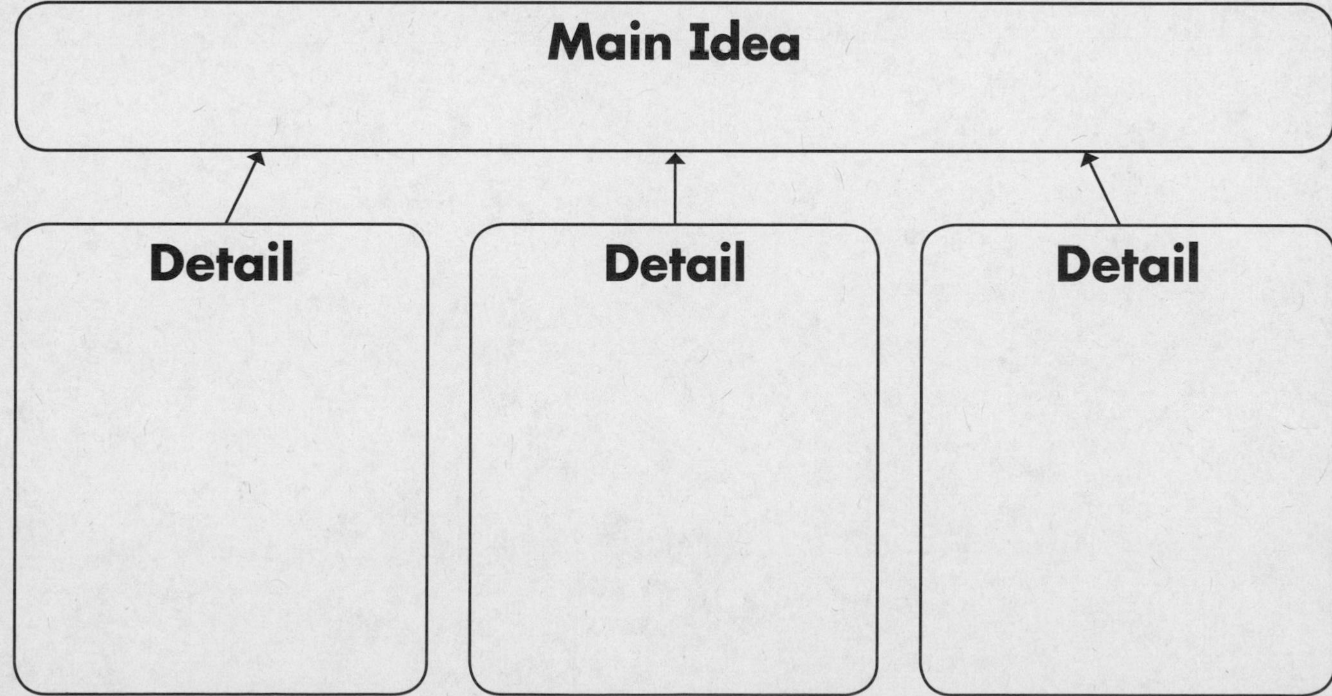

Vocabulary Activities and Word Cards

Copy the Word Cards on page 25 as needed for the following activities.
Use the blank cards for additional words that you want to teach.
Also see suggestions for teaching vocabulary in the ELL and Transition Handbook.

Word Card Jar	Definition Match	Word Hunt
• Put one set of Word Cards in a jar. • Ask a volunteer to pick a word out of the jar, read it, and chant the spelling. For example, if the word *early* is selected, the child will say *early, e-a-r-l-y*. The other children then repeat the word and the spelling. • The child with the card says a sentence using the word. The other children then repeat the sentence. • Continue with children taking turns drawing from the jar until all the Word Cards have been used. Also, make sure each child has had a turn selecting a word.	• Before play begins, write a brief definition for each high-frequency word on your own set of Word Cards. • Give each child a set of Word Cards. Have children arrange the cards face up in front of them. • Say the definition of a word. Do not say the word. • Children hold up the word that matches the definition. Have the first child to hold up the word read it aloud. • Continue until all the cards have been matched.	• Divide children into pairs. Give each pair one Word Card, saying each word aloud as you hand out the cards. • Challenge pairs to find their words in classroom books or other environmental print. Have them say where they find each word and then write the phrase or sentence in which they find it. • Invite pairs to share their findings with the class.

animals	**early**
eyes	**full**
warm	**water**

Multilingual Summaries

English

A Walk in the Desert

It is very hot and sunny in the desert. It almost never rains. Many plants and animals live in the desert.

Cactus is a plant that grows in the desert. There are many kinds of cactus.

Mice live in the desert. A large bird called a roadrunner lives there, too. Snakes and tortoises live in the desert. Jack rabbits live in the desert.

At night in the desert, the air gets cool. Other animals come out of their homes. Foxes and coyotes come out. Owls fly.

It is fun to visit the desert. There are deserts all over the world.

Spanish

Un paseo en el desierto

En el desierto hay mucho sol y hace mucho calor. Casi nunca llueve. Muchas plantas y animales viven en el desierto.

El cactus es una planta que crece en el desierto. Hay muchos tipos de cactus.

En el desierto viven ratones. También vive allí un pájaro grande llamado correcaminos. Además, viven serpientes, tortugas y liebres.

Por las noches, el aire del desierto es frío. Otros animales salen de sus refugios. Salen los zorros y los coyotes. Las lechuzas vuelan.

Es divertido visitar el desierto. Hay desiertos en muchas partes del mundo.

Multilingual Summaries

Chinese

漫步沙漠

沙漠非常熱，太陽很大，而且幾乎不下雨。很多植物和動物都住在沙漠裡。

仙人掌是生長在沙漠裡的植物，有很多不同種類。

沙漠裡有老鼠，還有一種叫做走鵑的大鳥。蛇、烏龜和傑克兔也都住在沙漠裡。

沙漠到了晚上會變冷，改換其他動物上場，你可以看到狐狸和土狼，天空還有貓頭鷹飛翔。

去沙漠玩很有趣。世界上到處都有沙漠。

Vietnamese

Đi Trong Sa Mạc

Trời rất nóng và nắng chói chan trong sa mạc. Hầu như là trời không bao giờ mưa. Có nhiều thú vật và thực vật sống trong sa mạc.

Xương rồng là một loại cây mọc trong sa mạc. Có nhiều loại xương rồng.

Chuột sống ở sa mạc. Một con chim to gọi là gà lôi đuôi dài (roadrunner) cũng sống trong sa mạc. Rắn và loại rùa trên cạn sống ở sa mạc. Thỏ lớn (jack rabbit) sống ở sa mạc.

Không khí trở nên mát mẻ vào buổi tối ở sa mạc. Các con thú khác ra khỏi hang ổ của chúng. Cáo và sói nhỏ bò ra. Chim cú bay ra.

Đi đến sa mạc là điều thú vị. Sa mạc có khắp nơi trên thế giới.

Multilingual Summaries

Korean

사막에서의 산책

사막은 매우 덥고 햇볕이 내리쬐며 비가 거의 오지 않지만 사막에는 많은 동식물이 살고 있다.

선인장은 사막에서 자라나는 식물로 종류가 아주 많다.

사막에는 쥐와 로드러너라고 불리는 뻐꾸기 종류의 큰 새, 뱀, 거북이, 그리고 잭 래빗이라는 토끼도 산다.

밤이 되면 사막의 공기가 시원해지고 여우와 코요테같이 집 밖으로 나오거나 부엉이 같이 하늘을 날아다니는 동물들이 있다.

사막은 재미난 곳으로 세계 곳곳에 있다.

Hmong

Taug Kev Mus Rau Hauv Lub Toj Roob Qhua

Yog ib hnub sov thiab kub hauv lub toj roob qhua. Yeej tsis tshua los nag rau ntawd li. Muaj ntau yam tsiaj thiab xyoob ntoo nyob rau hauv lub toj roob qhua.

Pos rau tshws yog ib yam xyoob ntoo uas nyob rau hauv lub toj roob qhua. Nws kuj muaj ntau yam pos rau tshws.

Cov nas tsuag kuj nyob hauv lub toj roob qhua. Ib tug noog loj hu ua tus noog dhia kev kuj nyob hauv thiab. Kuj muaj cua nab thiab vaubkib nyob rau hauv lub toj roob qhua. Cov kab tais kuj nyob rau hauv thiab.

Cov cua kuj txias zias thaum hmo ntuj nyob rau hauv lub toj roob qhua. Muaj ntau yam tsiaj kuj tawm hauv lawd cov tsev tuaj. Cov plis thiab cov hma kuj tawm tuaj. Kuj muaj cov plas ya.

Kuj muaj kev lom zem thaum mus xyuas lub toj roob qhua. Kuj muaj ntau ntau lub toj roob qhua nyob thoob plaws lub ntiajteb no.

The Strongest One Student Edition pages 132–149

Week at a Glance	Customize instruction every day for your English Language Learners.				
	Day 1	**Day 2**	**Day 3**	**Day 4**	**Day 5**
Teacher's Edition	Use the ELL Notes that appear throughout each day of the lesson to support instruction and reading.				
ELL Poster 5	• Assess Prior Knowledge • Develop Concepts and Vocabulary	• Preteach High-Frequency Words	• Where Can I Find Answers?	• Family Drama	• Monitor Progress
ELL Teaching Guide	• Picture It! Lesson, pp. 29–30 • Multilingual Summaries, pp. 33–35	• ELL Reader Lesson, pp. 220–221	• Vocabulary Activities and Word Cards, pp. 31–32 • Multilingual Summaries, pp. 33–35		
ELL Readers	• Reread *The Saguaro Cactus*	• Teach *Rabbit and Coyote*	• Reread *Rabbit and Coyote* and other texts to build fluency		
ELL and Transition Handbook	Use the following as needed to support this week's instruction and to conduct alternative assessments: • Phonics Transition Lessons • Grammar Transition Lessons • Assessment				

Picture It! Comprehension Lesson

Realism and Fantasy

Use this lesson to supplement or replace the skill lesson on pages 129a–129b of the Teacher's Edition.

Teach

Distribute copies of the Picture It! blackline master on page 30.

- Ask children to look at the picture and tell what is happening.
- Read the paragraph aloud. Ask: *Could this story really happen?*
- Share the Skill Points (at right) with children.
- Have children explain which clues told them that the story was a fantasy.

Skill Points

✓ There are two kinds of made-up stories: **realistic stories** and **fantasies.**

✓ A realistic story tells about something that could happen in real life.

✓ A fantasy is a story about something that could not happen.

Practice

Read aloud the directions on page 30. Have children answer the questions about realism and fantasy.

Answers for page 30: 1. a rain storm; people getting wet **2.** Great-Grandmother blows the clouds away. **3.** (Guide the children to talk about why this story is a fantasy.) Sample response: The story is a fantasy because a person could not blow away rain clouds.

Name ______________________________

Look at the picture. **Read** the story.

A Rainy Day

Great-Grandmother was a very strong woman. She could do anything! One day it was raining and everyone was wet. Great-Grandmother took a very deep breath and blew as hard as she could. She blew the clouds away and the Sun came out!

Write or **draw** your answers.

1. What is something from the story that could happen in real life?

2. What is something from the story that could not happen in real life?

3. Talk about why you think this is a realistic story or a fantasy.

Vocabulary Activities and Word Cards

Copy the Word Cards on page 32 as needed for the following activities.
Use the blank card for an additional word that you want to teach.
Also see suggestions for teaching vocabulary in the ELL and Transition Handbook.

Cloze Sentences	Bingo	Teacher's Chair
• Give each child a set of Word Cards. Have children place the cards face up in front of them. • Write these cloze sentences on the board, leaving a blank line in place of the high-frequency word: *The food is all [gone]. What did you [learn] today? I [often] go to the park. The glass broke into [pieces] when it fell. I am strong even [though] I am small. We will work on it [together]. The water is [very] cold.* • Read each sentence as a group and have children hold up the Word Card for the missing word. • Ask a volunteer to write the missing word on the board and reread the sentence with the word in place.	• Give each child a set of Word Cards and have them paste six of their cards on a piece of paper. The cards should be in two columns with three rows. • Pass out coins, beans, or other counters to use as bingo chips. • Tell children the definition of or a phrase that describes one of the words. For example: *This is something we do in school. (learn); When something breaks it is no longer whole. It is in ______. (pieces)* • Children who have the defined word on their bingo boards put a chip on the word. Allow children time to look for the word, then read aloud and show the correct word. • A child calls *bingo* and wins the game when he or she has placed chips on three words in a row. • You may wish to have children trade bingo boards and play the game again.	• Use one set of Word Cards. Invite a child to sit in your chair and "teach" the other children. • Ask the child to choose a Word Card, show it to the group, and read the word. Then have the child use the word in a sentence or define the word. Have the other children repeat after the "teacher." • Allow each child at least one turn in the teacher's chair.

gone	**learn**
often	**pieces**
though	**together**
very	

Multilingual Summaries

English

The Strongest One

Little Red Ant wants to know who is the strongest. Little Red Ant asks Snow. Snow says Sun is strongest. Sun says Wind is strongest. Wind says House is strongest. House says Mouse is strongest. Mouse says Cat is strongest. Cat says Stick is strongest. Stick says Fire is strongest. Fire says Water is strongest. Water says Deer is strongest. Deer says Arrow is strongest. Arrow says Big Rock is strongest. Big Rock says the Ants are strongest. Little Red Ant has learned that everything can be stronger than something else.

Spanish

El más fuerte

Hormiguita Roja quiere saber quién es el más fuerte. Hormiguita Roja le pregunta a Nieve. Nieve le dice que Sol es el más fuerte. Sol dice que Viento es el más fuerte. Viento dice que Casa es la más fuerte. Casa dice que Ratón es el más fuerte. Ratón dice que Gato es el más fuerte. Gato dice que Palo es el más fuerte. Palo dice que Fuego es el más fuerte. Fuego dice que Agua es la más fuerte. Agua dice que Ciervo es el más fuerte. Ciervo dice que Flecha es la más fuerte. Flecha dice que Piedra Grande es la más fuerte. Piedra Grande dice que las Hormigas son las más fuertes. Hormiguita Roja ha aprendido que cada cosa puede ser más fuerte que otra cosa.

Multilingual Summaries

Chinese

誰最厲害？

小紅螞蟻想知道誰最厲害，他問雪：「你是不是最厲害的？」雪說太陽最厲害，因為太陽會融化雪；太陽說風最厲害，因為風會把雲吹過來遮住太陽；風說房子最厲害，因為房子可以擋風；房子說老鼠最厲害，因為老鼠會在房子身上打洞；老鼠說貓最厲害，因為貓會抓老鼠；貓說棍子最厲害，因為棍子會打貓；棍子說火最厲害，因為火會燒棍子；火說水最厲害，因為水可以滅火；水說鹿最厲害，因為鹿會喝水；鹿說弓箭最厲害，因為弓箭可以獵鹿；弓箭說大石頭最厲害，因為大石頭可以把弓箭打壞；大石頭說小紅螞蟻最厲害，因為小紅螞蟻會把石頭一塊塊地搬走。小紅螞蟻回家後告訴大家，每個東西都可以比別的東西厲害。

Vietnamese

Người Mạnh Nhất

Chú Kiến Nhỏ Màu Đỏ muốn biết xem ai là người mạnh nhất. Chú Kiến Nhỏ Màu Đỏ hỏi Tuyết có phải là người mạnh nhất không. Tuyết trả lời Mặt Trời mạnh nhất vì mặt trời làm tan tuyết. Mặt Trời nói Gió mạnh nhất vì gió thổi mây bay ngang Mặt Trời. Gió nói Ngôi Nhà mạnh nhất vì Nhà dừng được Gió. Nhà nói Chuột mạnh nhất vì Chuột cắn lỗ trong nhà. Chuột nói Mèo mạnh nhất vì Mèo đuổi bắt Chuột. Mèo nói Gậy mạnh nhất vì Gậy đập Mèo. Gậy nói Lửa mạnh nhất vì Lửa đốt cháy Gậy. Lửa nói Nước mạnh nhất vì Nước dập tắt được Lửa. Nước nói Hươu mạnh nhất vì Hươu uống nước. Hươu nói Mũi Tên mạnh nhất vì nó có thể giết chết Hươu. Mũi Tên nói Hòn Đá To mạnh nhất vì nó làm gẫy Mũi Tên. Đá To nói Chú Kiến Nhỏ Màu Đỏ và đàn kiến của chú mạnh nhất vì họ khuân vác những mảnh nhỏ của Đá To đi nơi khác. Chú Kiến Nhỏ Màu Đỏ về nhà. Chú nói cho dân kiến biết rằng mọi vật đều có thể mạnh hơn một vật khác.

Multilingual Summaries

Korean

가장 힘센 것

작은 불개미는 누가 가장 힘이 센지 알고 싶어 눈에게 가장 힘이 세냐고 물어본다. 눈은 태양이 눈을 녹이기 때문에 가장 힘이 세다고 대답한다. 그런데 태양은 바람이 구름을 불어 자기를 가리기 때문에 바람을, 바람은 집이 바람을 막기 때문에 집을, 또 집은 쥐가 집에 구멍을 내기 때문에 쥐를, 쥐는 고양이가 자기를 쫓아버리기 때문에 고양이를, 고양이는 막대기가 자기를 때리기 때문에 막대기를, 막대기는 불이 자기를 태우기 때문에 불을, 불은 물이 자기를 끄기 때문에 물을, 물은 사슴이 자기를 마시기 때문에 사슴을, 사슴은 화살이 자기를 죽일 수 있기 때문에 화살을, 화살은 큰 바위가 자기를 부러뜨리기 때문에 큰 바위를, 큰 바위는 작은 불개미들이 큰 바위 조각들을 옮기기 때문에 작은 불개미가 가장 힘세다고 말한다. 작은 불개미는 집에 돌아가 친구들에게 누구나 자기보다 힘센 것은 있다고 말해준다.

Hmong

Tus Muaj Zog Tshaj

Tus Ntsaum Liab xav paub seb leejtwg muaj zog tshaj. Tus Ntsaum Liab tau nug Te seb nws puas yog tus muaj zog dua. Te teb tias lub Hnub yog tus muaj zog dua vim rau qhov lub hnub ua te yaj tag. Lub Hnub tias Cua yog tus muaj zog dua vim rau qhov nws tshuab cov huab cua tuaj plooj lub Hnub. Cua teb tias lub Tsev yog tus muaj zog dua vim rau qhov lub Tsev nres tau Cua. Tsev teb tias tus Nas yog tus muaj zog dua vim rau qhov Nas tho qhov hauv nws. Nas teb tias tus Miv yog tus muaj zog dua vim rau qhov tus Miv caum tus Nas. Tus Miv teb tias tus Pas Ntoo yog tus muaj zog dua vim rau thov tus Pas Ntoo ntaus tus Miv. Tus Pas Ntoo teb tias Hluavtaws yog tus muaj zog dua vim rau qhov nws hlawv tus Pas Ntoo. Hluavtaws teb tias Dej yog tus muaj zog dua vim rau qhov nws tua Hluavtaws. Dej teb tias tus Mos Lwj yog tus muaj zog dua vim rau qhov nws haus Dej. Mos Lwj teb tias tus Hneev muaj zog dua vim rau qhov nws tua tus Mos Lwj. Tus Hneev teb tias lub Pobzeb Loj yog tus muaj zog dua vim rau qhov nws ua kom tus Hneev dam. Lub Pobzeb Loj teb tias tus Ntsaum Liab thiab nws haivneeg yog cov muaj zog dua vim rau qhov lawm nqa lub Pobzeb Loj mus. Tus Ntsaum Liab thiaj mus tsev. Nws qhia rau nws haivneeg tias txhua yam yeej muaj zog dua lwm yam.

Tara and Tiree Student Edition pages 166–181

Week at a Glance	Customize instruction every day for your English Language Learners.				
	Day 1	**Day 2**	**Day 3**	**Day 4**	**Day 5**
Teacher's Edition	Use the ELL Notes that appear throughout each day of the lesson to support instruction and reading.				
ELL Poster 6	• Assess Prior Knowledge • Develop Concepts and Vocabulary	• Preteach High-Frequency Words	• Interview	• What Should You Do?	• Monitor Progress
ELL Teaching Guide	• Picture It! Lesson, pp. 36–37 • Multilingual Summaries, pp. 40–42	• ELL Reader Lesson, pp. 222–223	• Vocabulary Activities and Word Cards, pp. 38–39 • Multilingual Summaries, pp. 40–42		
ELL Readers	• Reread *Rabbit and Coyote*	• Teach *Sandy to the Rescue!*	• Reread *Sandy to the Rescue!* and other texts to build fluency		
ELL and Transition Handbook	Use the following as needed to support this week's instruction and to conduct alternative assessments: • Phonics Transition Lessons • Grammar Transition Lessons • Assessment				

Picture It! Comprehension Lesson

Sequence

Use this lesson to supplement or replace the skill lesson on pages 163a–163b of the Teacher's Edition.

Teach

Distribute copies of the Picture It! blackline master on page 37.

- Ask children to look at the picture story and describe what happens.
- Read the sentences aloud. Ask: *What happens first in the story? What happens next?*
- Review the Skill Points (at right) with children.
- Have children look at the pictures and words to find clues about the sequence of the story.

Practice

Read aloud the directions on page 37. Have children fill in the sequence chart.

Answers for page 37: *First:* Marie let Buster out to play. *Next:* It started to snow, so Marie called Buster. *Last:* Buster came home.

Skill Points

✓ **Sequence** is the order in which things happen.

✓ Think about what happens first, next, and last in a story.

✓ Look for words such as *then* and *next* to figure out sequence.

✓ As you read, think about the order of events so you can keep track of what happens.

Name ______________________________

Look at the pictures. **Read** the story.

- What happens first in the story? What happens next? What happens last? **Write** your answers in the chart.

Out in a Storm

Marie let Buster out to play in the yard.

Then it started to snow. Marie called Buster.

He came running. What a good dog!

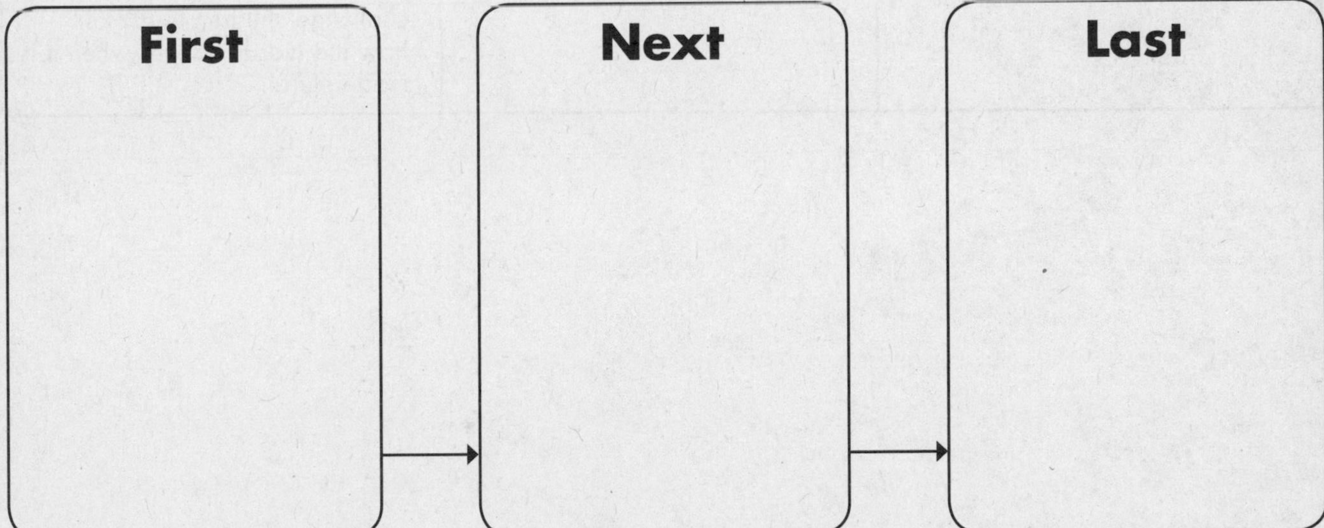

Vocabulary Activities and Word Cards

Copy the Word Cards on page 39 as needed for the following activities.
Use the blank cards for additional words that you want to teach.
Also see suggestions for teaching vocabulary in the ELL and Transition Handbook.

Everyday Game	Home Language Connection	Word Endings
• Give each child a set of Word Cards in alphabetical order. • Read the words aloud as a group. Then have each child tell what two of the words mean. • As a group, discuss how children might use these words every day. Ask volunteers to give example sentences: *I listen to the radio.* *I live with my family.* *I heard a noise.*	• Display a set of Word Cards for the group. • Have children take turns choosing a card, using the word in a sentence, and saying the sentence in the home language. • Continue until each child has been able to say at least one sentence.	• Give each child a set of Word Cards and two blank cards. Ask children to write the word endings *-s* and *-ing* on the blank cards. • Review the meaning of each word with children. Then discuss which of the word endings can be matched to which of the words. • Invite volunteers to hold up a Word Card and an ending and read the new word. Possible words are *breaks, breaking, listens, listening, pulls, pulling.* • Point out the word *family* as an exception. Write *families* and challenge children to explain how the word changes when it is made plural.

break	**family**
heard	**listen**
once	**pull**

Multilingual Summaries

English

Tara and Tiree

Jim and his family always had dogs. He loved them. When he grew up, Jim got two dogs of his own. They were named Tara and Tiree. Jim and the dogs liked the winter. They liked to go for walks in the snow.

One day, Jim and the dogs walked on the ice on a lake. The ice broke and Jim fell in. No one heard him calling for help. The dogs stayed near Jim. Tiree tried to help. But she fell in the water. Then Tara tried to help. But Jim was too big. Tiree walked on Jim's back and got out of the water. Together, the dogs pulled Jim out of the water. They saved his life! Jim loved his dogs even more.

Spanish

Tara y Tiree

Jim y su familia siempre tuvieron perros. Jim los quería mucho. Cuando creció, Jim tuvo dos perros propios. Sus nombres eran Tara y Tiree. A Jim y a sus perros les encantaba el invierno. Les gustaba salir a dar paseos en la nieve.

Un día, Jim y sus perros salieron a dar un paseo a un lago congelado. El hielo se rompió y Jim cayó adentro. Nadie lo oía gritar pidiendo ayuda. Tara y Tiree se quedaron cerca de Jim. Tiree trató de ayudarlo, pero también cayó al agua. Luego Tara trató de ayudarlo, pero Jim era demasiado grande. Tiree caminó sobre la espalda de Jim y salió del agua. Entre los dos, por fin lograron sacarlo del agua. ¡Ellos le salvaron la vida! Jim quiere aún más a sus perros.

Multilingual Summaries

Chinese

泰拉與泰利

吉姆和他的家人一直都有養狗，吉姆很喜歡狗，長大以後，他自己也養了兩隻狗，他們的名字叫泰拉和泰利。吉姆和狗狗都喜歡冬天，因為冬天可以在雪地上散步。

有一天，吉姆和狗狗走在結冰的湖面上，冰突然破了，吉姆掉進湖裡，沒有人聽到他的求救聲。狗狗留在吉姆附近，泰利想幫忙，可是也掉進水裡去。泰拉也試著要幫忙，可是吉姆太重了，拉不上來。泰利爬到吉姆的背上，跳出水面。兩隻狗狗同心協力把吉姆救了出來。狗狗救了吉姆一命！吉姆比以前更愛狗了。

Vietnamese

Tara và Tiree

Jim và gia đình lúc nào cũng có nuôi chó. Cậu bé yêu thương chó. Khi cậu lớn lên, Jim có hai con chó. Tên của chúng là Tara và Tiree. Jim và hai con chó đều thích mùa đông. Họ thích đi dạo khi có tuyết.

Ngày nọ, Jim và chó đi trên mặt hồ đóng băng. Băng vỡ và Jim bị rơi xuống nước. Không ai nghe tiếng Jim kêu cứu. Hai con chó ở quanh quẩn bên Jim. Tiree cố giúp. Nhưng nó bị rơi xuống nước. Kế đến Tara cố giúp. Nhưng Jim to quá. Tiree đi trên lưng của Jim và thoát ra khỏi hồ. Hai con chó cùng kéo Jim ra khỏi hồ nước. Chúng đã cứu sống Jim! Jim càng thương yêu hai con chó của mình nhiều hơn.

Multilingual Summaries

Korean

타라와 타이리

짐의 가족은 항상 개를 키워왔기 때문에 짐도 개를 사랑한다. 짐은 자라서 자기 개 두 마리를 얻어 타라와 타이리라고 이름 짓는다. 짐과 개들은 겨울과 눈 속에서 걷기를 좋아한다.

어느 날 짐은 개들과 호수의 얼음 위를 걷다가 얼음이 깨지면서 물에 빠진다. 아무도 그가 도와달라고 외치는 말을 듣지 못하는데 마침 개들이 가까이에 있다. 타이리가 짐을 도우려 하지만 물에 빠지고 타라가 이들을 구하려 하지만 그러기엔 짐의 덩치가 너무 크다. 타이리가 짐의 등 위로 기어올라가 물 밖으로 나와 타라와 함께 짐을 물 밖으로 끌어낸다. 개들이 짐의 생명을 구하게 되면서 짐은 개들을 더욱 사랑하게 된다.

Hmong

Tara thiab Tiree

Jim thiab nws tsevneeg yeej ib txwm muaj ib co dev. Nws hlub lawv. Thaum nws loj lawm, Jim kuj muaj ob tug dev uas yog nws tug. Nkawd ob lub npe yog Tara thiab Tiree. Jim thiab nws cov dev nyiam lub caij no. Lawv nyiam mus taug kev saum cov te.

Muaj ib hnub, Jim thiab nws cov dev mus taug kev tom ib lub pas dej uas khov tag. Cov naj kheem tawg ua rau Jim poob rau hauv lub pas dej. Tsis muaj leejtwg hnov nws hu. Cov dev kuj tseem nyob ze ze ntawm Jim. Tiree kuj pab nws. Tiamsis ua rau nws poob rau hauv lub pas dej. Ces Tara thiaj tau pab thiab. Tiamsis Jim nws loj heev. Tiree tau caij Jim lub nrob qaum kom nws tawm tau hauv lub pas dej. Ob tug dev ntawm thiaj uake rub Jim tawm hauv lub pas dej los. Nkawd cawm tau nws txojsia. Jim haj yam hlub nws ob tug dev ntxiv xwb.

Ronald Morgan Goes to Bat

Student Edition pages 194–211

Week at a Glance	Customize instruction every day for your English Language Learners.				
	Day 1	**Day 2**	**Day 3**	**Day 4**	**Day 5**
Teacher's Edition	Use the ELL Notes that appear throughout each day of the lesson to support instruction and reading.				
ELL Poster 7	• Assess Prior Knowledge • Develop Concepts and Vocabulary	• Preteach High-Frequency Words	• Let's Play Bingo!	• What's in the Scene Riddles	• Monitor Progress
ELL Teaching Guide	• Picture It! Lesson, pp. 43–44 • Multilingual Summaries, pp. 47–49	• ELL Reader Lesson, pp. 224–225	• Vocabulary Activities and Word Cards, pp. 45–46 • Multilingual Summaries, pp. 47–49		
ELL Readers	• Reread *Sandy to the Rescue!*	• Teach *The Soccer Picnic*	• Reread *The Soccer Picnic* and other texts to build fluency		
ELL and Transition Handbook	Use the following as needed to support this week's instruction and to conduct alternative assessments: • Phonics Transition Lessons • Grammar Transition Lessons • Assessment				

Picture It! Comprehension Lesson

Realism and Fantasy

Use this lesson to supplement or replace the skill lesson on pages 191a–191b of the Teacher's Edition.

Teach

Distribute copies of the Picture It! blackline master on page 44.

- Ask children to look at the picture and describe what is happening.
- Read the paragraph aloud. Ask: *Does anything happen in this story that could* not *happen in real life?*
- Share the Skill Points (at right) with children.
- Have children discuss what kinds of clues might tell them that a story is realistic.

Practice

Read aloud the directions on page 44. Have children answer the questions about realism and fantasy.

Answers for page 51: 1. playing soccer **2.** fly **3.** (Guide children to talk about why they think this is a realistic story or a fantasy.) Sample response: The story is realistic. Children can play soccer. The children in the story don't do anything that is not real.

Skill Points

✓ A **realistic story** tells about something that could happen in real life.

✓ A **fantasy** is a make-believe story. It could not happen in real life.

✓ To figure out if a story is realistic or a fantasy, ask: *Does anything happen in the story that could not happen in real life?*

Name ______________________________

Realism and Fantasy

Look at the picture. **Read** the paragraph.

An Exciting Game

What a great soccer game! Both teams have played very well. There are only three seconds left in the game. The score is tied—each team has one goal. Mara is trying to score another goal. If she scores a goal, her team will win. If she does not score, nobody will win. The final score will be one to one.

Answer the questions below.

1. What are the children doing?

O eating lunch O playing soccer O going to school

2. Which of these is something children <u>cannot</u> do in real life?

O run O play O fly

3. Talk about why you think this is a realistic story or a fantasy.

Vocabulary Activities and Word Cards

Copy the Word Cards on page 46 as needed for the following activities.
Use the blank card for an additional word that you want to teach.
Also see suggestions for teaching vocabulary in the ELL and Transition Handbook.

Word Match	Tell a Story	Fishing Game
• Organize children into groups of two or three. Give two sets of Word Cards to each group, and ask children to mix the cards together and then spread them out face down. • One child at a time picks up a card, reads it aloud, and tries to find its matching card. • When a child has a match, he or she tells what the word means. • The game ends when all the cards have been matched.	• Give two Word Cards to each child, and arrange children in a circle. • Start a story with a sentence that uses one of the words. For example: *We played a great game today.* • The next child continues the story, finding a way to use one of his or her words in a sentence. Children can help each other make sentences. • Children should take turns until all the Word Cards have been used and the group decides the story is complete.	• Use one or more sets of Word Cards. Attach a metal paper clip to each card, and put the words in a bucket. Tie a string to a short stick, and fasten a magnet to the end of the string. • Have children take turns "fishing" for words. • When a child "catches" a word, he or she reads it and either tells what it means or uses it in a sentence. If the word is used correctly, the child keeps the card. If not, the child returns the card to the bucket. • The child with the most "fish" when the bucket is empty wins the game.

certainly

either

great

laugh

second

worst

you're

Multilingual Summaries

English

Ronald Morgan Goes to Bat

Ronald and his classmates played baseball. Everyone could hit and catch the ball except for Ronald. Ronald tried, but he was afraid of the ball. He closed his eyes when he swung the bat. His teacher told him to keep trying. Ronald was good at cheering for the team.

One day, the team practiced running. Ronald ran in the wrong direction. Then Ronald could not catch the ball. Ronald said that maybe he would not play anymore. Ronald's father told him to open his eyes when he batted. The two practiced playing ball together, and Ronald hit the ball. Ronald felt better, and ran to play ball with the other children.

Spanish

Ronald Morgan va a batear

Ronald y sus compañeros de clase jugaban al béisbol. Todos le podían pegar la pelota y agarrarla excepto Ronald. Ronald trataba pero le tenía miedo a la pelota. Cerraba los ojos mientras bateaba. Su maestro le dijo que siguiera intentándolo. Ronald era bueno animando al equipo.

Un día, el equipo practicaba carreras. Ronald corrió en la dirección contraria. Luego, Ronald no pudo agarrar la pelota. Ronald dijo que quizás no volvería a jugar más. El papá de Ronald le dijo que abriera los ojos cuando bateara. Juntos, practicaron jugando a la pelota y por fin Ronald le pegó a la pelota. Ronald se sintió mejor y corrió a jugar a la pelota con los otros niños.

Multilingual Summaries

Chinese

羅南・摩根上場打球

羅南和同學一起打棒球，大家都打得到球，也接得到球，只有羅南不行。他試了好幾次，可是還是沒辦法，因為他怕球。揮棒的時候，羅南嚇得把眼睛閉起來。老師告訴他要堅持下去。羅南很會為棒球隊打氣。

有一天，棒球隊練習跑步，羅南跑錯了方向，之後又接不到球。他沮喪地說，以後可能都不會來打棒球了。羅南的爸爸告訴他，揮棒的時候要把眼睛睜開，爸爸陪他一起練習，練了好久，羅南終於打到球了。他覺得狀況好多了，所以又跑去跟其他小朋友一起打棒球。

Vietnamese

Đến Lượt Ronald Morgan Đánh Quả Bóng

Ronald và bạn học trong lớp chơi môn bóng chày. Mọi người đều có thể đánh và chụp được quả bóng ngoại trừ Ronald. Ronald cố gắng, nhưng nó sợ quả bóng. Nó nhắm mắt lại khi nó vung cây gậy đánh quả bóng. Thầy giáo bảo nó cứ tiếp tục cố gắng. Ronald thích reo hò cổ vũ cho đội của mình.

Một ngày kia, đội tập chạy. Ronald chạy ngược hướng. Rồi Ronald không bắt được quả bóng. Ronald nói là có thể cậu sẽ không chơi bóng nữa. Ba của Ronald bảo cậu mở mắt ra khi đánh quả bóng. Hai cha con tập chơi với nhau, và Ronald đánh trúng quả bóng. Ronald thấy vui hơn, và chạy đi chơi bóng với những trẻ khác.

Multilingual Summaries

Korean

야구공을 쳐낸 로널드 모건

반 친구들과의 야구 경기에서 공을 치지도 잡지도 못하는 것은 로널드뿐이다. 로널드는 잘 하려고 노력하지만 공이 무서워서 야구 방망이를 휘두를 때 눈을 감는다. 이에 선생님은 계속 노력하라고 말씀하신다. 로널드는 팀 응원은 잘한다.

어느 날 야구팀에서 달리기 연습을 하는데 로널드가 엉뚱한 방향으로 뛰어가 공을 잡지 못한다. 로널드가 이제 더 이상 야구 경기를 하지 않겠다고 하자 로널드의 아버지는 공을 칠 때 눈을 뜨라고 얘기해준다. 로널드는 아버지와 함께 야구 연습을 하다가 공을 쳐내고는 기분이 좋아져서 다른 아이들과 야구 경기를 하러 달려간다.

Hmong

Ronald Morgan Tau Mus Ntaus Npas

Ronald thiab cov tub ntxhais kawmntawv uake nrog nws ua si ntaus baseball. Sawvdaws puavleej txawj ntaus thiab txawj txais lub npas tsuas tshuav Ronald ib leeg xwb. Ronald kuj sim kawg, tiamsis lub npas ua rau nws ntsai. Nws kaw nws lub qhovmuag thaum nws ntaus lub npas. Nws tus nais khus hais kom nws rau siab ntaus ntxiv. Ronald nyiam qw rau nws pab heev.

Muaj ib hnub, nws pab tau mus xyaum dhia. Ronald dhia mus rau sab tsis yog. Ces Ronald txais tsis tau lub npas. Ronald hais tias tejzaum nws yuav tsis ua si ntxiv lawm. Ronald txiv hais rau nws hais tias thaum nws ntaus lub npas nws yuav tau nqe nws lub qhovmuag. Nkawd xyaum ntaus npas uake thiaj ua rau Ronald ntaus tau lub npas. Ua rau Ronald zoo siab me ntsis nws thiaj mus nrog lwm cov menyuam ua si ntaus npas.

Turtle's Race with Beaver

Student Edition pages 222–242

Week at a Glance	Customize instruction every day for your English Language Learners.				
	Day 1	**Day 2**	**Day 3**	**Day 4**	**Day 5**
Teacher's Edition	Use the ELL Notes that appear throughout each day of the lesson to support instruction and reading.				
ELL Poster 8	• Assess Prior Knowledge • Develop Concepts and Vocabulary	• Preteach High-Frequency Words	• Interaction Action	• Use Words	• Monitor Progress
ELL Teaching Guide	• Picture It! Lesson, pp. 50–51 • Multilingual Summaries, pp. 54–56	• ELL Reader Lesson, pp. 226–227	• Vocabulary Activities and Word Cards, pp. 52–53 • Multilingual Summaries, pp. 54–56		
ELL Readers	• Reread *The Soccer Picnic*	• Teach *Summer Returns to the Pond*	• Reread *Summer Returns to the Pond* and other texts to build fluency		
ELL and Transition Handbook	Use the following as needed to support this week's instruction and to conduct alternative assessments: • Phonics Transition Lessons • Grammar Transition Lessons • Assessment				

Picture It! Comprehension Lesson

Sequence

Use this lesson to supplement or replace the skill lesson on pages 219a–219b of the Teacher's Edition.

Teach

Distribute copies of the Picture it! blackline master on page 51.

- Ask children to look at the pictures and describe what happens.
- Read the sentences aloud. Ask: *What happened first in the story?*
- Share the Skill Points (at right) with children.
- Have children look at the pictures and words to find clues about the sequence of the story.

Practice

Read aloud the directions on page 51. Have children fill in the sequence chart.

Answers for page 44: *First:* The kids played at the park. *Next:* The children had lunch. Kari forgot hers. *Last:* Kari's friends shared their lunches.

Skill Points

✓ **Sequence** is the order in which things happen.

✓ As you read, think about what happens first, next, and last in a story.

✓ Look for words such as *then* and *next* to help you understand when things are happening.

Name ______________________________

Look at the pictures. **Read** the story.

- What is the first thing that happened in the story? What happened next? What happened last? **Write** your answers in the sequence chart.

Lunchtime

The three friends played at the park. They had a good time.

Soon it was time for lunch. Oh, no! Kari forgot to bring her lunch to the park. She was hungry.

Kari's friends helped her. Tomás gave her an apple. Then Gabby shared her sandwich. What nice friends!

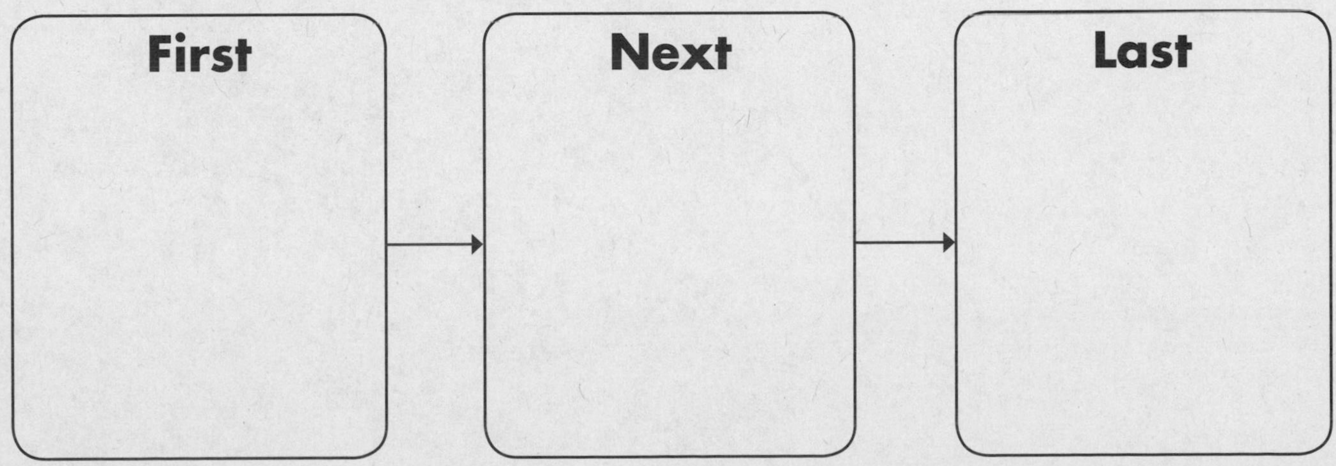

Vocabulary Activities and Word Cards

Copy the Word Cards on page 53 as needed for the following activities.
Use the blank cards for additional words that you want to teach.
Also see suggestions for teaching vocabulary in the ELL and Transition Handbook.

Word Card Jar	Speak or Be Silent	Mind Reader
• Put one set of Word Cards in a jar. • Ask a volunteer to pick a word out of the jar, read it, and chant the spelling. For example, if the word *whole* is selected, the child will say, *whole, w-h-o-l-e*. The other children repeat the word and the spelling. • The child with the card says a sentence using the word. The other children repeat the sentence. • Have children take turns drawing from the jar until all the Word Cards have been used.	• Divide children into pairs and give two sets of Word Cards to each child. Have each child mix up the cards and place them in a pile face down. • Players each turn one card face up at the same time. • If the words on the cards match, players say the word aloud. The player who says the word first gets the pair of cards. • If the words do not match, players should remain silent. If both players remain silent, no one gets the cards. If both players say a word when they should not, no one gets the cards. If one player accidentally says a word, the other player gets the pair of cards. • Play continues with unmatched cards until no more matches are possible. The player who has collected the most cards wins.	• Give each child a set of Word Cards. Have children spread out their cards face up so they can see them. • Write these sentence frames on the board: *This word starts with the letter _____. This word means _____. This word ends with the letter _____.* • Pick up a Word Card, and give children clues about the word by reading and completing the sentence frames. • Tell children to hold up the correct Word Card when they have the answer. • The child who correctly guesses the word may choose another card and provide the group with the next riddle. Allow children to use the sentence frames or make up their own clues.

above	**ago**
enough	**toward**
whole	**word**

Multilingual Summaries

English

Turtle's Race with Beaver

Turtle lived in a pond. She slept all winter in the mud at the bottom. While she slept, a beaver built a dam and a lodge. The dam made the pond much deeper. Turtle's favorite rocks were under water.

Turtle asked Beaver to share the pond. Beaver said no. He challenged Turtle to a race. The winner would stay in the pond.

The race began the next morning. The other animals watched. Beaver was ahead. Turtle bit onto Beaver's tail. Near the finish line, Turtle bit down hard and Beaver flipped his tail. Beaver's tail threw Turtle to the finish line. Turtle won the race. Beaver went to another pond, and shared it with another turtle.

Spanish

La carrera de Tortuga y Oso

Tortuga vivía en un estanque. Dormía todo el invierno en el barro del fondo. Mientras dormía, un castor construyó una presa y una madriguera. La presa hizo el lago más profundo. Las piedras favoritas de Tortuga quedaron debajo del agua.

Tortuga le pidió a Castor que compartiera el estanque. Castor le dijo que no. Él desafió a Tortuga a una carrera. El ganador podría quedarse en el estanque.

La carrera comenzó a la mañana siguiente. Los otros animales se reunieron a mirar. Castor iba ganando la carrera. Entonces, Tortuga mordió en la cola de Castor. Cuando iban a llegar a la meta, Tortuga mordió más duro y Castor tiró la cola hacia arriba. La cola de Castor lanzó a Tortuga a la meta. Tortuga ganó la carrera. Castor se fue para otro estanque y lo compartió con otra tortuga.

Multilingual Summaries

Chinese

烏龜和河狸的賽跑

烏龜住在池塘裡，一整個冬天她都窩在池塘底的泥巴堆睡覺。河狸趁烏龜睡覺的時候，偷偷蓋了一座水壩和一個小窩。因為建了水壩，所以池塘變深了，把烏龜最喜歡的那塊石頭淹在水底下了。

烏龜要河狸把池塘讓出來大家一起用，河狸不肯。他向烏龜下戰書賽跑，贏的就可以住在池塘裡。

第二天早上比賽開始，其他動物都跑來看熱鬧。河狸領先，烏龜從後面咬著河狸的尾巴。快要抵達終點的時候，烏龜用力咬下去，使河狸甩動尾巴，把烏龜甩向終點去了。最後，烏龜贏了這場比賽。河狸只好搬到其他池塘去，和另一隻烏龜一起住。

Vietnamese

Cuộc Đua Của Rùa Và Hải Ly

Rùa sống trong một cái ao. Suốt mùa đông nó ngủ trong lớp bùn dưới đáy ao. Khi nó ngủ, một con hải ly xây một cái đập và hang ở ao này. Cái đập làm cho ao trở nên sâu hơn trước. Những hòn đá mà rùa ưa thích bị chìm dưới nước.

Rùa kêu Hải Ly cùng chia sẻ cái ao cho Rùa ở chung. Hải Ly không chịu. Nó thách thức Rùa đua với nó. Người nào thắng sẽ được ở trong ao.

Cuộc đua bắt đầu vào sáng hôm sau. Các con thú khác đến xem. Hải Ly bơi nhanh hơn. Rùa cắn vào đuôi Hải Ly. Khi gần đến đích, Rùa cắn thật mạnh và Hải Ly vẩy đuôi của mình. Đuôi của Hải Ly ném Rùa đến đích. Rùa thắng cuộc đua. Hải Ly dọn đến một cái ao khác, và ở chung với một con rùa khác.

Multilingual Summaries

Korean

거북이와 비버의 경주

거북이는 연못에 사는데 겨울 내내 연못 바닥의 진흙 속에서 잠을 잔다. 거북이가 겨울잠을 자는 동안 비버가 댐과 집을 지었고 그 댐 때문에 연못이 훨씬 더 깊어져 거북이가 좋아하던 바위가 물 아래로 잠겨버렸다.

거북이는 비버에게 연못을 함께 쓰자고 하지만 비버는 싫다며 경주를 해서 이긴 쪽이 연못에 남자고 한다.

다음 날 아침 다른 동물들이 구경하는 가운데 경주가 시작된다. 비버가 앞서 나가자 거북이는 비버의 꼬리를 물어버린다. 결승선 가까이까지 와서 거북이는 비버의 꼬리를 세게 물어버리자 비버는 꼬리를 털어 거북이를 결승선에 던져버린다. 거북이는 경주에서 이기고 비버는 다른 연못으로 이사를 가 그곳에서 다른 거북이와 함께 연못을 쓰게 된다.

Hmong

Vaubkib Sib Xeem Nrog Nas Dej

Vaubkib nyob hauv ib lub pas dej. Nws pw hauv lub qab pag txhua lub caij ntuj no. Thaum nws tseem pw pw muaj ib tug Nas Dej tuaj tauv tau ib lub pag dej rau nws nyob. Pag dej ntawd txawm ua rau lub pas dej haj yam tob ntxiv xwb. Tus Vaubkib kuj muaj cov pobzeb uas nws nyiam tshaj plaws nyob rau hauv lub qab pag dej.

Vaubkib hais rau Nas Dej kom nws yuav tau koom lub pas dej. Nas Dej tsis kam. Nws hais kom Vaub Kib sib xeem nrog nws. Tus uas yeej tus ntawd thiaj tau nyob hauv lub pas dej.

Hnub tom qab kev sib xeem thiaj pib. Tsis muaj lwm tus tsiaj los saib. Nas Dej yog tus ua ntej. Vaubkib thiaj tom Nas Dej tus ko tw. Thaum mus yuav txog kab kawg, Vaubkib siv zog tom thiaj ua rau nws tus ko tw ntxeev hlo. Nas Dej tus ko tw thiaj tib txawb Vaubkib mus txog rau kab kawg. Vaubkib thiaj li yeej qhov kev sib xeem. Nas Dej thiaj li mus rau lwm lub pas dej thiab mus sib koom nyob nrog lwm tus vaubkib.

The Bremen Town Musicians

Student Edition pages 256–273

Week at a Glance	Customize instruction every day for your English Language Learners.				
	Day 1	**Day 2**	**Day 3**	**Day 4**	**Day 5**
Teacher's Edition	Use the ELL Notes that appear throughout each day of the lesson to support instruction and reading.				
ELL Poster 9	• Assess Prior Knowledge • Develop Concepts and Vocabulary	• Preteach High-Frequency Words	• What Can We Do Alone?	• Working Together with Skits	• Monitor Progress
ELL Teaching Guide	• Picture It! Lesson, pp. 57–58 • Multilingual Summaries, pp. 61–63	• ELL Reader Lesson, pp. 228–229	• Vocabulary Activities and Word Cards, pp. 59–60 • Multilingual Summaries, pp. 61–63		
ELL Readers	• Reread *Summer Returns to the Pond*	• Teach *Big News in the Barn*	• Reread *Big News in the Barn* and other texts to build fluency		
ELL and Transition Handbook	Use the following as needed to support this week's instruction and to conduct alternative assessments: • Phonics Transition Lessons • Grammar Transition Lessons • Assessment				

Picture It! Comprehension Lesson

Author's Purpose

Use this lesson to supplement or replace the skill lesson on pages 253a–253b of the Teacher's Edition.

Teach

Distribute copies of the Picture It! blackline master on page 58.

- Ask children to look at the pictures and tell what they see.
- Read the sentences aloud. Ask: *Why do you think the author wrote this story?*
- Share the Skill Points (at right) with children.
- Have children look at the pictures and sentences to find clues about the author's purpose.

Practice

Read aloud the directions on page 58. Have children answer the questions about the story.

Answers for page 58: 1. a pig and a cat **2.** Sample response: funny; The animals did funny things. **3.** Sample response: I think the author wrote the story to make people laugh.

Skill Points

✓ An author has a reason for writing. The author's reason is also called the **author's purpose.**

✓ An author can write to make you laugh, to explain something, to describe something, or to try to get you to think or act in a certain way.

✓ To figure out the author's purpose, ask yourself: *Is the story funny, serious, or sad? Why do I think so?*

Name ______________________

Look at the pictures. **Read** the sentences.

Going to the Fair

"The fair is very far away," said Cat. "You can ride on my back," said Pig. "That's silly," said Cat. "Cats don't ride pigs. I will meet you there."

"I told you cats don't ride pigs," Cat said. "They ride bikes!"

Answer the questions below.

1. What is the story about?

O a pig and a cat O a boy and a dog O a trip to the store

2. Do you think the story is funny or sad? Why do you think so?

____

____

3. Why do you think the author wrote the story?

____

____

Vocabulary Activities and Word Cards

Copy the Word Cards on page 60 as needed for the following activities.
Use the blank card for an additional word that you want to teach.
Also see suggestions for teaching vocabulary in the ELL and Transition Handbook.

Picture Match	Puzzle Pieces	What's the Word?
• Before children play, draw large picture cards for the words *bought, people, pleasant, scared (adj.),* and *sign*. For example, a drawing for *scared* might be a face with a frightened expression. • Give each child a set of Word Cards, leaving out the cards for *probably* and *shall*. Have children spread out their cards face up so they can see them. • Show children one of the picture cards, and ask them to hold up the matching Word Card. Have the first child who holds up the correct card read the word aloud. • Invite children to draw their own pictures and play the game with a partner.	• Give partners one set of Word Cards. • Have children cut each card into two differently shaped puzzle pieces. • Ask children to mix up the puzzle pieces, lay them face up, and take turns putting the words back together and reading them aloud. • Then have children write or say a sentence using each word.	• Give each child a set of Word Cards to look at during the activity. Keep another set at the front of the room. • Ask a volunteer to come to the front of the room and choose a Word Card without showing it to the group. • Have the child write the word where others can see it, leaving out two or three letters. The child should write an underscore for any missing letters, for example, s c _ r e _ *(scared)*. • Ask the other children to write the word and fill in the missing letters. Have a volunteer use the word in a sentence. • Continue until each child has had at least one turn at the front of the room and all the Word Cards have been used.

bought

people

pleasant

probably

scared

shall

sign

Multilingual Summaries

English

The Bremen Town Musicians

An old donkey could not work hard anymore. He ran away to Bremen to be a musician. On the way he met a dog, a cat, and a rooster. They went with the donkey.

The animals came to a house. They saw three robbers inside. The robbers had food. The animals were hungry. They sang. The robbers ran away. The animals ate the food and went to sleep.

The robbers returned. One robber woke the cat, who scratched him. He woke the dog, who bit him. He tripped over the donkey, who kicked him. The rooster began to crow. The robbers ran away. The animals stayed. They sang together every night.

Spanish

Los músicos del pueblo de Bremen

Un burro viejo ya no podía trabajar más. Se escapó a Bremen a hacerse músico. En el camino conoció a un perro, a un gato y a un gallo. Ellos decidieron irse a acompañar al burro.

Los animales llegaron a una casa. Dentro de la casa había tres ladrones. Los ladrones tenían comida. Los animales estaban hambrientos. Comenzaron a cantar y los ladrones se fueron. Los animales comieron la comida y se fueron a dormir.

Los ladrones regresaron. Un ladrón despertó al gato y éste lo arañó. Despertó al perro y éste lo mordió. Tropezó con el burrito y éste lo pateó. El gallo comenzó a cantar. Todos los ladrones se fueron y los animales se quedaron. Ellos cantaban juntos todas las noches.

Multilingual Summaries

Chinese

不來梅鎮的音樂家

老驢子無法再賣命工作，所以主人不想養牠了。驢子決定逃走，到不來梅鎮當音樂家。途中牠遇到了一隻狗、一隻貓和一隻公雞，他們也很老了，跟隨驢子一起走。

動物們到了不來梅鎮，看到一棟房子，裡面有三個強盜，正在吃豐富的晚餐。動物們已很餓，牠們也想吃，於是靈機一動，開始唱歌，強盜以為有人來了，所以嚇得逃跑。動物們進了屋子，享用晚餐，吃完後便舒服地睡覺。

夜裡強盜們偷偷溜回來，其中一個進了屋子。他嚇到貓了，貓抓了他一把；他嚇到狗了，狗咬了他一口；他被驢子絆倒，驢子踢了他一腳。公雞開始大聲啼叫。那個強盜跌跌撞撞地逃出屋外，說房子裡有妖怪。所有強盜都嚇跑了，動物們於是就安心住了下來，每天晚上都一起快樂地唱歌。

Vietnamese

Các Nhạc Sĩ Phố Bremen

Một chú lừa già không thể làm việc nặng nhọc được nữa. Chủ không muốn giữ chú. Chú bỏ đi. Chú đi đến Bremen để làm nhạc sĩ. Trên đường đi chú gặp chó, mèo, và gà trống. Chúng cũng già nữa. Chúng cùng đi với lừa.

Các con thú này đến Bremen. Chúng thấy một căn nhà. Chúng thấy có ba tên trộm trong nhà. Ba tên trộm đang ăn một bữa ăn tối thịnh soạn. Các con thú đang đói bụng. Chúng ca hát, và các tên trộm bỏ đi. Các con thú vào nhà và ăn uống. Kế đến chúng đi ngủ.

Ba tên trộm quay trở lại. Một tên vào nhà. Nó làm mèo giật mình, mèo cào nó. Nó làm chó giật mình, chó cắn nó. Nó giẫm lên lừa, lừa đá nó. Gà trống bắt đầu gáy. Tên trộm nói là có ba yêu quái ở trong nhà. Tất cả mấy tên trộm bỏ chạy, nhưng các con thú ở lại. Chúng cùng nhau ca hát mỗi đêm.

Multilingual Summaries

Korean

브레멘의 음악대

당나귀가 늙어 더 이상 일을 못하자 주인은 당나귀가 필요 없어진다. 당나귀는 도망쳐서 음악가가 되려고 브레멘으로 가는 도중 개와 고양이, 수탉을 만나게 된다. 이들도 당나귀와 같이 모두 늙었고 같이 떠나기로 한다.

브레멘에 온 동물들은 집을 하나 발견하는데 그 안에는 저녁을 배불리 먹고 있는 도둑 세 명이 있다. 배가 고픈 동물들은 노래를 해서 도둑들을 쫓아내고 집 안에 들어가 음식을 먹고 잠이 든다.

도둑들이 돌아온다. 그 중 한 명이 집 안으로 들어와서 고양이를 놀래 키자 고양이가 그를 할퀸다. 또 개를 놀래 켜 개에게 물리고 당나귀에 발이 걸려 넘어지자 이번엔 당나귀가 그를 차버린다. 수탉은 울기 시작하고… 도둑은 집에 괴물이 있다고 말하고 모두 도망을 가지만 남아 있는 동물들은 매일 밤 함께 노래를 부른다.

Hmong

Lub Zos Bremen Tus Tub Txawj Suab Nkauj

Ib tug zag laus laus ua tsis taus haujlwm hnyav ntxiv lawm. Nws tus tswv los tsis yuav nws lawm thiab. Nws thiaj khiav mus rau lub zos Bremen mus ua ib tug tub txawj suab nkauj. Thaum nws tabtom mus nws ntsib ib tug dev, ib tug miv, thiab ib tug lau qaib. Lawv kuj laus laus lawm thiab. Lawv thiaj nrog zag mus.

Cov tsiaj tuaj mus txog lub zos Bremen. Lawv pom ib lub tsev. Lawv pom peb tug tub sab nyob rau hauv lub tsev. Cov tub sab noj ib pluag hmo loj kawg nkaus. Cov tsiaj no kuj tshaib plab. Lawv hu nkauj ces cov tub sab thiaj li tawm mus lawm. Cov tsiaj mus sab hauv mus noj mov. Ces lawv thiaj li mus pw.

Cov tub sab rov qab los. Ib tug tub sab xub nkag mus hauv tsev ua ntej. Nws ua rau tus miv ceeb tus miv thiaj li khawb nws. Nws ua rau tus dev ceeb tus dev thiaj li tom nws. Nws dawm ko taw ntawm tus zag, tus zag thiaj li ncaws nws. Tus lau qaib thiaj li qua. Cov tub sab hais tias muaj dab nyob rau hauv lub tsev. Tagnrho cov tub sab thiaj li khiav tas lawm, tiamsis cov tsiaj nyob. Lawv hu nkauj txhua txhua hmo.

A Turkey for Thanksgiving

Student Edition pages 286–302

Week at a Glance	Customize instruction every day for your English Language Learners.				
	Day 1	**Day 2**	**Day 3**	**Day 4**	**Day 5**
Teacher's Edition	Use the ELL Notes that appear throughout each day of the lesson to support instruction and reading.				
ELL Poster 10	• Assess Prior Knowledge • Develop Concepts and Vocabulary	• Preteach High-Frequency Words	• Let's Celebrate!	• Fourth of July Riddles	• Monitor Progress
ELL Teaching Guide	• Picture It! Lesson, pp. 64–65 • Multilingual Summaries, pp. 68–70	• ELL Reader Lesson, pp. 230–231	• Vocabulary Activities and Word Cards, pp. 66–67 • Multilingual Summaries, pp. 68–70		
ELL Readers	• Reread *Big News in the Barn*	• Teach *A Thanksgiving Party*	• Reread *A Thanksgiving Party* and other texts to build fluency		
ELL and Transition Handbook	Use the following as needed to support this week's instruction and to conduct alternative assessments: • Phonics Transition Lessons • Grammar Transition Lessons • Assessment				

Picture It! Comprehension Lesson

Draw Conclusions

Use this lesson to supplement or replace the skill lesson on pages 283a–283b of the Teacher's Edition.

Teach

Distribute copies of the Picture It! blackline master on page 65.

- Ask children to look at the picture and tell what is happening.
- Read the paragraph aloud. Ask: *How do the children feel? How do you know?*
- Share the Skill Points (at right) with children.
- Have children look at the picture and paragraph to draw conclusions about the story.

Practice

Read aloud the directions on page 65. Have children answer the questions about drawing conclusions.

Answers for page 65: 1. Tabitha is eight years old. There are eight candles on her cake. **2.** Tabitha is happy because it is her birthday, and she is having fun at her party. **3.** Tabitha might wish for a horse. There are horses on her t-shirt and on all of her party decorations.

Skill Points

✓ When you **draw a conclusion,** you figure out something about the characters and what happens in a story.

✓ To draw conclusions, use what you already know and what you read.

✓ Look for clues in the story to help you draw conclusions.

✓ Ask: *Does my conclusion make sense?*

Name ______________________________

Look at the picture. **Read** the paragraph.

A Birthday Party

Today is Tabitha's birthday. Her friends have come for a party. Everybody is having a good time. They have played games, and now it is time for cake. The cake looks very tasty. Before they eat, they will sing *Happy Birthday.* Then Tabitha will blow out the candles and make a wish.

Answer the questions below.

1. How old is Tabitha? How do you know?

____

____

2. Why is Tabitha happy?

____

____

3. What do you think Tabitha might wish for? Why do you think that?

____

____

Vocabulary Activities and Word Cards

Copy the Word Cards on page 67 as needed for the following activities.
Use the blank card for an additional word that you want to teach.
Also see suggestions for teaching vocabulary in the ELL and Transition Handbook.

Word Hunt	Cloze Sentences	Word Toss
• Divide children into pairs. Give each pair one Word Card, saying each word aloud as you hand out the cards. • Challenge pairs to find their words in classroom books or other environmental print. Have them show where they find each word and write the phrase or sentence where they find it. • Invite pairs to share their findings with the class.	• Give each child a set of Word Cards. Have children place the cards face up in front of them. • Write these cloze sentences on the board, leaving out the high-frequency word: *I stand [behind] Ana in line. We [brought] snacks to eat. The [door] is open. [Everybody] is here now. We will start in one [minute]. I made a [promise] to my friend. I am [sorry] that I am late.* • Read each sentence as a group, and have children hold up the Word Card for each missing word. • Ask a volunteer to write the missing word on the board and reread the sentence with the word in place.	• Tape one set of Word Cards onto an open space on the floor. Provide a mini beanbag or a small stuffed toy. • Have a child gently toss the beanbag onto one of the words on the floor. If the bag does not fall directly on a word, have the child use the word that is closest to the bag. • Ask the child to read the word and then use it in a sentence. • Play the game until each child has had at least one turn to throw the beanbag and use a word in a sentence.

behind

brought

door

everybody

minute

promise

sorry

Multilingual Summaries

English

A Turkey for Thanksgiving

Mr. and Mrs. Moose were setting the table for Thanksgiving dinner. Sheep, the Goats, Porcupine, and Rabbit were coming. Mrs. Moose wanted a turkey. Mr. Moose went to find one.

He met his friends while he looked for a turkey. They helped him to look. They came to Turkey's house. He tried to get away but could not. The friends took Turkey to Mr. Moose's house.

Inside, Mrs. Moose had everything ready. She was happy to see Turkey. She pulled up a chair for him. Turkey was confused. He thought that he would be the dinner. Mrs. Moose welcomed all her friends, including Turkey, to dinner. Turkey was happy to be sitting at the table.

Spanish

Pavo para el Día de Acción de Gracias

Los Alce preparaban la mesa para la cena del Día de Acción de Gracias. Oveja, las Cabras, Puercoespín y Conejo iban a llegar. La señora Alce quería un pavo. El señor Alce salió a buscar uno.

Mientras buscaba el pavo se encontró con sus amigos. Ellos ayudaron a buscarlo. Cuando llegaron a la casa de Pavo él trató de escaparse, pero no pudo. Los amigos lo agarraron y lo llevaron a la casa del señor Alce.

Adentro, la señora Alce tenía todo preparado. Ella estaba muy contenta de ver a Pavo. Le buscó una silla y lo invitó a sentarse. Pavo estaba confundido. Pensaba que él iba a ser la cena. La señora Alce les dio la bienvenida a la cena a todos sus amigos, incluyendo a Pavo. Pavo estaba feliz de estar sentado a la mesa.

Multilingual Summaries

Chinese

感恩節的火雞

摩斯夫婦正在佈置感恩節晚餐的餐桌。綿羊、山羊、豪豬和兔子都來了。摩斯太太想要一隻火雞，於是摩斯先生出門找火雞。

正在找的時候，摩斯先生遇到了朋友，他們全都要幫他找火雞。大家一起去到火雞家，火雞試著要逃跑，可是卻找不到出路，於是大家就把火雞帶到摩斯家去。

屋子裡，摩斯太太已經把所有東西都準備好了。看到火雞的時候，她非常高興，連忙為他拉了張椅子，請他坐。火雞滿頭霧水，他原本以為自己會變成感恩節的大餐。摩斯太太熱情招待所有朋友一起吃晚餐，也招待了火雞。火雞很高興自己也可以坐下來吃感恩節晚餐。

Vietnamese

Một Con Gà Lôi cho Lễ Tạ Ơn

Ông và Bà Nai đang đặt bàn cho bữa ăn tối vào Lễ Tạ Ơn. Cừu, Dê, Nhím, và Thỏ sắp đến. Bà Nai muốn có một con gà lôi. Ông Nai đi ra tìm một con.

Ông gặp hết thảy bạn bè của mình khi ông đi tìm gà lôi. Ai cũng giúp ông tìm. Họ đến nhà của Gà Lôi, Gà Lôi muốn thoát đi nhưng không thoát được. Những người bạn mang Gà Lôi đến nhà Ông Nai.

Bên trong nhà, Bà Nai đã chuẩn bị mọi thứ sẵn sàng. Bà vui mừng được gặp Gà Lôi. Bà kéo ghế mời Gà Lôi. Gà Lôi lúng túng. Nó đã tưởng là mình sẽ bị làm thịt cho bữa ăn tối. Bà Nai đón tiếp tất cả bạn bè của bà ấy, kể cả Gà Lôi, đến bữa ăn. Gà Lôi vui mừng được ngồi ăn tại bàn.

Multilingual Summaries

Korean

추수감사절 칠면조

무스 부부는 추수감사절 식사를 위해 식탁을 차리고 있고 식사엔 양과 염소, 고슴도치, 토끼가 참석하기로 했다. 무스 부인이 칠면조도 왔으면 좋겠다고 해서 무스씨는 칠면조를 찾아 나선다.

칠면조를 찾는 동안 무스씨는 친구들을 만나 모두 함께 칠면조를 찾아 나선다. 그들이 칠면조의 집에 도착하자 칠면조는 도망가려 하지만 실패한다. 친구들은 칠면조를 무스씨의 집에 데리고 간다.

집 안에서 모든 준비를 마친 무스 부인은 칠면조를 보고 반가워하며 칠면조를 위해 의자를 빼어 자리를 내준다. 칠면조는 자기가 저녁 식사로 먹힐 줄 알았기 때문에 어리둥절해하지만 무스 부인은 저녁 식사에 온 칠면조를 포함한 모든 친구들을 환영한다. 칠면조는 함께 식탁에 앉게 되어 행복해한다.

Hmong

Noj Qaib Ntxw Rau Thanksgiving

Ob niam txiv Moose rau hmo noj rau Thanksgiving. Tus Yaj, tus tshis, tus tsaug, thiab tus kab tais yuav tuaj thiab. Tus niamtsev Moose nws xav yuav ib tug qaib ntxw. Ces tus txivtsev Moose thiaj li mus nrhiav ib tug.

Nws kuj pom tagnrho nws cov phoojywg thaum nws mus yos ib tug qaib ntxw. Lawv kuj pab nws nrhiav thiab. Lawv mus txog rau Qaib Ntxw lub tsev. Nws twb yuav tawm khiav tiamsis nws tawm tsis tau. Cov phoojywg coj Qaib Ntxwv rau tom tus txivtsev Moose lub tsev.

Thaum mus txog sab hauv tsev, tus niamtsev Moose twb npaj tau txhua yam tiav lawm. Nws zoo siab thaum nws pom tus Qaib Ntxwv. Nws rub ib lub rooj rau nws zaum. Ua rau Qaib Ntxw ntxov siab. Nws xav tias lawv yuav muab nws ua lawv pluas hmo. Tus Niamtsev Moose tos txias tagnrho nws cov phoojywg txhua tus thiab rau Qaib Ntxw uas tau tuaj nrog nkawd noj hmo. Qaib Ntxw zoo siab uas tau zaum ntawm lub rooj noj mov.

Pearl and Wagner

Student Edition pages 320–337

Week at a Glance	Customize instruction every day for your English Language Learners.				
	Day 1	**Day 2**	**Day 3**	**Day 4**	**Day 5**
Teacher's Edition	Use the ELL Notes that appear throughout each day of the lesson to support instruction and reading.				
ELL Poster 11	• Assess Prior Knowledge • Develop Concepts and Vocabulary	• Preteach High-Frequency Words	• Mad Scientists	• Inventions at Home	• Monitor Progress
ELL Teaching Guide	• Picture It! Lesson, pp. 71–72 • Multilingual Summaries, pp. 75–77	• ELL Reader Lesson, pp. 232–233	• Vocabulary Activities and Word Cards, pp. 73–74 • Multilingual Summaries, pp. 75–77		
ELL Readers	• Reread *A Thanksgiving Party*	• Teach *Ada's Castle*	• Reread *Ada's Castle* and other texts to build fluency		
ELL and Transition Handbook	Use the following as needed to support this week's instruction and to conduct alternative assessments: • Phonics Transition Lessons • Grammar Transition Lessons • Assessment				

Picture It! Comprehension Lesson

Author's Purpose

Use this lesson to supplement or replace the skill lesson on pages 317a–317b of the Teacher's Edition.

Teach

Distribute copies of the Picture It! blackline master on page 72.

- Ask children to look at the pictures and describe what happens.
- Read the sentences aloud. Ask: *Was this story funny, serious, or sad? Why do you think so?*
- Share the Skill Points (at right) with children.
- Have children look at the pictures and sentences to find clues about the author's purpose.

Practice

Read aloud the directions on page 72. Have children answer the questions about the story.

Answers for page 72: 1. Her glasses get wet and she cannot see. **2.** He thinks of glasses that have wipers on them. **3.** (Guide children in a discussion of the author's purpose.) Sample response: I think the author wrote this story to entertain me because the glasses are a funny invention. I also think the author wrote the story to show me that children can have good ideas.

Skill Points

- ✓ Keep in mind that the author has a **reason** or **purpose** for writing.
- ✓ An author can write to explain something.
- ✓ An author can write to tell a funny story.
- ✓ An author can write to try to get the reader to think or act in a certain way.

Name ______________________

Look at the pictures. **Read** the sentences.

A Creative Idea

It was raining hard outside, so Amy and Amir stayed inside. They drew pictures of their last soccer game. "I don't like to play soccer in the rain," said Amy. "My glasses get all wet and I can't see."

That gave Amir a great idea. If Amy's glasses had wipers like a car, she would never have to worry about the rain again!

Amy's mom is an inventor. She made Amy a pair of the glasses with wipers, and they worked. Amir's idea was very good. Maybe he will be an inventor too!

Answer the questions below.

1. What problem does Amy have in the rain?

____

____

2. What does Amir think of to solve Amy's problem?

____

3. Talk about why you think the author wrote this story.

Vocabulary Activities and Word Cards

Copy the Word Cards on page 74 as needed for the following activities.
Use the blank card for an additional word that you want to teach.
Also see suggestions for teaching vocabulary in the ELL and Transition Handbook.

Word Card Jar	Teacher's Chair	Home Language Connection
• Put one set of Word Cards in a jar. • Ask a volunteer to pick a word out of the jar, read it, and chant the spelling. For example, if the word *village* is selected, the child will say *village, v-i-l-l-a-g-e*. The other children repeat the word and the spelling. • The child with the card says a sentence using the word. The other children then repeat the sentence. • Continue with children taking turns drawing from the jar until all the Word Cards have been used. Also, make sure each child has had a turn selecting a word.	• Use one set of Word Cards. Invite a child to sit in your chair and "teach" the other children. • Ask the child to choose a Word Card, show it to the group, and read the word. Then have the child use the word in a sentence or define the word. Have the other children repeat after the "teacher." • Allow each child at least one turn in the teacher's chair.	• Pair children with the same home language and give each pair one set of Word Cards. • Ask one child to choose a card and say a sentence using the high-frequency word. • Have the other child translate the sentence into their home language. • Have children take turns using both languages.

guess	**pretty**
science	**shoe**
village	**watch**
won	

Multilingual Summaries

English

Pearl and Wagner: Two Good Friends

Pearl wants to make a robot for the Science Fair. Wagner says that he will win a prize.

Pearl makes a robot. Its mouth opens when Pearl pulls a string.

Wagner did not make anything. Pearl shows the robot to their teacher. Its head falls off. Pearl and Wagner fix it.

The judge comes to see the robot. It breaks again. Wagner climbs inside the robot. He speaks to the judge. She thinks that the robot talks! Then she finds Wagner inside.

The friends do not win a prize. Pearl knows that Wagner wanted to help. She is happy that she and Wagner are friends.

Spanish

Pearl y Wagner: Dos buenos amigos

Pearl quiere hacer un robot para la Feria de ciencias. Wagner dice que él ganará un premio.

Pearl hace un robot. Cuando Pearl tira de una cuerda, al robot se le abre la boca.

Wagner no hizo nada. Pearl le muestra el robot a la maestra. Al robot se le cae la cabeza. Pearl y Wagner se la arreglan.

La jueza llega a ver el robot. Éste se vuelve a romper. Wagner se mete dentro del robot y le habla a la jueza. ¡Ella piensa que el robot habla! Luego encuentra a Wagner adentro.

Los amigos no ganan el premio. Pearl sabe que Wagner quería ayudar. Ella está feliz porque Wagner y ella son amigos.

Multilingual Summaries

Chinese

珮兒和華格納是好朋友

珮兒想做個機械人參加科學比賽，華格納說他一定會贏。

珮兒的機械人做好了，只要繩子一拉，機械人的嘴巴就會張開。

華格納沒有做出任何東西來。珮兒把機械人拿給老師看，但是機械人的頭掉了下來。珮兒和華格納一起把它修好。

的時候，評判走過來看珮兒的機械人，可是機械人又壞了。華格納趕緊爬到機械人裡面去，躲在裡面跟評審說話。評審以為機械人會說話！不過後來她發現了躲在裡面的華格納。

比賽輸了，不過珮兒知道華格納只是想幫忙。珮兒很開心，因為她知道華格納是她的好朋友。

Vietnamese

Pearl và Wagner
Hai Người Bạn Thân

Cô bé Pearl muốn làm một người máy cho buổi Triển Lãm Khoa Học. Wagner nói là cậu sẽ đoạt giải thưởng.

Pearl làm một người máy. Khi Pearl kéo một sợi dây thì miệng của người máy mở ra.

Wagner không làm vật gì hết. Pearl đưa người máy cho thầy giáo xem. Đầu của người máy bị rớt. Pearl và Wagner sửa lại.

Vị giám khảo đến xem người máy. Người máy bị hư lần nữa. Wagner leo vào bên trong người máy. Cậu nói chuyện với vị giám khảo. Bà giám khảo nghĩ là người máy biết nói! Sau đó bà tìm ra là Wagner ở bên trong.

Đôi bạn không được giải thưởng. Pearl biết là Wagner muốn giúp mình. Cô bé vui mừng rằng mình và Wagner là bạn.

Multilingual Summaries

Korean

펄과 와그너는 좋은 친구

펄은 과학박람회에 낼 로봇을 만들고 싶어한다. 친구 와그너는 펄이 상을 탈 것이라고 얘기해준다.

펄은 줄을 잡아당기면 입이 벌어지는 로봇을 만든다.

와그너는 아무것도 만들지 않는다. 펄이 선생님께 로봇을 보여드리다가 그만 로봇의 머리가 떨어지자 와그너는 펄과 함께 로봇을 고친다.

박람회에서 심사위원이 로봇을 보러 왔지만 로봇이 또 고장 난다. 그러자 와그너는 로봇 안으로 기어올라가 심사위원에게 말을 한다. 펄은 로봇이 말을 하는 줄 알고 놀라지만 곧 그 안에 들어있는 와그너를 발견한다.

두 친구는 상을 타지는 못했지만 펄은 와그너가 자신을 도와주려 했다는 걸 알고는 그와 친구라는 사실에 기뻐한다.

Hmong

Pearl thiab Wagner Ob Tug Phoojywg Zoo

Pearl xav txua ib tug hlau uas txawj mus kev rau lub Science Fair. Wagner hais tias nws yuav yeej ib qho nqi zog.

Pearl txua tau ib tug hlau mus kev. Tus hlau no rua nws lub qhov ncauj thaum Pearl rub txoj hlua.

Wagner tsis ua ib yam dabtsi li. Pearl muab tus hlau no rau nws tus nais khus saib. Nws lub taubhau cia li hle los. Pearl thiab Wagner nkawd thiaj li kho rau.

Tus txiavtxim thiaj los saib tus hlau no. Lub taubhau rov qab hle dua thiab. Wagner thiaj li nce mus nyob sab hauv tus hlau no. Nws hais lus rau tus txiavtxim. Tus txiavtxim xav tias tus hlau no txawj hais lus. Ces nws txawm pom Wagner nyob sab hauv.

Ob tug phoojywg tsis yeej nqi zog. Pearl paub tias Wagner yeej txaus siab pab nws. Nws zoo siab tias nws thiab Wagner nkawd yog phoojywg.

Dear Juno Student Edition pages 348–365

Week at a Glance	Customize instruction every day for your English Language Learners.				
	Day 1	**Day 2**	**Day 3**	**Day 4**	**Day 5**
Teacher's Edition	Use the ELL Notes that appear throughout each day of the lesson to support instruction and reading.				
ELL Poster 12	• Assess Prior Knowledge • Develop Concepts and Vocabulary	• Preteach High-Frequency Words	• Let's Make New Friends	• Review Draw Conclusions	• Monitor Progress
ELL Teaching Guide	• Picture It! Lesson, pp. 78–79 • Multilingual Summaries, pp. 82–84	• ELL Reader Lesson, pp. 234–235	• Vocabulary Activities and Word Cards, pp. 80–81 • Multilingual Summaries, pp. 82–84		
ELL Readers	• Reread *Ada's Castle*	• Teach *Letters from Here to There*	• Reread *Letters from Here to There* and other texts to build fluency		
ELL and Transition Handbook	Use the following as needed to support this week's instruction and to conduct alternative assessments: • Phonics Transition Lessons • Grammar Transition Lessons • Assessment				

Picture It! Comprehension Lesson

Draw Conclusions

Use this lesson to supplement or replace the skill lesson on pages 345a–345b of the Teacher's Edition.

Teach

Distribute copies of the Picture It! blackline master on page 79.

- Ask children to look at the pictures and tell what is happening.
- Read the sentences aloud. If necessary, tell what a pen pal is. Ask: *What can you tell about the children in the story?*
- Share the Skill Points (at right) with children.
- Have children look at the pictures to draw a conclusion about the characters in the story.

Practice

Read aloud the directions on page 79. Have children answer the questions about drawing conclusions.

Answers for page 79: 1. He has a dog and two cats. **2.** Possible answer: She has a big family. **3.** Possible answer: Yes, they like being pen pals. They are friends even though they live far apart. They are excited to send and receive the letters.

Skill Points

✓ When you **draw a conclusion**, you figure out more about the characters and what happens in the story.

✓ Use what you read and what you know from real life to draw conclusions.

✓ When you draw a conclusion, ask yourself: *Does that make sense?*

Name ______________________________

Look at the pictures. **Read** the sentences.

Pen Pals

Ignacio is from Mexico City. He is drawing a picture of his pets to send to his pen pal in the United States.

Karen is from California. She is drawing a picture of her family to send to her pen pal in Mexico.

Karen and Ignacio are mailing their letters. They can't wait to learn more about each other!

Answer the questions below.

1. What does Ignacio's drawing tell you about him?

____

2. What does Karen's drawing tell you about her?

____

3. Do you think Karen and Ignacio like being pen pals? Why?

____

Vocabulary Activities and Word Cards

Copy the Word Cards on page 81 as needed for the following activities.
Use the blank card for an additional word that you want to teach.
Also see suggestions for teaching vocabulary in the ELL and Transition Handbook.

Mind Reader	Tell a Story	Everyday Game
• Give each child a set of Word Cards. Have children spread out their cards face up so they can see them. • Write these sentence frames on the board: *This word starts with the letter _____. This word means ______. This word ends with the letter _____.* • Pick up a Word Card and give children clues about the word by reading and completing the sentence frames. • Children hold up the correct Word Card when they believe they have the answer. • The child who correctly guesses the word may choose another card and provide the group with the next riddle. Allow children to use the sentence frames or make up their own clues.	• Give two Word Cards to each child and arrange the children in a circle. • Start a story with a sentence that uses one of the words. For example: *My parents came home early.* • The next child continues the story, finding a way to use one of his or her words in a sentence. Children can help each other make sentences. • Children take turns until all the Word Cards have been used and the group decides that the story is complete.	• Give each child a set of Word Cards in alphabetical order. • Read the words aloud as a group. Then have each child tell what two of the words mean. • As a group, discuss how children might use these words every day. Ask volunteers to give example sentences: *I will write my answer here. My dog keeps me company. We lived in a faraway place.*

answer	**company**
faraway	**parents**
picture	**school**
wash	

Multilingual Summaries

English

Dear Juno

Juno's grandmother lives in Korea. One day, Juno gets a letter from her. He cannot read Korean. He looks at the photograph and the flower that come in the letter. He knows what the letter is about.

Juno writes back to his grandmother. He draws pictures of his family and his dog. He puts in a leaf from his swinging tree. Juno's grandmother writes back. She sends colored pencils, a photograph, and a toy airplane. Juno knows that his grandmother is coming to visit. He is very happy.

Spanish

Querido Juno

La abuela de Juno vive en Corea. Un día, Juno recibe una carta de su abuela. Él no sabe leer coreano. Mira la fotografía y la flor que vienen en la carta. Él sabe de qué se trata la carta.

Juno le contesta la carta a su abuela. Dibuja a su familia y a su perro. Le pone una hoja del árbol donde él se columpia. La abuela de Juno le vuelve a escribir. Le manda lápices de colores, una fotografía y un avión de juguete. Juno sabe que la abuela va a venir a visitarlos. Él está muy feliz.

Multilingual Summaries

Chinese

親愛的朱諾

朱諾的祖母住在韓國。有一天，朱諾收到祖母寄給他的信。他看不懂韓文，不過看到和信一起寄過來的照片和小花，朱諾就明白信的內容了。

朱諾回了一封信給祖母，他畫了一張全家福，連狗狗也畫進去了，還從鞦韆樹上摘了片葉子，一起寄給祖母。不久之後，祖母回信了，她寄了顏色筆、一張照片和一架玩具飛機給朱諾。朱諾知道，祖母要來看他了，他很高興。

Vietnamese

Juno Yêu Quý

Bà của Juno sống ở Hàn Quốc. Một ngày nọ, Juno nhận được một lá thư của bà. Cậu bé không đọc được Hàn ngữ. Cậu nhìn vào tấm ảnh và cành hoa gởi trong thư. Cậu bé hiểu lá thư viết gì.

Juno viết thư lại cho bà. Cậu vẽ hình của gia đình và con chó của cậu. Cậu để vào thư một chiếc lá từ cây treo xích đu của mình. Bà của Juno viết thư lại. Bà gởi bút chì màu, một tấm ảnh, và một chiếc máy bay đồ chơi. Juno hiểu là bà của mình sắp đến thăm. Cậu rất vui mừng.

Multilingual Summaries

Korean

준오에게

어느 날 준오는 한국에 계신 할머니가 보낸 편지를 받지만 한국어를 몰라 편지와 같이 온 사진과 꽃을 보고 편지의 내용을 이해하게 된다.

준오는 할머니에게 답장으로 가족과 개를 그린 그림과 그네가 매달려 있는 나무의 잎을 하나 넣어 보낸다. 할머니는 다시 답장으로 색연필과 사진, 장난감 비행기를 보내준다. 준오는 할머니가 자신을 보러 올 것이라는 것을 알고 매우 행복해한다.

Hmong

Hmov Tshua Txog Juno

Juno pog nyob rau Kauslim tebchaws. Muaj ib hnub Juno txais ib tsab ntawv tuaj ntawm nws. Nws nyeem tsis tau lus Kauslim. Nws tsuas ntsia cov duab thiab cov paj uas nyob rau hauv daim ntawv. Nws paub hais tias daim ntawv ntawd hais txog dabtsi lawm.

Juno sau ntawv teb nws pog daim ntawv. Nws teeb duab txog nws tsevneeg thiab nws tus dev. Nws ntsaws ib daim nplooj uas nyob rau ntawm tsob ntoo nws ua si. Juno pog rov qab sau ntawv tuaj dua. Nws xa tau ib cov xaum thas xim, ib daim duab, thiab ib lub dav hlau ua si tuaj rau nws. Juno paub tias nws pog yuav tuaj xyuas nws. Ua rau nws zoo siab heev.

Anansi Goes Fishing

Student Edition pages 376–394

Week at a Glance	Customize instruction every day for your English Language Learners.				
	Day 1	**Day 2**	**Day 3**	**Day 4**	**Day 5**
Teacher's Edition	Use the ELL Notes that appear throughout each day of the lesson to support instruction and reading.				
ELL Poster 13	• Assess Prior Knowledge • Develop Concepts and Vocabulary	• Preteach High-Frequency Words	• Review Cause and Effect	• Creative Ideas	• Monitor Progress
ELL Teaching Guide	• Picture It! Lesson, pp. 85–86 • Multilingual Summaries, pp. 89–91	• ELL Reader Lesson, pp. 236–237	• Vocabulary Activities and Word Cards, pp. 87–88 • Multilingual Summaries, pp. 89–91		
ELL Readers	• Reread *Letters from Here to There*	• Teach *Webs and Other Catchers*	• Reread *Webs and Other Catchers* and other texts to build fluency		
ELL and Transition Handbook	Use the following as needed to support this week's instruction and to conduct alternative assessments: • Phonics Transition Lessons • Grammar Transition Lessons • Assessment				

Picture It! Comprehension Lesson

Cause and Effect

Use this lesson to supplement or replace the skill lesson on pages 373a–373b of the Teacher's Edition.

Teach

Distribute copies of the Picture It! blackline master on page 86.

- Ask children to look at the pictures and describe what happens.
- Read the sentences aloud. Ask: *Why does Abby get up from the table?* (She needs to get a clip for her hair.)
- Share the Skill Points (at right) with children.
- Have children look at the pictures and sentences to find causes and effects in the story.

Practice

Read aloud the directions on page 86. Have children draw lines to match causes and effects.

Answers for page 86: 1. c **2.** a **3.** b

Skill Points

✓ Keep in mind that most things happen for a reason.

✓ As you read, think about what is happening and why it is happening.

✓ Why something happens is the **effect**. What happens is the **cause**.

Name ______________________________

Look at the pictures. **Read** the sentences.

Champ Has a Snack

Abby sat down to eat her ice cream, but her hair kept getting in the way!

Abby got a clip to hold her hair up. She wanted to taste her ice cream, not her hair. But when she left the table, Champ had a snack!

Abby sent Champ outside. Now she can have some ice cream, but she'll have to get a clean bowl first!

Draw lines to match the causes and effects.

1. Because Abby's hair was in her face,

2. Because Abby left the table,

3. Because Champ ate the ice cream,

a. Champ had a snack.

b. Abby sent Champ out.

c. Abby got a clip.

Vocabulary Activities and Word Cards

Copy the Word Cards on page 88 as needed for the following activities.
Use the blank card for an additional word that you want to teach.
Also see suggestions for teaching vocabulary in the ELL and Transition Handbook.

Cloze Sentences	Go Fish	Poster Descriptions
• Give each child a set of Word Cards. Have children place the cards face up in front of them. • Write these cloze sentences on the board, leaving a blank line in place of the high-frequency word: *We have [been] working hard. Do you [believe] his story? I [caught] a fish in the pond. It is [finally] time to go home. We played at the park [today]. We will go back to the park [tomorrow]. We can play [whatever] game you like.* • Read each sentence as a group and have children hold up the Word Card for the missing word. • Ask a volunteer to write the missing word on the board and reread the sentence with the word in place.	• Have small groups of children play Go Fish. Give each group four sets of Word Cards. • One child mixes the cards, gives five cards to each child, and places the remaining cards face down in a stack. • Before play begins, children look at their cards and lay down any matching pairs, saying the high-frequency words aloud. • Then the first player chooses a card in his or her hand and asks one other player for a matching card. For example: *Do you have the word* been? • If the other player has the card, he or she must give it up. The first player then puts down the pair, says the high-frequency word, and uses it in a sentence. If not, the other player says *Go Fish*, and the first player picks a card from the pile. • Play continues until all the pairs have been made.	• Give one set of Word Cards to each child. Have children place the cards face up so they can see them during the activity. • Make sure the ELL Poster for Unit 3, Week 3 is visible. • Ask children to say an original sentence that uses one of the words and describes an aspect of the Poster. • Continue until each child has had the opportunity to make up a sentence.

been	**believe**
caught	**finally**
today	**tomorrow**
whatever	

Multilingual Summaries

English

Anansi Goes Fishing

Turtle will teach Anansi to fish. Anansi is lazy. He plans to make Turtle do all the work.

Turtle says that when he works, he becomes tired. Turtle says that now he can work, and Anansi can become tired. Because lazy Anansi doesn't want to be tired, he decides to work.

Anansi makes a net, catches a fish, and cooks the fish. While Anansi works, Turtle sleeps.

Turtle says that when he eats, he becomes full. Turtle says that now he will eat and Anansi will become full. Because greedy Anansi wants to be full, he lets Turtle eat the fish. Turtle is full. Anansi is not.

Spanish

Anansi va a pescar

Tortuga le va a enseñar a Anansi a pescar. Anansi es perezoso. Planea dejar que Tortuga haga todo el trabajo.

Tortuga dice que cuando trabaja, se siente cansado. Tortuga le dice que ahora él va a trabajar y Anansi va a sentirse cansado. Como Anansi no quiere sentirse cansado, decide trabajar.

Anansi hace una red, atrapa un pescado y lo cocina. Mientras Anansi trabaja, Tortuga duerme.

Tortuga dice que cuando come, se siente lleno. Tortuga le dice que ahora él va a comer y Anansi va a sentirse lleno. Como el glotón Anansi quiere estar lleno, deja que Tortuga se coma el pescado. Tortuga está lleno, pero Anansi no.

Multilingual Summaries

Chinese

蜘蛛捕魚

烏龜要教蜘蛛捕魚，可是蜘蛛很懶惰，他想叫烏龜做所有的工作。

烏龜說只要他一工作，蜘蛛就會很累，現在他可以工作，不過累的是蜘蛛。因為懶惰的蜘蛛不想很累，所以他決定自己去工作。

蜘蛛結了一張網，捕到了魚，還把魚煮好。蜘蛛在工作的時候，烏龜卻在睡覺。

烏龜說只要他一吃東西，蜘蛛就會覺得飽，現在他要吃東西，不過會覺得飽的是蜘蛛。因為貪心的蜘蛛想吃得很飽，所以就讓烏龜吃魚。結果是烏龜飽了，蜘蛛卻還是很餓。

Vietnamese

Anansi Đi Câu Cá

Rùa sẽ dạy cho Anansi câu cá. Anansi lười biếng. Nó dự định là sẽ để cho Rùa làm hết mọi việc.

Rùa nói là khi nào Rùa làm việc, nó bị mệt. Rùa nói rằng bây giờ nó có thể làm việc và Anansi có thể bị mệt mỏi. Vì Anansi lười biếng không muốn bị mệt, nó quyết định đi làm việc.

Anansi làm một cái lưới, bắt được một con cá, và nấu con cá này. Trong khi Anansi làm việc thì Rùa ta ngủ.

Rùa nói khi nào nó ăn, nó bị no. Rùa nói bây giờ nó sẽ ăn và Anansi sẽ được no. Vì Anansi tham lam muốn được no, nó để Rùa ăn con cá. Rùa no bụng. Anansi bị đói.

Multilingual Summaries

Korean

낚시하러 간 아난시

거북이는 아난시에게 낚시하는 법을 가르쳐주려 하지만 게으른 아난시는 거북이가 모든 일을 다 하게 만들 계획이다.

거북이는 일을 하면 피곤해진다면서, 이제는 자기가 일을 하고 아난시가 피곤해질 차례라고 말한다. 게으른 아난시는 피곤해지고 싶지 않아 일을 하기로 하는데…

그물을 만들어 물고기를 잡고 요리를 하는 아난시. 아난시가 일하는 동안 거북이는 잠을 잔다.

거북이는 음식을 먹으면 배가 불러진다면서, 이제는 자기가 음식을 먹고 아난시의 배가 불러질 차례라고 말한다. 욕심 많은 아난시는 배불러지고 싶어 거북이가 생선을 먹도록 해 준다. 결국 거북이는 배가 부르지만 아난시는 그렇지 않다.

Hmong

Anansi Mus Nuv Ntses

Vaubkib yuav qhia Anansi nuv ntses. Anansi tub nkeeg. Nws xav kom Vaubkib ua tagnrho cov haujlwm rau nws.

Vaubkib hais tais thaum nws ua haujlwm ces ua rau nws nkees nkees. Vaubkib hais tias cia nws mam li ua haujlwm es cia Anansi mam li ua tus nkees nkees. Vim rau qhov Anansi tsis xav ua tus nkees nkees nws thiaj txiavtxim mus ua haujlwm.

Anansi mus ua ib lub zes, mus nuv ntses, thiab muab ntses coj los ua noj. Thaum Anansi ua haujlwm, Vaubkib pw.

Vaubkib hais tias nws tsau plam heev thaum nws noj mov tag. Vaubkis hais tias ziag no nws yuav noj xwb es Anansi mam ua tus tsau plab. Vim rau qhov Anansi yog ib tug neeg cuaj khaum nws mam li cia Vaubkib noj tus ntses. Vaubkib thiaj tsau plab. Anansi thiaj li tsis tsau plab.

Rosa and Blanca

Student Edition pages 406–417

Week at a Glance	Customize instruction every day for your English Language Learners.				
	Day 1	**Day 2**	**Day 3**	**Day 4**	**Day 5**
Teacher's Edition	Use the ELL Notes that appear throughout each day of the lesson to support instruction and reading.				
ELL Poster 14	• Assess Prior Knowledge • Develop Concepts and Vocabulary	• Preteach High-Frequency Words	• Fruit Market Skits	• Problems and Solutions	• Monitor Progress
ELL Teaching Guide	• Picture It! Lesson, pp. 92–93 • Multilingual Summaries, pp. 96–98	• ELL Reader Lesson, pp. 238–239	• Vocabulary Activities and Word Cards, pp. 94–95 • Multilingual Summaries, pp. 96–98		
ELL Readers	• Reread *Webs and Other Catchers*	• Teach *American Hero Day*	• Reread *American Hero Day* and other texts to build fluency		
ELL and Transition Handbook	Use the following as needed to support this week's instruction and to conduct alternative assessments: • Phonics Transition Lessons • Grammar Transition Lessons • Assessment				

Picture It! Comprehension Lesson

Theme and Plot

Use this lesson to supplement or replace the skill lesson on pages 403a–403b of the Teacher's Edition.

Teach

Distribute copies of the Picture It! blackline master on page 93.

- Ask children to look at the pictures and tell what is happening.
- Read the sentences aloud. Ask: *What happens first in the story?*
- Share the Skill Points (at right) with children.
- Have children look at the pictures and sentences to determine what the theme of the story is.

Practice

Read aloud the directions on page 93. Have children fill in the chart and answer the question about theme.

Answers for page 93: *First:* Damon's dad carries a big bag. Damon offers to help with his wagon. *Next:* His dad drops the bag and spills the plant food. *Last:* His dad borrows the wagon. Sample response: The big idea of this story is that sometimes we can all use a little help.

Skill Points

✓ The **plot** is what happens in the beginning, middle, and end of a story.

✓ Every story has one big idea, or **theme.**

✓ Pay attention to what happens and the order in which it happens. What happens in the story can help you figure out the big idea.

Name ______________________________

Look at the pictures. **Read** the sentences.

- **Fill** in the boxes below. **Write** what happens first, next, and last in the story. Then answer the question.

Damon's Wagon

Damon's father bought plant food to help the grass grow. The bag was very heavy! Damon offered his wagon to help his father, but his father said no.

The bag was too heavy. Damon's father dropped it and it broke. Plant food spilled all over the driveway.

Damon's father decided to use the wagon after all. Damon was very happy to help!

What do you think is the big idea of this story? Talk about it.

Vocabulary Activities and Word Cards

Copy the Word Cards on page 95 as needed for the following activities.
Use the blank card for an additional word that you want to teach.
Also see suggestions for teaching vocabulary in the ELL and Transition Handbook.

Puzzle Pieces	Concentration	Bingo
• Give pairs of children one set of Word Cards. • Have children cut each of the cards into two puzzle pieces of different shapes. • Ask children to mix up the puzzle pieces, lay them face up, and take turns putting words back together. As they do so, they should read the words aloud. • Once all the Word Cards have been reassembled, have children write or say sentences using each word.	• Divide children into pairs and give each pair one set of Word Cards. Also give seven (or eight) blank cards to each pair. • Have children write one of the words on each blank card. • When they finish writing, have children mix all the cards together and spread them out face down. • Children take turns picking up a card, reading it aloud, and trying to find its match. • When a child finds a match, he or she says a sentence using that word and keeps the cards. • The game ends when all the cards have been matched.	• Give each child a set of Word Cards. Have children paste six of their cards on a piece of paper in two columns with three rows. • Pass out coins, beans, or other counters to use as bingo chips. • Say the definition of or a phrase that describes one of the words. For example: *This is the opposite of* oldest. *(youngest); The opposite of* sell *is* ______. *(buy)* Have children look for the correct word and cover it with a chip. If necessary, announce the answer before moving on to the next word. • A child calls *bingo* and wins the game when he or she has placed bingo chips on three words in a row. • You may wish to have children trade bingo boards and play the game again.

alone	**buy**
daughters	**half**
many	**their**
youngest	

Multilingual Summaries

English

Rosa and Blanca

Rosa and Blanca are sisters. The sisters help each other. This makes their mother happy.

The sisters grow up. The sisters still help each other. Each wants to give half of her vegetables from her garden to the other. At night, each leaves vegetables in the other sister's kitchen. The sisters pass each other in the dark. In the morning, each sister is surprised. There are so many vegetables!

One day, Rosa is home when Blanca brings vegetables to her kitchen. Now the sisters understand. They tell their mother. Their mother is very happy. She says that she is the luckiest mother in the world.

Spanish

Rosa y Blanca

Rosa y Blanca son hermanas. Las hermanas se ayudan la una a la otra. Esto hace a su mamá muy feliz.

Las hermanas crecen. Ellas todavía se ayudan. Cada una quiere darle a la otra la mitad de los vegetales de su jardín. Por la noche, cada una le deja a la otra vegetales en la cocina. Las hermanas se cruzan en la oscuridad. En la mañana, cada hermana se sorprende. ¡Hay tantos vegetales!

Un día, Rosa está en la casa cuando Blanca lleva los vegetales a su cocina. Ahora las hermanas comprenden lo que pasa. Le cuentan a su mamá. Su mamá está muy feliz. Dice que es la mamá más afortunada del mundo.

Multilingual Summaries

Chinese

羅莎與布蘭卡

羅莎和布蘭卡是姊妹，兩人相親相愛，彼此幫忙，這讓媽媽覺得很高興。

兩姊妹長大後，還是一樣互相幫忙。兩個人都想把自己園子裡的蔬菜分一半給對方，於是就利用晚上，偷偷地把菜放到對方家裡的廚房。兩人在黑暗中擦身而過，彼此都沒有發覺。第二天一早醒來，兩姊妹都嚇了一跳，因為家裡竟然有很多蔬菜！

有一天，羅莎在家，剛巧看見布蘭卡把蔬菜放在她家廚房裡，這時兩姐妹才明白到底是怎麼一回事。她們把事情告訴媽媽，媽媽非常開心，並說自己是全世界最幸運的媽媽。

Vietnamese

Rosa và Blanca

Rosa và Blanca là hai chị em gái. Hai chị em này giúp đỡ nhau. Điều này làm cho mẹ của hai người rất vui lòng.

Hai chị em lớn lên. Họ vẫn còn giúp đỡ nhau. Mỗi người đều muốn cho phân nửa rau quả trồng ở vườn của mình cho người kia. Ban đêm, mỗi người mang rau quả đến để trong bếp của người kia. Hai chị em đi ngang nhau trong đêm tối. Đến sáng, mỗi chị đều ngạc nhiên. Có nhiều rau quả quá!

Một ngày nọ, Rosa đang ở nhà khi Blanca mang rau quả vào bếp của mình. Bấy giờ, hai chị em chợt hiểu. Họ nói cho mẹ nghe. Mẹ rất vui. Mẹ nói rằng bà là người mẹ may mắn nhất đời.

Multilingual Summaries

Korean

로사와 블랑카

로사와 블랑카 자매는 서로를 도와줘 엄마를 기쁘게 해드린다.

자매는 자라서도 여전히 서로를 도와준다. 각자의 정원에서 키운 야채의 반을 서로에게 주고 싶어 밤이 되면 서로의 부엌으로 가 야채를 놓고 온다. 어두운 밤이라 두 사람은 서로 알아보지 못하고 스쳐 지난다. 아침이 되면 부엌에 야채가 많이 쌓여있는 것을 보고 놀란다.

어느 날 로사가 집에 있는 동안 블랑카가 부엌에 야채를 몰래 가져다 놓는 것을 본다. 자매는 이제 모든 것을 이해하게 되고 엄마에게 이 이야기를 한다. 엄마는 이런 딸들을 두어 세상에서 가장 행복한 엄마라며 기뻐한다.

Hmong

Rosa thiab Blanca

Rosa thiab Blanca nkawd yog viv ncaus. Ob tug viv ncaus no ib leeg pab ib leeg. Qhov no ua rau nkawd niam zoo siab.

Ob tug viv ncaus tau loj los. Nkawd yeej tseem ib leeg pab ib leeg. Nkawd ib leeg xav faib ib leeg ib nrab zaub uas nyob hauv nkawd lub vaj. Thaum tsaus ntuj, nkawd ib leeg zais ib leeg ib cov zaum nqa tuaj tso rau hauv chav ua noj haus. Hmo ntuj nkawd ua li no los nkawd tsis sib pom li. Thaum sawv ntxov, ob tug viv ncaus ceeb. Ua cas yuav muaj cov zaub ntau ua luaj li.

Muaj ib hnub, Rosa nyob hauv tsev thaum nws pom Blanca nqa cov zaub tuaj tso rau nws chav ua noj haus. Ziag no ob tug viv ncaus no mam li totaub. Nkawd mus qhia rau nkawd niam. Nkawd niam zoo siab heev. Nws hais tias nws yog ib leej niam uas muaj hmoo tshaj plaws nyob rau hauv lub ntiajteb no.

A Weed Is a Flower

Student Edition pages 430–451

Week at a Glance	Day 1	Day 2	Day 3	Day 4	Day 5
	Customize instruction every day for your English Language Learners.				
Teacher's Edition	Use the ELL Notes that appear throughout each day of the lesson to support instruction and reading.				
ELL Poster 15	• Assess Prior Knowledge • Develop Concepts and Vocabulary	• Preteach High-Frequency Words	• Creative Sandwich Ideas	• Cooking Shows	• Monitor Progress
ELL Teaching Guide	• Picture It! Lesson, pp. 99–100 • Multilingual Summaries, pp. 103–105	• ELL Reader Lesson, pp. 240–241	• Vocabulary Activities and Word Cards, pp. 101–102 • Multilingual Summaries, pp. 103–105		
ELL Readers	• Reread *American Hero Day*	• Teach *Inventions Help People*	• Reread *Inventions Help People* and other texts to build fluency		
ELL and Transition Handbook	Use the following as needed to support this week's instruction and to conduct alternative assessments: • Phonics Transition Lessons • Grammar Transition Lessons • Assessment				

Picture It! Comprehension Lesson

Cause and Effect

Use this lesson to supplement or replace the skill lesson on pages 427a–427b of the Teacher's Edition.

Teach

Distribute copies of the Picture It! blackline master on page 100.

- Ask children to look at the pictures and talk about what they see.
- Read the sentences aloud. Ask: *What is different between the first picture and the last picture?*
- Share the Skill Points (at right) with children.
- Have children look at the pictures and sentences to find cause and effect in the story.

Skill Points

✓ Keep in mind that most things happen for a reason.

✓ As you read, ask yourself: *What is happening? Why is it happening?*

Practice

Read aloud the directions on page 100. Have children answer the questions about cause and effect.

Answers for page 100: 1. He wanted to make the world brighter. **2.** He worked hard to make electricity safe and cheap to use. **3.** Bulbs lasted longer than candles. Electric light made it easier to see at night.

Name ____________________

Look at the pictures. **Read** the sentences.

A Bright Idea

Thomas Edison was an inventor. He wanted to make the world brighter.

He worked very hard to make electricity safe and cheap to use.

Thomas Edison made his dream come true. Soon electricity and lightbulbs were in many homes. The bulbs lasted longer than candles, and electric light made it much easier to see at night.

Answer the questions below.

1. What did Thomas Edison want to do?

____

2. How did he make his dream come true?

____

3. Why were electricity and lightbulbs in many homes?

____

Vocabulary Activities and Word Cards

Copy the Word Cards on page 102 as needed for the following activities.
Use the blank card for an additional word that you want to teach.
Also see suggestions for teaching vocabulary in the ELL and Transition Handbook.

Creative Poster	Everyday Game	Word Hunt
• Divide children into groups of two or three, and give each group one set of Word Cards. • Give each group a large piece of construction paper or a poster board and a variety of drawing materials. • Ask children to design a poster that illustrates at least four of the words. They may use all of the words if they wish. • Ask children to paste the Word Cards they use onto their poster. • Have each group present its poster to the class. Encourage each child in the group to use a complete sentence to describe an aspect of the poster.	• Give each child a set of Word Cards and ask children to arrange their cards in alphabetical order. • Read the words aloud as a group. Then have each child tell what two of the words mean. • As a group, discuss how children might use these words every day. Ask volunteers to give example sentences: *I washed my dirty clothes. We played outside for hours. My neighbor is nice.*	• Divide children into pairs. Give each pair one Word Card, saying each word aloud as you hand out the cards. • Challenge pairs to find their words in classroom books or other environmental print. Have them say where they find each word and then write the phrase or sentence in which they find it. • Invite pairs to share their findings with the class.

clothes

hours

money

neighbor

only

question

taught

Multilingual Summaries

English

A Weed is a Flower

George Washington Carver was born a slave. As a boy, George asked questions about everything. He grew plants. He wanted to go to school. When he was ten, slavery ended. When he was older, George left home.

He worked hard. He saved money for college. At college, he studied plants. George learned so much that he later taught agriculture.

George taught farmers to plant new crops. Farmers did not believe that the new crops would sell. George discovered how to make many things with the new crops. The crops became important to the state of Alabama. George had become a great scientist.

Spanish

La mala hierba es una flor

George Washington Carver nació esclavo. De niño, hacía muchas preguntas sobre todo. Cultivaba plantas. Quería ir a la escuela. Cuando George tenía diez años se terminó la esclavitud. Cuando se hizo mayor, George se fue de su casa.

Trabajó duro. Ahorró dinero para ir a la universidad. En la universidad, estudió las plantas. Aprendió tanto que después enseñó agricultura.

George les enseñó a los granjeros a sembrar nuevos cultivos. Los granjeros no creían que estos cultivos se podían vender. George descubrió cómo hacer muchas cosas con los nuevos cultivos. Los cultivos se volvieron muy importantes en Alabama. George se había convertido en un gran científico.

Multilingual Summaries

Chinese

植物教授

喬治・華盛頓・卡佛的一生

喬治・華盛頓・卡佛出身於奴隸家庭。小時候，他對每一樣東西都充滿了好奇，他喜歡栽種植物，而且一直渴望能夠上學唸書。喬治十歲時，美國的奴隸制度被廢除了。稍微年長之後，喬治就離家出外工作。

他辛勤地工作，打算儲錢上大學。上了大學之後，他選擇研究植物。喬治讀了非常多的書，變得很有學問，後來他開始教授農業。

喬治教導農夫種植新作物，可是農夫不相信那可以賣錢。喬治於是想出了很多方法，利用新作物製造出其他東西。結果新作物變成了阿拉巴馬州的重要作物，喬治也成為了偉大的科學家。

Vietnamese

Ngọn Cỏ Dại là một Cành Hoa

Cuộc Đời của George Washington Carver

George Washington Carver sanh ra bị làm nô lệ. Từ khi còn là một cậu bé, George thắc mắc về mọi điều. Cậu bé trồng cây. Cậu bé muốn được đi học. Khi cậu được mười tuổi, chế độ nô lệ chấm dứt. Khi lớn lên, George rời nhà.

George cần cù làm việc. Ông để dành tiền đi học đại học. Ở trường đại học, ông học về thực vật. Ông học hỏi được nhiều đến nỗi sau này ông dạy môn nông nghiệp.

George dạy các nông phu trồng một loại cây nông nghiệp mới. Các nông phu đã không tin là loại cây nông nghiệp mới sẽ bán chạy. George khám phá cách chế biến ra nhiều thứ từ loại cây nông nghiệp mới. Loại cây này trở nên quan trọng ở Alabama. George trở thành một nhà bác học vĩ đại.

Multilingual Summaries

Korean

잡초도 꽃이다

조지 워싱턴 카버의 삶

노예로 태어난 조지 워싱턴 카버는 소년 시절 궁금한 것이 많았다. 그는 식물을 키웠으며 학교에 다니고 싶어했다. 조지가 열 살이 되던 해 노예 제도가 없어졌고, 성장한 조지는 집을 떠났다.

그는 열심히 일해 대학에 갈 돈을 모았다. 대학에서 식물을 공부한 조지는 많은 것을 배워 나중에 농업을 가르쳤다.

조지는 농부들에게 새 품종을 재배하는 법을 가르쳤지만 농부들은 새 품종이 잘 팔리지 않을 것이라고 생각했다. 조지는 새 품종으로 많은 것을 만드는 법을 알아냈고 이 품종은 앨라배마에서 중요한 작물이 되었다. 조지는 훌륭한 과학자가 된 것이다.

Hmong

Nroj Yog Paj

George Washington Carver Lub Neej

George Washington Carver yug los ua ib tug tub qhe. Thaum nws yog ib tug menyuam tub, George muaj lus nug txog txhua yam. Nws cog qoob cog loo. Nws xav mus kawm ntawv. Thaum nws muaj kaum xyoo ces kev ua qhev thiaj li tu. Thaum nws hlob tiav neeg, George thiaj li tawm hauv tsev mus lawm.

Nws ua haujlwm hnyav heev. Nws khaws nyiaj tseg yuav mus kawm ntawv qib siab. Nws mus kawm txog kev cog qoob cog loo thaum nws mus kawm ntawv qib siab. George kawm tau ntau yam nws thiaj li tau mus qhia ntawv txog kev ua liaj ua teb.

George qhia cov tub ua liaj ua teb kom lawv txawj cog cov qoob loo tshiab. Cov tub ua liaj ua teb tsis ntseeg tias lawv yuav muag tau nyiaj rau cov qoob loo tshiab no. George tau kawm ntxiv txog ntau yam ua nws tsim tau thaum nws siv cov qoob loo tshiab no. Cov qoob loo no tseem ceeb heev nyob rau Alabama. George los mus ua ib tug tibneeg kawm txujci zoo kawg.

The Quilt Story

Student Edition pages 16–30

Week at a Glance	Customize instruction every day for your English Language Learners.				
	Day 1	**Day 2**	**Day 3**	**Day 4**	**Day 5**
Teacher's Edition	Use the ELL Notes that appear throughout each day of the lesson to support instruction and reading.				
ELL Poster 16	• Assess Prior Knowledge • Develop Concepts and Vocabulary	• Preteach Tested Vocabulary	• Review Compare and Contrast	• Familiar Things Riddles	• Monitor Progress
ELL Teaching Guide	• Picture It! Lesson, pp. 106–107 • Multilingual Summaries, pp. 110–112	• ELL Reader Lesson, pp. 242–243	• Vocabulary Activities and Word Cards, pp. 108–109 • Multilingual Summaries, pp. 110–112		
ELL Readers	• Reread *Inventions Help People*	• Teach *For Good Luck!*	• Reread *For Good Luck!* and other texts to build fluency		
ELL and Transition Handbook	Use the following as needed to support this week's instruction and to conduct alternative assessments: • Phonics Transition Lessons • Grammar Transition Lessons • Assessment				

Picture It! Comprehension Lesson

Compare and Contrast

Use this lesson to supplement or replace the skill lesson on pages 12–13 of the Teacher's Edition.

Teach

Distribute copies of the Picture It! blackline master on page 107.

- Ask children to look at the pictures and tell what is happening.
- Read the story aloud. Ask: *Are the pancakes the same?* (no)
- Share the Skill Points (at right) with children.
- Have children look at the pictures and sentences to find clues about comparing and contrasting.

Practice

Read aloud the directions on page 107. Have children fill in the compare-and-contrast chart.

Answers for page 107: *Alike:* fluffy, taste good. *Different:* Sister's pancakes are small and round. Dad's pancakes are big and shaped like animals.

Skill Points

✓ When you **compare** things, you tell how they are alike. When you **contrast** things, you tell how they are different.

✓ Words such as *like* and *also* are clues that something is being compared.

✓ Words such as *but* and *unlike* are clues that something is being contrasted.

Name ______________________________

Look at the pictures. **Read** the story.

- **Fill in** the chart. **Write** how the pancakes are alike. **Write** how the pancakes are different.

Great Pancakes!

Every Saturday, Niki's dad made big, fluffy pancakes. He shaped them like animals. Niki loved to eat Dad's pancakes.

One Saturday, Dad was not home to make breakfast. Niki's sister made the pancakes. But these pancakes were not like Dad's. They were small and round.

Niki took a bite. The pancakes were fluffy and they tasted great, just like Dad's!

Dad's and Sister's Pancakes

How They Are Alike	How They Are Different

Vocabulary Activities and Word Cards

Copy the Word Cards on page 109 as needed for the following activities.
Use the blank card for an additional word that you want to teach.
Also see suggestions for teaching vocabulary in the ELL and Transition Handbook.

Word Pictures	Word Sorting	Word Toss
• Divide children into pairs or small groups, and give each group two or three Word Cards. Do not include the card for *pretended*. • Have groups take turns drawing pictures to show the meaning of one of their words for the other groups to guess. If children need additional support, post a set of Word Cards where they can be seen. • Continue until each child has had a turn drawing.	• Give each child one set of Word Cards. • Review the meaning of each word with children. Then give children categories that the words can be sorted into. For example, children can sort the words into *Actions* and *Things.* (Note that in this unit, *stuffing* is used as a noun.) • Continue the activity by providing additional categories such as *Ends in -ed* and *Ends in -ing.* • Discuss the answers as a group. Invite volunteers to tell how they knew where to put each card.	• Use one set of Word Cards. You will also need a mini beanbag or a small stuffed toy. • Tape the Word Cards on an open space on the floor. • Have a child gently toss the beanbag onto one of the words on the floor. If the bag does not fall directly on a word, have the child use the word that is closest to the bag. • Ask the child to read the word and then use it in a sentence. • Play the game until each child has had at least one turn to throw the beanbag and create a sentence.

blankets	**pretended**
quilt	**stuffing**
trunks	**unpacked**
wrapped	

Multilingual Summaries

English

The Quilt Story

A long time ago, Abigail's mother made a quilt. The quilt kept Abigail warm. When it tore, her mother fixed it. When Abigail was sick, she slept under the quilt.

Abigail's family moved far away. They took the quilt with them. The quilt made Abigail feel at home.

One day, Abigail put the old quilt in the attic. Everyone forgot about it. A mouse had babies on the quilt. A raccoon used the quilt. A cat rested on the quilt. The cat's owner found the quilt. She took it home, and her mother fixed it.

That girl's family moved to a new house. They took the quilt with them. The quilt made that girl feel at home too.

Spanish

La historia del edredón

Hace muchos años, la mamá de Abigail hizo un edredón. El edredón arropaba a Abigail. Cuando se rompió, la mamá lo volvió a coser. Cuando Abigail estaba enferma, dormía con el edredón.

La familia de Abigail se mudó muy lejos. Se llevaron con ellos el edredón. El edredón ayudaba a Abigail a sentirse a gusto.

Un día, Abigail puso el viejo edredón en el ático. Todos se olvidaron de él. Una ratona tuvo ratoncitos en el edredón. Un mapache usó el edredón. Un gato descansó en el edredón. La dueña del gato encontró el edredón. Se lo llevó a casa y su mamá lo arregló.

La niña se mudó a otra casa. Ella y su familia se llevaron el edredón. El edredón también ayudaba a la niña a sentirse a gusto.

Multilingual Summaries

Chinese

被子的故事

很久以前，愛碧蓋爾的母親縫了一張被子。被子讓愛碧蓋爾覺得很溫暖。被子如果破了，母親會把它補好。愛碧蓋爾生病的時候，也蓋著這張被子。

後來，愛碧蓋爾一家搬到很遠的地方去，他們把被子也一起帶走。愛碧蓋爾的父親蓋了一棟新房子，但是真正讓愛碧蓋爾有回家感覺的是被子。

有一天，愛碧蓋爾把舊被子收到閣樓去。不久之後，大家都忘記了被子的存在。 老鼠媽媽在被子上生了一窩鼠寶寶，浣熊也用過被子。貓跑到被子上休息，貓的主人才發現這張被子，她把被子拿回家，請母親把它縫補好。

後來，女孩一家搬到新房子去，他們把被子也一起帶走。這張被子也讓女孩有回家的感覺。

Vietnamese

Chuyện Tấm Chăn Bông

Cách đây đã lâu, mẹ của Abigail may một tấm chăn bông. Chăn này giữ Abigail được ấm. Khi chăn rách, mẹ của cô may vá nó lại. Khi Abigail bị bệnh, cô bé đắp chăn bông này.

Gia đình của Abigail dọn đi xa. Họ mang theo tấm chăn bông. Ba của Abigail xây một ngôi nhà mới. Tấm chăn làm Abigail cảm thấy dễ chịu như ở trong một ngôi nhà thân quen.

Đến một ngày kia, Abigail đem tấm chăn bông cũ kỹ để lên gác xép. Mọi người đều quên tấm chăn này. Một con chuột lắc đẻ con trên đó. Một con chồn Mỹ dùng chăn đó. Một con mèo nghỉ ngơi trên chăn đó. Cô chủ của con mèo tìm gặp tấm chăn bông. Cô bé mang về nhà và mẹ may vá chăn lại.

Gia đình của cô gái dọn đến nhà mới. Họ mang theo tấm chăn. Tấm chăn bông cũng làm cho cô gái thấy dễ chịu như ở trong một ngôi nhà thân quen.

Multilingual Summaries

Korean

누비 이불 이야기

옛날에 에비게일의 어머니는 누비 이불을 만들었고 이 이불 덕분에 에비게일은 따뜻하게 지낸다. 어머니는 이불이 낡아지면 다시 꿰매주고 에비게일은 아플 때면 누비 이불을 덮고 잔다.

에비게일의 가족은 누비 이불을 가지고 멀리 이사를 간다. 그곳에서 에비게일의 아버지가 새 집을 지었고 누비 이불 덕분에 에비게일은 편안함을 느낀다.

어느 날 에비게일이 그 낡은 이불을 다락방에 두었는데 사람들은 그 사실을 잊어버린다. 쥐 한 마리가 그 누비 이불에 새끼를 낳고 너구리가 그 이불을 사용한다. 고양이가 이불에서 쉬고 있는데 고양이 주인이 그 누비 이불을 발견하고는 집으로 가져갔고 소녀의 어머니가 그 이불을 수선한다.

소녀의 가족도 누비 이불과 함께 새 집으로 이사를 가고 그 이불 덕분에 소녀도 편안함을 느낀다.

Hmong

Zaj Dab Neeg Txog Daim Pam

Puag thaum ub, Abigail niam tau xaws ib daig pam. Daim pam tau ua rau Abigail so. Thaum daim pam tau ntuag, nws niam tau muab ntxiv. Thaum Abigail mob, nws tau kauv daim pam pw.

Abigail tsev neeg tau siv mus deb deb. Lawv tau nqa daim pam nrog lawv. Abigail txiv tau ua ib lub tsev tshiab. Daim pam ua kom Abigail nyob swm.

Muaj ib hnub, Abigail tau muab daim pam qub tso rau saum qaum tsev. Txhua tus tsis nco qab txog daim pam. Ib tug nas tau yug nws cov me nyuam rau saum daim pam. Ib tug mab tau siv daim pam. Ib tug miv tau pwm saum daim pam. Tus miv tus tswv tau khaws tau daim pam. Nws tau nqa mus tsev thiab nws niam tau muab daim pam xaws.

Tus me nyuam ntxhais ntawd tsev neeg tau tsiv mus rau ib lub tsev tshiab… Lawv tau nqa daim pam nrog lawv. Daim pam ua kom tus me nyuam ntxhais ntawd nyob swm.

Life Cycle of a Pumpkin Student Edition pages 46–59

Week at a Glance	Customize instruction every day for your English Language Learners.				
	Day 1	**Day 2**	**Day 3**	**Day 4**	**Day 5**
Teacher's Edition	Use the ELL Notes that appear throughout each day of the lesson to support instruction and reading.				
ELL Poster 17	• Assess Prior Knowledge • Develop Concepts and Vocabulary	• Preteach Tested Vocabulary	• Review Fact and Opinion	• Five Questions Game	• Monitor Progress
ELL Teaching Guide	• Picture It! Lesson, pp. 113–114 • Multilingual Summaries, pp. 117–119	• ELL Reader Lesson, pp. 244–245	• Vocabulary Activities and Word Cards, pp. 115–116 • Multilingual Summaries, pp. 117–119		
ELL Readers	• Reread *For Good Luck!*	• Teach *The Tomato Times*	• Reread *The Tomato Times* and other texts to build fluency		
ELL and Transition Handbook	Use the following as needed to support this week's instruction and to conduct alternative assessments: • Phonics Transition Lessons • Grammar Transition Lessons • Assessment				

Picture It! Comprehension Lesson

Fact and Opinion

Use this lesson to supplement or replace the skill lesson on pages 42–43 of the Teacher's Edition.

Teach

Distribute copies of the Picture It! blackline master on page 114.

- Ask children to look at the picture and tell how the people are using pumpkins.
- Read the paragraph aloud. Ask: *Can you find a fact in the paragraph?*
- Share the Skill Points (at right) with children.
- Have children look at the picture and paragraph to find facts and opinions.

Practice

Read aloud the directions on page 114. Have children answer the questions about fact and opinion in the paragraph.

Answers for page 114: 1. Pumpkins are large, orange fruits. **2.** Pumpkin pies make the best dessert! **3.** They make a tasty snack.

Skill Points

✓ A **fact** can be proven true or false. You can check in a book, ask someone who knows, or see for yourself.

✓ An **opinion** tells someone's ideas or feelings. Clue words such as *best* and *should* show statements of opinion.

✓ As you read, ask yourself: *Can this sentence be proven true or false?*

Name ______________________________

Look at the picture. **Read** the paragraph.

Hooray for Pumpkins!

Pumpkins are large, orange fruits. They have many uses. Kara is drawing a funny face on her pumpkin. It will look great outside on the porch! Mark is eating pumpkin seeds. He baked them in the oven and put salt on them. They make a tasty snack. Mom used cooked pumpkin to make a pie. Pumpkin pies make the best dessert!

Answer the questions below.

1. Which sentence is a **fact**?
- O Pumpkin pies make the best dessert!
- O It will look great outside on the porch!
- O Pumpkins are large, orange fruits.

2. Which sentence is an **opinion**?
- O Mom used cooked pumpkin to make a pie.
- O Pumpkin pies make the best dessert!
- O Pumpkins have many uses.

3. Find another opinion in the paragraph. Write it.

____

Vocabulary Activities and Word Cards

Copy the Word Cards on page 116 as needed for the following activities.
Use the blank card for an additional word that you want to teach.
Also see suggestions for teaching vocabulary in the ELL and Transition Handbook.

Guess the Word	Fishing Game	What's the Word?
• Give each child two or three Word Cards. • Ask children to use the back of the card to draw a picture, write a synonym, write a definition, or write a cloze sentence using the word from the front of the card. Assist children as necessary. • Collect the completed cards and stack them word side down. • Have each child draw a card (not the child's own), look at the clue, and name the vocabulary word on the front of the card. • Continue until all the cards have been used.	• Use one or more sets of Word Cards. Attach a metal paper clip to each card and put the cards in a bucket. Tie a string to a short stick and fasten a magnet to the end of the string. • Have children take turns "fishing" for words. • When a child "catches" a word, he or she reads it and either tells what it means or uses it in a sentence. If the word is used correctly, the child keeps the card. If not, the child returns the card to the bucket. • The child with the most "fish" when the bucket is empty wins the game.	• Give each child a set of Word Cards to look at during the activity. Keep another set at the front of the room. • Ask a volunteer to come to the front of the room and choose a Word Card without showing it to the group. • Have the child write the word on the board, leaving out two or three letters. The child should write an underscore for any missing letters, for example, _ a r _ e s _ *(harvest)*. • Ask the other children to write down the word and fill in the missing letters. Have a volunteer use the word in a sentence. • Continue until each child has had at least one turn at the front of the room and all the Word Cards have been used.

bumpy	**fruit**
harvest	**root**
smooth	**soil**
vine	

Multilingual Summaries

English

Life Cycle of a Pumpkin

A seed is planted in soil. A root grows out of the seed and into the soil. Leaves grow, and the plant becomes a vine. It grows longer and longer. The vine grows flowers. Bees bring pollen to the flowers. Parts of the flowers grow into pumpkins.

Pumpkins need water and sun. Insects can hurt pumpkins, so farmers protect the plants. The pumpkins grow bigger. Seeds and pulp grow inside. The outsides turn from green to orange. The vines turn brown in the fall. Then it is time to pick the pumpkins.

The farmers sell the pumpkins. People cook them.

Spanish

El ciclo de vida de una calabaza

Una semilla se siembra en la tierra. Una raíz crece fuera de la semilla y debajo de la tierra. Las hojas crecen y la planta se hace una enredadera. La planta crece más y más. De la enredadera, salen flores. Las abejas le traen polen a las flores. Algunas de las flores se convierten en calabazas.

Las calabazas necesitan agua y sol. Los insectos pueden dañar las calabazas, por eso los granjeros protegen las plantas. Las calabazas crecen mucho. Las semillas y la pulpa crecen dentro de ellas. La parte de afuera cambia de verde a color naranja. Las enredaderas se vuelven marrones en el otoño. Entonces, ya es tiempo de cosechar las calabazas.

Los granjeros venden las calabazas. Las personas las cocinan.

Multilingual Summaries

Chinese

南瓜的一生

南瓜從小種子開始發芽成長。種子種在泥土裡，根從種子長出來，然後慢慢伸進泥土裡。不久之後，葉子也長出來，變成了一種藤蔓植物。藤蔓越長越長，然後開出花朵來。蜜蜂把花粉帶到花朵裡，有些花朵就結出南瓜來。

南瓜需要澆水和曬太陽。昆蟲會吃南瓜，所以農夫要保護南瓜。南瓜越長越大，種子和果肉都長在南瓜裡面，南瓜的外面會從綠色變成橘色。藤蔓到了秋天會變成棕色，這便是收割南瓜的時候。

農夫把南瓜賣出去，人們把南瓜煮來吃。

所有南瓜都收割以後，農夫開始耕地。他會在春天的時候種下更多南瓜種子。

Vietnamese

Chu Kỳ Đời Sống của Quả Bí Đỏ

Quả bí đỏ bắt đầu từ hạt. Một hạt được trồng trong đất. Rễ mọc ra từ hạt và đâm vào đất. Lá mọc ra, và cái cây nhỏ trở thành dây leo. Dây mọc càng dài ra. Dây trổ nhiều hoa. Ong mang phấn đến cho các cánh hoa. Những phần của hoa trở thành những quả bí.

Bí đỏ cần có nước và ánh nắng mặt trời. Các côn trùng có thể làm hại những quả bí, vì vậy các bác nông phu bảo vệ những dây bí. Những quả bí to lớn thêm. Hạt và phần cơm của bí phát triển ở bên trong quả bí. Phần vỏ ngoài chuyển từ màu xanh sang màu cam. Dây bí ngả sang màu nâu vào mùa thu. Rồi đến lúc để hái những quả bí đó.

Các bác nông phu bán những quả bí đỏ. Người ta nấu những quả bí này.

Sau khi tất cả những quả bí đã được hái đi, bác nông phu cày bừa cánh đồng. Ông ấy sẽ gieo trồng thêm những hạt bí đỏ vào mùa xuân.

Multilingual Summaries

Korean

호박의 생명 주기

호박은 씨앗부터 출발한다. 씨앗이 땅에 뿌려지고 뿌리가 씨앗에서 나와 땅속으로 자라며 잎사귀들이 자라고 묘목이 줄기로 바뀐다. 줄기는 무럭무럭 자라나서 꽃을 피우고 벌들이 꽃에 꽃가루를 옮긴다. 그리고 나서 꽃의 일부가 자라 호박이 된다.

호박은 물과 태양을 필요로 한다. 벌레들이 호박을 상하게 할 수 있기 때문에 농부들은 묘목을 보호한다. 호박은 무럭무럭 자라 씨앗과 과육이 호박 안쪽에서 자라며 호박 바깥쪽이 녹색에서 오렌지색으로 변한다. 가을이 되면 줄기가 갈색으로 변하고 그러면 호박을 딸 때가 된 것이다.

농부들은 호박을 팔고 사람들은 그 호박으로 요리를 한다.

호박을 다 수확하게 되면 농부는 밭을 일구고 봄이 되면 더 많은 호박씨를 뿌린다.

Hmong

Lub Neej Ntawm Ib Lub Taub

Cov taub pib los ntawm cov noob. Ib lub noob raug muab cog rau hauv av. Ib tug cag tawg kaus mus rau hauv av. Cov nplooj hlav, thiab tsob taub pib muaj hmab. Nws pib hlav ntev zuj zus. Tsob hmab pib tawg paj. Cov ntseeb nqa tej paj ntoos los rau cov paj. Tej txhia paj hlob los ua taub.

Cov taub yuav tsum muaj dej thiab lub hnub. Tej kab yeej ua kom cov taub hlob tsis tau, ces cov neeg ua teb thiaj li tiv thaiv cov taub. Cov taub loj hlob zuj zus. Tej noob pib muaj nyob hauv lub taub thiab daim tawv tuab zuj zus. Daim tawv xim ntshiab rais mus ua daim tawv xim xob. Cov hmab pauv mus ua xim ka-fas hauv lub caij nplooj ntoos zeeg. Ces txog lub sij hawm de cov taub.

Cov neeg ua teb muab cov taub muag. Cov neeg muab cov taub ua noj.

Tom qab cov taub raug muab de, tus neeg ua teb rov muab daim teb ncaws. Nws yuav rov cog dua lwm cov noob taub hauv lub caij nplooj ntoos hlav.

Frogs Student Edition pages 70–87

Week at a Glance	Customize instruction every day for your English Language Learners.				
	Day 1	**Day 2**	**Day 3**	**Day 4**	**Day 5**
Teacher's Edition	Use the ELL Notes that appear throughout each day of the lesson to support instruction and reading.				
ELL Poster 18	• Assess Prior Knowledge • Develop Concepts and Vocabulary	• Preteach Tested Vocabulary	• Review Compare and Contrast	• What Is Happening in the Pond?	• Monitor Progress
ELL Teaching Guide	• Picture It! Lesson, pp. 120–121 • Multilingual Summaries, pp. 124–126	• ELL Reader Lesson, pp. 246–247	• Vocabulary Activities and Word Cards, pp. 122–123 • Multilingual Summaries, pp. 124–126		
ELL Readers	• Reread *The Tomato Times*	• Teach *The Panda Gift*	• Reread *The Panda Gift* and other texts to build fluency		
ELL and Transition Handbook	Use the following as needed to support this week's instruction and to conduct alternative assessments: • Phonics Transition Lessons • Grammar Transition Lessons • Assessment				

Picture It! Comprehension Lesson

Compare and Contrast

Use this lesson to supplement or replace the skill lesson on pages 66–67 of the Teacher's Edition.

Teach

Distribute copies of the Picture It! blackline master on page 121.

- Ask children to look at the pictures and describe what they see.
- Read the paragraph aloud. Ask: *How are the bears alike?*
- Share the Skill Points (at right) with the children.
- Have children look at the picture and paragraph to compare and contrast grizzlies and polar bears.

Practice

Read aloud the directions on page 121. Have children fill in the Venn diagram.

Answers for page 121: *Grizzly Bears*: brown; eat plants; live in woods in North America; *Both:* are bears; eat meat; have fur, claws, and sharp teeth; *Polar Bears*: white; live in Arctic

Skill Points

✓ When you **compare** things, you tell how they are alike. When you **contrast** things, you tell how they are different.

✓ Clue words such as *like* and *both* show comparisons.

✓ Clue words such as *but* and *different* show contrasts.

Name ________________________________

Look at the pictures. **Read** the paragraph.

- In the Grizzly Bears circle, **write** things that are true only about grizzly bears. In the Polar Bears circle, **write** things that are true only about polar bears. In the middle section, **write** how the two animals are alike.

Grizzly Bears and Polar Bears

Do you know how a grizzly bear and a polar bear are alike? They are both bears. They both have fur, sharp teeth, and claws. Grizzlies and polar bears are also different from each other. Grizzly bears are brown. They eat plants and meat. They live in woods in North America. Polar bears are white and only eat meat. They live in the Arctic.

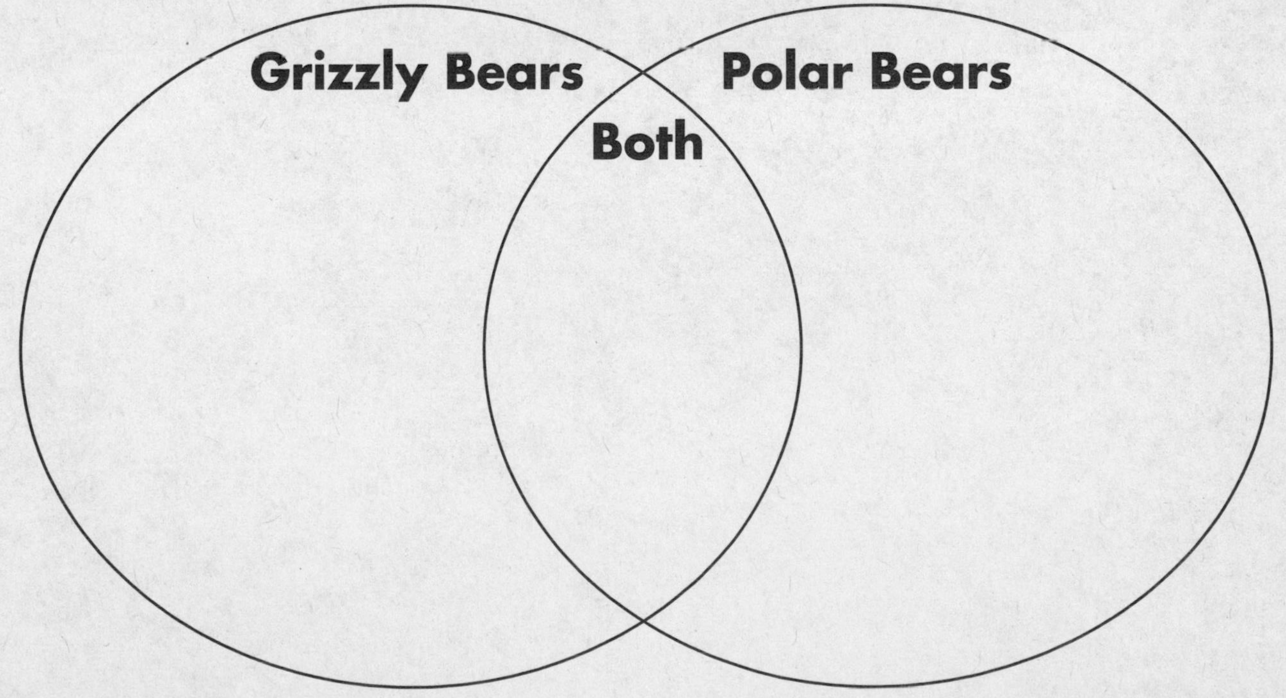

Vocabulary Activities and Word Cards

Copy the Word Cards on page 123 as needed for the following activities.
Use the blank card for an additional word that you want to teach.
Also see suggestions for teaching vocabulary in the ELL and Transition Handbook.

Definition Match	Tick-Tack-Toe	Tell a Story
• Before play begins, write a brief definition for each high-frequency word on your own set of Word Cards. • Give each child a set of Word Cards. Have children arrange their cards face up in front of them. • Say the definition of a word. Do not say the word. • Children hold up the word that matches the definition. Have the first child to hold up the word read it aloud. • Continue until all the cards have been matched.	• Use one set of Word Cards plus several Word Cards from previous weeks. Divide children into teams of X and O. • Draw a tick-tack-toe grid on the board. Tape the Word Cards next to the grid. • Players take turns taking a Word Card off the board and using the word in a complete sentence. If a player uses the word correctly, he or she draws an X or O on the grid and gives you the Word Card. If the player uses the word incorrectly, the card is put back on the board, and the other team takes a turn. • The game ends when a team has three Xs or Os in a row, or all the grid spaces have been filled.	• Give two Word Cards to each child, and arrange the children in a circle. • Start a story with a sentence that uses one of the vocabulary words. For example: *I walked by the pond.* • The next child continues the story, finding a way to use one of his or her words in a sentence. Encourage children to help each other make up sentences. • Children take turns until all the Word Cards have been used and the group decides that the story is complete.

crawls

insects

pond

powerful

shed

skin

wonderful

Multilingual Summaries

English

Frogs

Frogs lay their eggs in a pond. Most of the eggs grow into tadpoles. Tadpoles are baby frogs. The tadpoles hatch and begin to swim. They can breathe in the water. They eat very small plants called algae.

The tadpoles grow little teeth. Their back legs grow. The tadpoles swim to the surface to breathe air. Finally, the front legs grow. The frogs move to land. They eat insects by catching them with their tongues.

Some frogs live in the water and on land. They are good jumpers. Frogs can be different sizes. There are many different kinds of frogs.

Spanish

Las Ranas

Las ranas ponen huevos en el lago. La mayoría de los huevos crecen y se vuelven renacuajos. Los renacuajos son los bebés de las ranas. Los renacuajos salen del cascarón y empiezan a nadar. Ellos pueden respirar en el agua. Se alimentan con plantas pequeñitas llamadas algas.

A los renacuajos les crecen dientes pequeños. Les crecen patas traseras. Los renacuajos nadan a la superficie para respirar aire. Finalmente, las patas delanteras crecen. Las ranas se mudan para la tierra. Comen insectos cazándolos con su lengua.

Algunas ranas viven en el agua y en la tierra. Son buenas saltadoras. Las ranas pueden ser de diferentes tamaños. Hay muchos tipos de ranas.

Multilingual Summaries

Chinese

青蛙

青蛙在池塘裡產卵。有時其他動物會吃掉一些卵，剩下的卵會變成蝌蚪，蝌蚪就是青蛙寶寶。蝌蚪孵化出來後會開始游泳，牠們有腮，可以在水裡呼吸。蝌蚪吃一種很小的植物，叫做水藻。

蝌蚪會長出牙齒，牠們的後腿會變長和變得強壯，使牠們游泳時更加有力。蝌蚪還會長出肺部，需要浮到水面呼吸新鮮空氣。最後，前腿也會長出來。這時候，青蛙就會搬到陸地上居住，用牠們又長又黏的舌頭捉昆蟲吃。

有些青蛙會同時住在水裡和陸地上。青蛙很會跳，牠們有不同的大小，也有很多不同的品種。

Vietnamese

Ếch

Ếch đẻ trứng trong ao. Đôi khi có các thú vật khác ăn mất vài trứng này. Phần còn lại sẽ phát triển thành nòng nọc. Nòng nọc là ếch con. Nòng nọc nở và bắt đầu bơi lội. Chúng có thể thở trong nước bằng mang. Chúng ăn những loài cây rất nhỏ gọi là rong tảo.

Nòng nọc mọc những cái răng nhỏ. Chúng bắt đầu bơi lội mạnh hơn. Mọc hai chân sau. Nòng nọc bắt đầu phát triển phổi. Nòng nọc bơi lên mặt nước để thở không khí. Cuối cùng, hai chân trước mọc ra. Ếch lên sống trên bờ. Chúng ăn côn trùng bằng cách bắt chúng bằng chiếc lưỡi dài và dính như keo.

Có vài loại ếch sống ở trong nước và trên bờ. Chúng nhảy giỏi. Ếch có thể có nhiều kích thước khác nhau. Có nhiều loại ếch khác nhau.

Multilingual Summaries

Korean

개구리

개구리는 연못에 알을 낳고 때때로 그 알을 다른 동물들이 먹지만 남은 알들은 부화하여 올챙이가 된다. 올챙이는 아기 개구리이다. 이 올챙이들은 부화 후에 수영을 시작하고 아가미가 있어서 물 속에서도 숨을 쉴 수 있으며 조류라고 불리는 아주 작은 바다 식물을 먹는다.

올챙이들에겐 작은 이빨이 생기고 더욱 힘차게 수영을 하게 된다. 뒷다리가 나오고 허파도 생겨서 공기를 마시기 위해 물 표면으로 수영하여 올라온다. 마침내 앞다리가 생긴 개구리는 육지로 올라와 길고 끈끈한 혀로 곤충들을 잡아먹는다.

어떤 개구리들은 물과 땅에서 살아가는데 점프 실력이 대단하다. 개구리의 크기가 다른 것은 종류가 다양하기 때문이다.

Hmong

Cov Qav

Cov qav tso lawv tej qe rau saum ib lub me nyuam pas dej. Qee zaus lwm cov tsiaj muab tej txhia qe noj. Cov qee uas tsheem hlob mus ua tej qas taub. Cov qas taub yog cov me nyuam qav. Cov qas taub nraug thiab pib ua luam dej. Lawv siv lawv daim xiab ua pa hauv dej. Lawv noj tej nroj nyom me me hu ua algae.

Cov qas taub tuaj cov hneev me me. Lawv pib muaj zog ua luam dej. Lawv ob txhais ceg muaj zog tuaj. Cov qas taub hlav ntsws. Cov qas taub ua luam dej mus saum nplaim dej mus ua pas. Ces kawg nkaus, lawv ob txhais caj npaj hlav tuaj. Cov qav tsiv mus nyob saum nruab nqhuab. Lawv noj tej kab ntsaum thaum lawv siv lawv tus mlaig uas mlaum mlaum txog cov kab.

Ib txhia qav nyob hauv dej thiab saum av. Lawv txawj dhia. Yeej muaj cov qav me thiab cov qav loj. Yeej muaj ntau hom qav.

I Like Where I Am Student Edition pages 100–115

Week at a Glance	Customize instruction every day for your English Language Learners.				
	Day 1	**Day 2**	**Day 3**	**Day 4**	**Day 5**
Teacher's Edition	Use the ELL Notes that appear throughout each day of the lesson to support instruction and reading.				
ELL Poster 19	• Assess Prior Knowledge • Develop Concepts and Vocabulary	• Preteach Tested Vocabulary	• Changes	• What Am I?	• Monitor Progress
ELL Teaching Guide	• Picture It! Lesson, pp. 127–128 • Multilingual Summaries, pp. 131–133	• ELL Reader Lesson, pp. 248–249	• Vocabulary Activities and Word Cards, pp. 129–130 • Multilingual Summaries, pp. 131–133		
ELL Readers	• Reread *The Panda Gift*	• Teach *Adam's New Soccer Team*	• Reread *Adam's New Soccer Team* and other texts to build fluency		
ELL and Transition Handbook	Use the following as needed to support this week's instruction and to conduct alternative assessments: • Phonics Transition Lessons • Grammar Transition Lessons • Assessment				

Picture It! Comprehension Lesson

Theme and Plot

Use this lesson to supplement or replace the skill lesson on pages 96–97 of the Teacher's Edition.

Teach

Distribute copies of the Picture It! blackline master on page 128.

- Ask children to look at the pictures and describe what is happening.
- Read the story aloud. Ask: *What happens at the beginning of the story? How does Miguel feel?*
- Share the Skill Points (at right) with children.
- Have children look at the pictures and sentences and discuss what the theme of the story is.

Practice

Read aloud the directions on page 128. Have children answer the questions about plot and theme.

Answers for page 128: 1. Miguel starts his first day at his new school. He is sad. **2.** Miguel's teacher and his classmates are nice to him. **3.** (Guide children to discuss the big idea of the story.) Sample response: The big idea of this story is that a big change can be a good thing even if it is not easy.

Skill Points

✓ Keep in mind that every story has one big idea or **theme.**

✓ Use what you know from your own life to understand the theme of a story.

✓ The **plot** is what happens at the beginning, middle, and end of a story.

✓ Characters' actions help make up the plot of a story.

Name ______________________________

Look at the pictures. **Read** the story.

A New School

Today is Miguel's first day at his new school. He feels sad. He does not know anyone here, and he misses his old school.

Miguel's new teacher seems nice. But Miguel is still a little shy and scared. Then his teacher smiles at him. He smiles too.

At recess, a boy in Miguel's class asks him to play. Miguel is having fun. Maybe this new school will be just as good as the old one!

Answer the questions below.

1. Tell what happens at the beginning of the story. How does Miguel feel?

____

____

2. What happens to change how Miguel feels?

____

3. Talk about what you think is the big idea of this story.

Vocabulary Activities and Word Cards

Copy the Word Cards on page 130 as needed for the following activities. Use the blank card for an additional word that you want to teach. Also see suggestions for teaching vocabulary in the ELL and Transition Handbook.

Word Card Jar	Speak or Be Silent	Poster Clues
• Put one set of Word Cards in a jar. • Ask a volunteer to pick a word out of the jar, read it, and chant the spelling. For example, if the word *block* is selected, the child will say *block, b-l-o-c-k*. The other children then repeat the word and the spelling. • The child with the card says a sentence using the word. The other children then repeat the sentence. • Continue with children taking turns drawing from the jar until all the Word Cards have been used. Make sure each child has a turn selecting a word.	• Divide children into pairs and give two sets of Word Cards to each child. Have each child mix up their cards and place them in a pile face down. • Players each turn one card face up at the same time. • If the words on the cards match, players say the word aloud. The player who says the word first gets the pair of cards. • If the words do not match, players should remain silent. If both players remain silent, no one gets the cards. If both players say a word when they should not, no one gets the cards. If one player accidentally says a word, the other player gets the pair of cards. • Play continues with the unmatched cards until no more matches are possible. The player with the most cards wins.	• Use one set of Word Cards. Display this week's ELL Poster. • Have children take turns choosing a card without showing it to the others, and pointing to a scene or detail on the Poster that illustrates the word on the card. The child should talk about the scene and give clues about the vocabulary word without saying the word. • The first child to correctly guess the word takes the next turn.

block	**chuckle**
fair	**giant**
strong	**tears**
trouble	

Multilingual Summaries

English

I Like Where I Am

A boy likes his house. He likes playing with his sister's kitten. He is happy where he is. One day, a moving truck comes. The movers pack up everything in the house. The boy doesn't want to leave. There is a swimming pool nearby. His best friend lives nearby.

The family moves. The boy makes a new friend in the new town. The friend has a swimming pool. The boy gets a kitten of his own. He still thinks of his old house, but he likes where he is now.

Spanish

Me gusta donde estoy

A un niño le gusta su casa. Le gusta jugar con el gatito de su hermana. Él está contento donde está. Un día, llega un camión de mudanzas. Los trabajadores empacan todo lo que hay en la casa. El niño no quiere irse. Cerca de allí hay una piscina. Su mejor amigo vive cerca.

La familia se muda. El niño encuentra un nuevo amigo en el nuevo pueblo. Este amigo tiene una piscina. El niño recibe de regalo su propio gatito. Él todavía se acuerda de su otra casa, pero le gusta donde está ahora.

Multilingual Summaries

Chinese

我喜歡我居住的地方

小男孩喜歡他的家，也喜歡跟他妹妹的小貓玩，他很滿意現在居住的地方。有一天，家門口來了一輛搬家公司的卡車，搬運工人把房子裡所有東西都打包了。小男孩不想搬家，因為這附近有一個游泳池，他最好的朋友也住在這裡。

最後小男孩的家還是搬走了。不久之後，他在新家附近交到了一個新朋友，朋友家裡有一個游泳池，而且小男孩也有了自己的小貓。雖然小男孩還是會想起舊家，但是他喜歡現在居住的地方。

Vietnamese

Tôi Thích Nơi Tôi Đang Ở

Một cậu bé thích ngôi nhà của mình. Cậu thích chơi với con mèo con của chị mình. Cậu bé hài lòng với nơi mình đang ở. Một ngày kia, một chiếc xe dọn nhà đến. Những người khuân dọn chất mọi thứ ở trong nhà vào thùng. Cậu bé không muốn đi. Gần nhà có một hồ bơi. Người bạn thân nhất của cậu sống gần nhà.

Gia đình dọn đi. Cậu bé quen với một bạn mới trong thành phố mới. Người bạn này có hồ bơi. Và cậu bé được riêng cho mình một chú mèo con. Cậu bé vẫn còn nhớ ngôi nhà cũ, nhưng cậu bé thích nơi mình đang ở.

Multilingual Summaries

Korean

지금 있는 곳이 좋아

한 소년이 지금 살고 있는 집을 좋아한다. 이 소년은 자기 누나의 고양이와 노는 것을 좋아하고 지금 있는 곳을 참 좋아한다. 어느 날 이사 차가 와서 짐꾼들이 집에 있는 모든 물건들을 포장한다. 소년은 떠나기가 싫다. 근처에는 수영장도 있고 제일 친한 친구도 살고 있기 때문이다.

가족은 이사를 하고 소년은 새 마을에서 새로운 친구들을 사귀게 된다. 친구 집에는 수영장도 있고 소년은 고양이도 기르게 돼서 여전히 옛날에 살던 집이 생각나지만 이제는 새 집이 좋다.

Hmong

Kuv Nyiam Nyob Qhov Uas Kuv Nyob

Ib tug me nyuam tub nyaim nws lub tsev. Nws nyiam ua siv nrog nws tus muam tus me myuam miv. Muaj ib hnub ib lub rhuav tsiv tsev tau tuaj. Cov neeg tsiv neeg tau ntim txhua yam nyob hauv lub tsev. Tus me nyuam tub tsis xav tsiv tsev li. Muaj ib lub pas dej ua luam dej nyob ze. Nws tus phooj ywm zoo nyob ze nws.

Tsev neeg no tau tsiv tsev. Tus me nyuam tub tau muaj ib tug phooj ywg tshiab hauv lub zos tshiab. Tus phooj ywg muaj ib lub pas dej ua luam dej. Thiab tus me nyuam tub tau ib tug me nyuam miv rau nws tus kheej. Nws xav txog nws lub qub tsev, tiam sis nws nyiam nyob qhov uas nws nyob niam no.

Helen Keller and the Big Storm

Student Edition pages 128–141

Week at a Glance	Customize instruction every day for your English Language Learners.				
	Day 1	**Day 2**	**Day 3**	**Day 4**	**Day 5**
Teacher's Edition	Use the ELL Notes that appear throughout each day of the lesson to support instruction and reading.				
ELL Poster 20	• Assess Prior Knowledge • Develop Concepts and Vocabulary	• Preteach Tested Vocabulary	• Review Fact/ Opinion	• Weather Report	• Monitor Progress
ELL Teaching Guide	• Picture It! Lesson, pp. 134–135 • Multilingual Summaries, pp. 138–140	• ELL Reader Lesson, pp. 250–251	• Vocabulary Activities and Word Cards, pp. 136–137 • Multilingual Summaries, pp. 138–140		
ELL Readers	• Reread *Adam's New Soccer Team*	• Teach *How Is the Weather?*	• Reread *How Is the Weather?* and other texts to build fluency		
ELL and Transition Handbook	Use the following as needed to support this week's instruction and to conduct alternative assessments: • Phonics Transition Lessons • Grammar Transition Lessons • Assessment				

Picture It! Comprehension Lesson

Fact and Opinion

Use this lesson to supplement or replace the skill lesson on pages 124–125 of the Teacher's Edition.

Teach

Distribute copies of the Picture It! blackline master on page 135.

- Ask children to look at the picture and describe it.
- Read the paragraph aloud. Ask: *Can you find an opinion in the paragraph?*
- Share the Skill Points (at right) with children.
- Have children look at the picture and paragraph to find clues about facts and opinions in the story.

Practice

Read aloud the directions on page 135. Have children fill in the *Fact-and-Opinion* chart.

Answers for page 135: Possible answers: *Facts:* Helen Keller could not see or hear. She learned to do many things. She used her hands to read and write. She used her nose to smell flowers. She tasted food. *Opinions:* She was very brave. She was a very good student. Annie was the best teacher in the world. Helen lived a very full life.

Skill Points

✓ A **fact** can be proven true or false. You can check in a book, ask someone who knows, or see for yourself.

✓ An **opinion** tells what someone thinks or feels. Clue words such as *best* show statements of opinion.

✓ As you read, ask yourself: *Can this sentence be proven true or false?*

Name ______________________________

Look at the picture. **Read** the paragraph.

- **Fill in** the chart. Write two facts and two opinions from the story.

A Full Life

Helen Keller could not see or hear. But she was very brave. She was also a very good student. Her teacher Annie Sullivan helped her learn. Annie was the best teacher in the world! Throughout her life, Helen learned to do many things. She used her hands to read and write in Braille, a special language for the blind. She used her nose to smell flowers. She tasted good food. She lived a very full life.

Facts	Opinions

Vocabulary Activities and Word Cards

Copy the Word Cards on page 137 as needed for the following activities.
Use the blank card for an additional word that you want to teach.
Also see suggestions for teaching vocabulary in the ELL and Transition Handbook.

Another Way to Say It	Word Hunt	Mind Reader
• Give one set of Word Cards to each child. • Write context sentences on the board, but substitute other words for the vocabulary words. Underline the substituted words. For example: *The tree frog* <u>*held on tightly*</u> *to the tree. (clung); The* <u>*tree parts*</u> *moved in the wind. (branches)* • Invite volunteers to read each sentence aloud once, then read it again, substituting a vocabulary word for the underlined word or words.	• Divide children into pairs. Give each pair one Word Card, saying each word aloud as you hand out the cards. • Challenge pairs to find their words in classroom books or other environmental print. Have them say where they find each word and then write the phrase or sentence in which they find it. • Invite pairs to share their findings with the class.	• Give each child a set of Word Cards. Have children spread out their cards face up so they can see them. • Write these sentence frames on the board: *This word starts with the letter _____. This word means _____. This word ends with the letter _____.* • Pick up a Word Card and give children clues about the word by reading and completing the sentence frames. • Children hold up the correct Word Card when they believe that they have the answer. • The child who correctly guesses the word may choose another card and provide the group with the next riddle. Allow children to use the sentence frames or make up their own clues.

angry

branches

clung

fingers

picnic

pressing

special

Multilingual Summaries

English

Helen Keller and the Big Storm

Helen Keller was blind. She could not hear or speak. Sometimes she threw tantrums. Helen's parents found her a special teacher, Annie Sullivan. Annie taught Helen to read. Annie spelled out words with her fingers. Helen felt the words that Annie spelled. Then she could understand the words.

Helen and Annie went for walks outside. One summer day, they climbed a tree. Annie went inside to make lunch. Helen stayed in the tree. Suddenly, Helen felt a strong wind. A storm was coming. Helen was afraid. She could not see. She could not call for help. Then, Helen felt a hand. It was Annie. Helen was safe. Helen knew Annie would always be her friend.

Spanish

Helen Keller y la gran tormenta

Helen Keller era ciega. Tampoco podía oír ni hablar. A veces hacía pataletas. Los papás de Helen le encontraron una maestra especial, Annie Sullivan. Annie le enseñó a leer. Annie deletreaba palabras con sus dedos. Helen sentía las palabras que Annie deletreaba. Así pudo entender las palabras.

Helen y Annie salían a dar paseos. Un día de verano se subieron a un árbol. Annie regresó para hacer el almuerzo. Helen se quedó en el árbol. De repente, Helen sintió vientos muy fuertes. Una tormenta se avecinaba. Helen sintió miedo. No podía ver. No podía llamar por ayuda. Entonces, Helen sintió el contacto de una mano. Era Annie. Helen estaba a salvo. Helen supo que Annie iba a ser siempre su amiga.

Multilingual Summaries

Chinese

海倫・凱勒與暴風雨

海倫・凱勒的眼睛看不見東西，耳朵聽不到聲音，嘴巴也不會說話。她喜歡惡作劇，有時還會亂發脾氣。海倫的父母幫她請了一個專門的老師，她的名字叫安妮・沙利文。安妮教海倫閱讀，她用手指拼出單字，讓海倫感受她拼的單字，然後海倫就能明白這些單字的意思。

海倫和安妮喜歡到戶外散步。某個夏日，她們爬到樹上乘涼。後來安妮回家做午餐，讓海倫一個人待在樹上。突然之間，海倫感覺有一陣大風，原來是暴風雨要來了。海倫很害怕，可是她看不見，也無法開口求救。就在這個時候，海倫感到有人伸出手來救她，原來是安妮！海倫安全了，她知道安妮永遠也是她的朋友。

Vietnamese

Helen Keller và Trận Bão Lớn

Helen Keller bị mù. Cô bé không thể nghe hoặc nói. Cô thích nghịch phá. Đôi khi cô nổi cơn giận dữ. Ba mẹ của Helen tìm cho cô một cô giáo đặc biệt. Tên của cô giáo là Annie Sullivan. Annie dạy cho Helen đọc. Annie đánh vần những chữ với các ngón tay của mình. Helen sờ những chữ mà Annie đã đánh vần. Sau đó cô bé có thể hiểu chữ.

Helen và Annie thường đi dạo bên ngoài. Một ngày hè, họ leo lên cây. Annie đi nấu món ăn trưa. Helen ở lại trên cây. Thình lình, Helen cảm thấy một luồng gió mạnh. Một trận bão đang kéo đến. Helen sợ hãi. Cô bé không thể thấy. Cô bé không thể kêu cứu. Lúc ấy, Helen cảm thấy có một bàn tay. Tay của Annie. Helen được bình an. Helen biết Annie sẽ luôn là người bạn tốt nhất của mình.

Multilingual Summaries

Korean

헬렌 켈러와 대폭풍

헬렌 켈러는 앞을 볼 수 없었고, 듣지도 말하지도 못했다. 헬렌은 장난치며 노는 것을 좋아했지만 가끔씩 짜증을 내기도 했다. 헬렌의 부모님은 그녀를 가르칠 애니 설리반이라는 이름의 특별한 선생님 한 분을 찾았다. 애니는 헬렌에게 읽기를 가르치고 손가락으로 단어를 구별하게 했다. 헬렌은 애니가 발음하는 단어를 느끼며 그 뜻을 이해할 수 있었다.

헬렌과 애니는 밖으로 산책을 나갔는데 어느 여름 날 그들은 나무를 타고 올라갔다. 애니는 점심 식사를 준비하러 가고 헬렌은 나무에 머물러 있었다. 갑자기 헬렌은 강한 바람이 부는 것을 느꼈다. 폭풍이 몰려오고 있었던 것이다. 헬렌은 무서웠지만 앞을 볼 수도, 도와달라고 소리칠 수도 없었다. 그 때 헬렌은 누군가의 손길을 느꼈다. 그건 바로 애니였다. 헬렌은 무사했으며 애니가 늘 그녀의 친구가 되어 줄 것임을 알 수 있었다.

Hmong

Helen Keller thiab Kob Nag Loj

Helen Keller tau dig muag. Nws lag ntseg thiab hais tsis tau lus. Nws nyiam tso dag rau luag tej. Txhia zaus nws npaw taws heev. Helen niam txiv nrhiav tau ib tug nais khus zoo. Tus nais khus lub npe hu ua Annie Sullivan. Annie qhia Helen nyeem ntawv. Annie sau ntawv nrog nws cov ntiv tes. Helen xuas tau cov ntawv uas Annie sau. Ces nws to taub cov lus.

Helen thiab Annie mus kev nraum zoov. Muaj ib hnub thaum lub caij so, nkawv mus nce ntoo. Annie tau mus tsev mus npaj su. Helen nyob saum tsob ntoo. Helen txawm hnov kob cua hlob hlob. Ib kob nag yuav los. Helen tau ntshai. Nws tsis pom kev. Nws qw tsis tau kom luag tej los pab nws. Ces, Helen xuas tau ib txhais tes. Txhais tes yog Annie txhais. Helen tsis ntshia lawm. Helen paub tias Annie yeej yuav yog nws tus phooj ywg.

Firefighter! Student Edition pages 158–171

Week at a Glance	Customize instruction every day for your English Language Learners.				
	Day 1	**Day 2**	**Day 3**	**Day 4**	**Day 5**
Teacher's Edition	Use the ELL Notes that appear throughout each day of the lesson to support instruction and reading.				
ELL Poster 21	• Assess Prior Knowledge • Develop Concepts and Vocabulary	• Preteach Tested Vocabulary	• Do a Good Job Skits	• Community Job Chart	• Monitor Progress
ELL Teaching Guide	• Picture It! Lesson, pp. 141–142 • Multilingual Summaries, pp. 145–147	• ELL Reader Lesson, pp. 252–253	• Vocabulary Activities and Word Cards, pp. 143–144 • Multilingual Summaries, pp. 145–147		
ELL Readers	• Reread *How Is the Weather?*	• Teach *At the Fire Station*	• Reread *At the Fire Station* and other texts to build fluency		
ELL and Transition Handbook	Use the following as needed to support this week's instruction and to conduct alternative assessments: • Phonics Transition Lessons • Grammar Transition Lessons • Assessment				

Picture It! Comprehension Lesson

Main Idea

Use this lesson to supplement or replace the skill lesson on pages 154–155 of the Teacher's Edition.

Teach

Distribute copies of the Picture It! blackline master on page 142.

- Ask children to look at the picture and describe it.
- Read the paragraph aloud. Ask: *What is the paragraph mostly about?* (having a fire drill at school)
- Review the Skill Points (at right) with children.
- Have children tell you which sentence contains the main idea. Ask them to find details that tell more about it.

Practice

Read aloud the directions on page 142. Have children write the main idea and details in the graphic organizer.

Answers for page 142: *Main Idea*: Today we had a fire drill at school. *Details*: Accept any three details from the paragraph.

Skill Points

✓ The **main idea** is the most important idea in a selection.

✓ You can often find the main idea near the beginning of a selection.

✓ Look for the sentence that answers the question: *What is this paragraph mostly about?*

✓ **Details** tell more about the main idea.

Name ______________________________

Look at the pictures. **Read** the paragraph.

- Which sentence tells the main idea of the paragraph? **Write** that sentence in the top box.
- Which sentences give details? **Write** one detail in each box.

Fire Drill

Today we had a fire drill at school. We practiced what to do if there is a real fire. We heard the fire bell ring. We stood up quietly and went to the door. We followed our teacher in a line to our place outside. We waited until we heard the bell ring again. Then we went back inside. We have a good plan. If there is a fire, we will be safe.

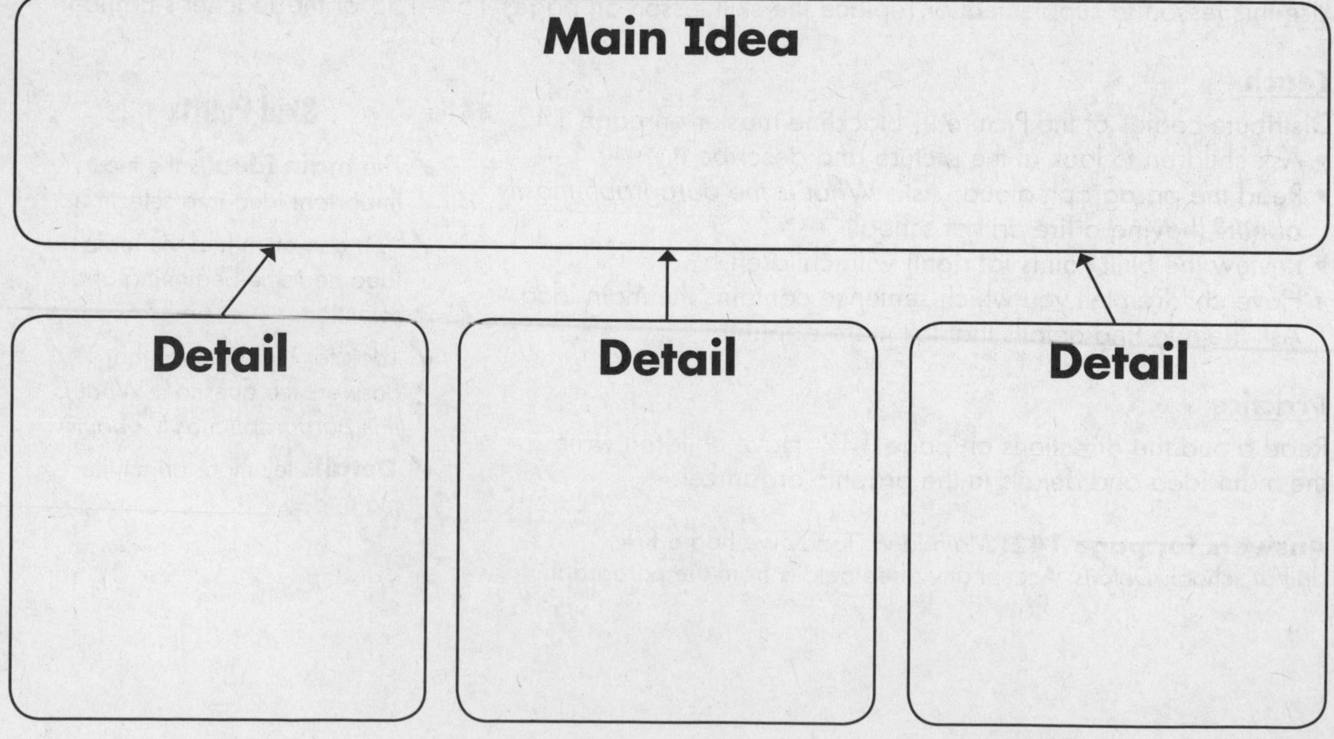

Vocabulary Activities and Word Cards

Copy the Word Cards on page 144 as needed for the following activities.
Use the blank card for an additional word that you want to teach.
Also see suggestions for teaching vocabulary in the ELL and Transition Handbook.

Mind Reader	Illustrating Word Cards	Puzzle Pieces
• Give each child a set of Word Cards. Have children spread out their cards face up so they can see them. • Write these sentence frames on the board: *This word starts with the letter ____. This word means _____. This word ends with the letter ____.* • Pick up a Word Card and give children clues about the word by reading and completing the sentence frames. • Children hold up the correct Word Card when they believe they have the answer. • The child who correctly guesses the word may choose another card and provide the group with the next riddle. Allow children to use the sentence frames or make up their own clues.	• Give one set of Word Cards to each child. • Ask children to draw a picture on the back of each Word Card to represent the tested word. Assist children as necessary with *quickly* and *tightly*, or do not use those cards. • When children have finished drawing, divide them into groups of two or three. • One child lays out his or her Word Cards with the illustrations facing up for the others in the group to see. The others figure out which word each illustration represents. • Continue until each child in each group has displayed his or her illustrations.	• Give pairs of children sets of Word Cards. • Have the children cut each card into two puzzle pieces of different shapes. • Ask children to mix up the puzzle pieces, lay them face up, and take turns putting words back together. As they do so, the children should read the words aloud. • Ask the children to write or say a sentence using each word.

building	**burning**
masks	**quickly**
roar	**station**
tightly	

Multilingual Summaries

English

Firefighter!

Firefighters work in the fire station. The alarm rings! Liz, Dan, and Anthony slide down the pole. They put on fireproof clothes. They ride to the fire in a fire truck.

An old house is on fire. No one lives there now. But someone saw a boy playing there this morning. Liz hooks up the hose to a fire hydrant. She helps to spray the fire. Dan and Anthony search for the boy. They can't find him. They run out before the roof falls. Someone tells them that the boy is safe.

Later, the fire is out. Anthony sprays water on the coals. Liz winds up the hoses. They go back to the station. They are tired and hungry. They sit down to eat, but the alarm rings again!

Spanish

¡Bomberos!

Los bomberos trabajan en la estación. ¡Suena la alarma! Liz, Dan y Anthony bajan por el poste. Se visten con ropas a prueba de fuego. Van rumbo al incendio en el camión de bomberos.

Una casa vieja está ardiendo. Ahora nadie vive allí. Pero alguien vio a un niño jugando allí en la mañana. Liz enrosca la manguera a una boca de incendios. Ella ayuda a echarle agua al fuego. Dan y Anthony buscan al niño. No lo pueden encontrar. Salen corriendo antes de que el techo se derrumbe. Alguien les dice que el niño está a salvo.

Después, se apaga el incendio. Anthony riega con agua los maderos quemados. Liz enrolla las mangueras. Regresan a la estación. Están cansados y hambrientos. Se sientan a comer, pero ¡la alarma suena otra vez!

Multilingual Summaries

Chinese

勇敢的消防員！

消防員在消防站工作。警報響了！ 麗茲、丹和安東尼沿著消防滑竿滑下去，然後穿上防火衣，跳上消防車趕到失火的地方去。

原來是一棟舊房子著火了，幸好現在已沒有人住在裡面，但有人說今天早上看到一個男孩在那裡玩耍。麗茲把消防水管接到消防栓上，幫忙噴水滅火。丹和安東尼衝進失火的房子裡找小男孩，但是找不到。屋頂要塌下來了，他們才不得已趕緊離開。後來有人告訴他們，小男孩沒事。

不久之後，火滅了。安東尼在焦炭上灑水，麗茲把消防水管收好，然後返回消防站。他們又累又餓，正坐下來吃飯的時候，警報又響了！

Vietnamese

Lính Cứu Hỏa!

Các người lính cứu hỏa làm việc ở trạm cứu hỏa. Chuông báo động reo vang! Liz, Dan, và Anthony tuột xuống cây cột. Họ mặc quần áo chống cháy vào. Họ lên xe cứu hỏa để đi đến nơi có hỏa hoạn.

Một căn nhà cũ đang bốc cháy. Không có ai đang sống ở đó. Nhưng có người thấy một đứa bé trai chơi ở đó hồi sáng này. Liz gắn vòi nước chữa lửa vào ống nước. Cô giúp phun nước vào lửa. Dan và Anthony đi tìm đứa bé. Họ không tìm thấy nó. Họ chạy ra trước khi mái nhà đổ sập xuống. Có người nói là đứa bé được bình an.

Lát sau, lửa được dập tắt. Anthony phun nước vào các đống than. Liz cuộn các vòi nước lại. Họ trở về trạm. Họ đều mệt và đói. Họ ngồi xuống để ăn, nhưng chuông báo động lại reo vang lần nữa!

Multilingual Summaries

Korean

소방관

소방관들은 소방서에서 일한다. 경보음이 울리고 리즈와 댄 그리고 안소니가 기둥을 타고 내려가 방화복을 입는다. 이들은 소방차를 타고 화재 현장으로 달려간다.

오래된 집 한 채가 불에 타고 있다. 지금은 그 집에 아무도 살고 있지 않지만 오늘 아침 한 소년이 그 집에서 놀고 있는 것을 누군가가 보았다. 리즈가 소화전에 호스를 연결시켜 물 뿌리는 것을 돕는다. 댄과 앤소니는 그 소년을 찾아보지만 찾지 못하고 지붕이 무너지기 전에 밖으로 나온다. 누군가가 그 소년은 무사하다고 말해준다.

나중에 화재가 정리되자 앤소니는 타고 남은 재에 물을 뿌린다. 리즈가 호스를 감은 후 모두 소방서로 돌아간다. 지치고 배고픈 이들은 허기를 채우려고 앉았지만 다시 경보음이 울린다.

Hmong

Cov Neeg Tua Hluav Taws

Cov neeg tua hluav taws ua hauj lwm hauv lub tsev tua hluav taws. Lub tswb quaj. Liz, Dan, thiab Anthony nqis mus sab hauv qab siv ib tug pas. Lawv hnav cov khaub ncaws tiv tau hluav taws. Lawv caij lub tsheb tua hluav taws mus rau qhov chaw muaj hluav taws.

Ib lub tsev qub qub tau kub hnyiab. Tsis muaj leej twg nyob hauv. Tiam sis muaj ib tug neeg uas tau pom ib tug me nyuam tub ua siv nyob hauv tag kis ntawd. Liz tau muab txoj hlua dej mus tauj tus kais dej tua hluav taws. Nws pab tsuag dej mus rau cov hluav taws. Dan thiab Anthony nrhiav tus me nyuam tub. Nkawd nrhiav tsis tau nws. Nkawd tau tawm hauv lub tsev ua ntev lub tsev tau vau. Ib tug neeg tau hais tias tus me nyuam tub yeej nyob zoo.

Tom qab ntawd, cov hluav taws tau tuag. Anthony tau tsuag dej rau cov ncaig. Liz muab txoj hlua dej kauv. Lawv rov qab mus tom lub tsev tua hluav taws. Lawv tau nkees thiab tshaib plab. Lawv zaum noj mov, tiam sis lub tswb tau quaj dua.

One Dark Night Student Edition pages 184–201

Week at a Glance	Customize instruction every day for your English Language Learners.				
	Day 1	**Day 2**	**Day 3**	**Day 4**	**Day 5**
Teacher's Edition	Use the ELL Notes that appear throughout each day of the lesson to support instruction and reading.				
ELL Poster 22	• Assess Prior Knowledge • Develop Concepts and Vocabulary	• Preteach Tested Vocabulary	• Review Sequence	• Descriptive Riddles	• Monitor Progress
ELL Teaching Guide	• Picture It! Lesson, pp. 148–149 • Multilingual Summaries, pp. 152–154	• ELL Reader Lesson, pp. 254–255	• Vocabulary Activities and Word Cards, pp. 150–151 • Multilingual Summaries, pp. 152–154		
ELL Readers	• Reread *At The Fire Station*	• Teach *Save the Ducks!*	• Reread *Save the Ducks!* and other texts to build fluency		
ELL and Transition Handbook	Use the following as needed to support this week's instruction and to conduct alternative assessments: • Phonics Transition Lessons • Grammar Transition Lessons • Assessment				

Picture It! Comprehension Lesson

Sequence

Use this lesson to supplement or replace the skill lesson on pages 180–181 of the Teacher's Edition.

Teach

Distribute copies of the Picture It! blackline master on page 149.

- Ask children to look at the pictures and describe what is happening in each one.
- Read the sentences aloud. Ask: *What happens first in the story? What happens next?*
- Share the Skill Points (at right) with children.
- Have children look at the pictures and words to find clues about the order of events in the story.

Practice

Read aloud the directions on page 149. Have children fill in the sequence chart.

Answers for page 149: *First:* Max runs to the window and barks loudly. *Next:* Max jumps on the boy's lap and covers his ears. *Then:* Max hides. *Finally:* Max comes out when the storm ends.

Skill Points

✓ **Sequence** is the order of events in a story.

✓ Think about what happens first, next, and last.

✓ Look for words such as *first, next, then, now,* and *finally* to help you figure out the order of events.

Name ____________________________________

Look at the pictures. **Read** the sentences.

- **Fill in** the sequence chart. **Write** the events of the story in order.

Weather Dog

I always know when a storm is coming. My dog Max lets me know. First, he runs to the window and barks loudly. Next, Max jumps onto my lap and covers his ears. Then, when the thunder gets loud, Max hides. He will not even come out for a treat! Finally, Max comes out when the storm ends. He is glad to see the Sun!

First

↓

Next

↓

Then

↓

Finally

Vocabulary Activities and Word Cards

Copy the Word Cards on page 151 as needed for the following activities.
Use the blank card for an additional word that you want to teach.
Also see suggestions for teaching vocabulary in the ELL and Transition Handbook.

Charades	Poster Clues	Word Hunt
• Divide children into small groups and give each group one or two Word Cards. Do not use the word *rolling*. • Give groups time to discuss how to act out the meanings of the words. Allow children to use sounds as they act out each word. • Have groups take turns acting while others guess the word. • Continue until each group has acted out at least one word.	• Use one set of Word Cards. Display this week's ELL Poster. • Have children take turns choosing a card without showing it to the others, and pointing to a scene or detail on the Poster that illustrates the word on the card. The child should talk about the scene and give clues about the vocabulary word without saying the word. • The first child to correctly guess the word takes the next turn.	• Divide children into pairs. Give each pair one or two Word Cards, and ask children to say the words aloud as you hand them the cards. • Challenge pairs to find their words in classroom books or other environmental print. Have them say where they find each word and then write the phrase or sentence in which they find it. • Invite pairs to share their findings with the class.

flashes

lightning

pounds

pours

rolling

storm

thunder

Multilingual Summaries

English

One Dark Night

A thunderstorm is coming. There is lightning and thunder. Jonathan is home with Grandmother and Grandfather. A stray cat comes indoors. The cat is carrying a kitten. She puts the kitten down. She goes outside again. Jonathan wraps the kitten in his bathrobe. The cat comes back. She brings another kitten. Then she goes outside again.

The storm comes. It rains hard. There is more thunder and lightning. The cat comes back. She brings another kitten. The stray cat and her kittens fall asleep in Jonathan's bathrobe. They are all safe from the storm.

Spanish

Una noche oscura

Se avecina una tormenta. Hay relámpagos y truenos. Jonathan está en casa con Abuela y Abuelo. Una gata callejera entra a la casa. La gata lleva un gatito. Después lo pone en el piso y vuelve a salir. Jonathan envuelve el gatito en la bata. La gata regresa. Va llevando otro gatito. Luego, vuelve a salir.

La tormenta llega. Llueve muy fuerte. Hay más relámpagos y truenos. La gata regresa. Va llevando otro gatito. La gata perdida y los gatitos se acuestan a dormir en la bata de Jonathan. Están protegidos de la tormenta.

Multilingual Summaries

Chinese

一個月黑風高的夜晚

大雷雨要來了，天空不斷閃電和打雷。強納生和祖父母一起待在家裡。有隻貓跑進他們的屋裡，身邊還帶著一隻小貓。貓媽媽放下小貓，然後走出去了。強納生用浴袍把小貓包好。貓媽媽回來了，這次帶來了另一隻小貓，然後又走出去了。

暴風雨來了，雨很大，閃電和打雷比剛才還多。貓媽媽又回來了，帶來了第三隻小貓。迷路的貓媽媽和小貓在強納生的浴袍裡睡著了。他們都很安全，不用再怕暴風雨。

Vietnamese

Một Đêm Tối

Một cơn mưa bão sắp đến. Có sấm sét. Jonathan đang ở nhà với Ông Bà. Một con mèo vào nhà. Con mèo này mang theo một con mèo con. Mèo mẹ đặt mèo con xuống. Mèo mẹ đi trở ra ngoài. Jonathan quấn con mèo con trong áo choàng tắm của mình. Mèo mẹ trở lại. Nó mang theo một mèo con khác. Rồi nó lại trở ra ngoài lần nữa.

Bão đến. Mưa to. Sấm sét nhiều hơn. Mèo mẹ trở lại. Nó mang theo một con mèo con khác. Con mèo hoang và các con của nó ngủ thiếp trong chiếc áo choàng tắm của Jonathan. Tất cả chúng đều được an toàn.

Multilingual Summaries

Korean

어느 어두운 밤

번개와 천둥을 동반한 폭우가 몰려오고 있다. 조나단은 할아버지 할머니와 함께 집에 있었는데 한 고양이가 새끼 고양이를 데리고 집안으로 들어온다. 고양이가 새끼를 내려놓고는 다시 밖으로 나가버린다. 조나단이 목욕 타월로 새끼 고양이를 감싸준다. 고양이가 다른 새끼 고양이를 데리고 돌아왔다. 그리고는 다시 밖으로 나간다.

폭풍이 몰려온다. 비가 심하게 내리고 천둥과 번개도 더 심해진다. 고양이는 또 다른 새끼 고양이를 데리고 다시 돌아온다. 길을 잃은 엄마 고양이와 새끼 고양이들이 조나단의 목욕 타월 속에서 잠이 든다. 모두들 폭풍우에도 불구하고 무사하다.

Hmong

Ib Hmo Tsaus Ntuj Ntiv

Ib kob nag xob nag cua yuav los. Muaj xob laim thiab xob quaj. Jonathan nyob tsev nrog nws Niam Tais thiab Yawm Txiv. Ib tug miv tau los tsev. Tus miv nqa ib tug me nyuam miv. Nws tso tus me nyuam miv hauv av. Nws rov qab mus nraum zoov. Jonathan muab ib daim phuam los qhwv tus me nyuam miv. Tus miv rov qab los. Nws nqa ib tug me nyuam miv ntxiv. Ces nws rov mus nraum zoov dua.

Kob nag tau los. Nws los nag hlob heev. Yeej muaj ntau tshaj xob quaj thiab xob laim. Tus miv rov qab los. Nws rov qab nqa ib tug me nyuam miv los. Tus miv uas tsis muaj tsw tau pw zaug zog hauv Jonathan txoj phuam. Lawv sawv daws nyob zoo hauv lub tsev tsis ntub nag.

Bad Dog, Dodger! Student Edition pages 212–225

Week at a Glance	Customize instruction every day for your English Language Learners.				
	Day 1	**Day 2**	**Day 3**	**Day 4**	**Day 5**
Teacher's Edition	Use the ELL Notes that appear throughout each day of the lesson to support instruction and reading.				
ELL Poster 23	• Assess Prior Knowledge • Develop Concepts and Vocabulary	• Preteach Tested Vocabulary	• Review Character/ Setting/Plot	• Guidebooks for Pets	• Monitor Progress
ELL Teaching Guide	• Picture It! Lesson, pp. 155–156 • Multilingual Summaries, pp. 159–161	• ELL Reader Lesson, pp. 256–257	• Vocabulary Activities and Word Cards, pp. 157–158 • Multilingual Summaries, pp. 159–161		
ELL Readers	• Reread *Save the Ducks!*	• Teach *Puppy Show*	• Reread *Puppy Show* and other texts to build fluency		
ELL and Transition Handbook	Use the following as needed to support this week's instruction and to conduct alternative assessments: • Phonics Transition Lessons • Grammar Transition Lessons • Assessment				

Picture It! Comprehension Lesson

Plot and Theme

Use this lesson to supplement or replace the skill lesson on pages 208–209 of the Teacher's Edition.

Teach

Distribute copies of the Picture It! blackline master on page 156.

- Ask children to look at the pictures and describe what is happening in them.
- Read the story aloud. Ask: *What does Jack do?* (He misbehaves.)
- Share the Skill Points (at right) with the children.
- Have children look at the pictures and sentences and think about the theme of the story.

Skill Points

✓ The **theme** is the big idea of a story.

✓ Look at the title and the pictures. Ask yourself: *What do I think the story will be about? Do I know anything about this?*

✓ The **plot** is what happens at the beginning, middle, and end of a story.

Practice

Read aloud the directions on page 156. Have children answer the questions about plot and theme.

Answers for page 156: 1. Nana babysits. She and the girl try to play a game. Jack throws the pieces. **2.** Jack has to go to bed early. He does not get ice cream because he did not behave. **3.** (Guide children to discuss the story's big idea.) Sample response: The big idea of this story is that if you don't behave you may not get the things you want.

Name ______________________________

Look at the pictures. **Read** the story.

Oh Brother!

Mom and Dad went out to dinner. Nana stayed with Jack and me. We tried to play a game, but Jack took the pieces.

Then Nana and I painted pictures. Jack painted his face!

Finally, Nana sent Jack to bed early. She and I ate ice cream. Jack loves ice cream. I know next time he will behave!

Answer the questions below.

1. Explain what happens at the beginning of the story.

____

____

2. What happens to Jack at the end of the story? Why does this happen?

____

____

3. Talk about what you think is the big idea of this story.

Vocabulary Activities and Word Cards

Copy the Word Cards on page 158 as needed for the following activities.
Use the blank card for an additional word that you want to teach.
Also see suggestions for teaching vocabulary in the ELL and Transition Handbook.

Pet Poster	Home Language Lesson	Word Endings
• Divide children into groups of two or three, and give each group one set of Word Cards. • Give each group a large piece of construction paper or a poster board and a variety of drawing materials. • Have children design a poster that illustrates at least five of the vocabulary words. They may use all of the words if they wish. • Ask children to paste the Word Cards they use onto their poster. • Have each group present its poster to the class. Encourage children to use complete sentences when describing the poster. Each child should say at least one sentence.	• Give each child a set of Word Cards. Have children place the cards face up in front of them. • Hold up one of the Word Cards and invite a volunteer to use it in a sentence, such as *The dog is chewing on a bone.* Write the sentence on the board. • Continue until you have written a sentence using each of the vocabulary words. • Then ask children to translate one of the sentences into their home language and write it on a piece of paper. • Invite volunteers to read their sentences. Encourage all children to repeat what they hear.	• Give each child a set of Word Cards. Write *-s*, *-ed*, and *-ing* at the top of the board. • Review the meaning of each word with children. • Then invite volunteers to hold up a Word Card, read the word, and tell what ending it has. Write the word on the board under the appropriate heading. • When all the words with inflected endings are on the board, discuss with children each base word. Write the base words on the board. • Finally, write *practice* and *treat* on the board. Ask children to make new words by adding endings. Discuss how an ending changes the meaning of a word.

chased

chewing

dripping

grabbed

practice

treat

wagged

Multilingual Summaries

English

Bad Dog, Dodger!

Sam gets a puppy for his birthday. He names the dog Dodger. Dodger does many bad things. Dodger knocks over the trash. Dodger jumps in the bathtub with Molly. Dodger chews Sam's baseball cap. Dodger pulls down the curtains.

Sam's mom puts Dodger outside. Dodger jumps over the fence. He follows Sam to school. Dodger makes a mess in the classroom. Dodger runs onto the field at Sam's baseball game. He grabs a bat and runs away with it.

Now, Sam gets up early. He trains Dodger. Sam teaches Dodger to fetch. Sam teaches Dodger how to stay. Sam brings Dodger to a baseball game. Dodger catches a foul ball. Dodger is a good dog.

Spanish

¡Dodger, perro malcriado!

A Sam le regalan un perrito el día de su cumpleaños. Su nombre es Dodger. Dodger hace muchísimas picardías. Dodger voltea la basura. Dodger salta en la bañera con Molly. Dodger mastica la gorra de béisbol de Sam. Dodger arranca las cortinas.

La mamá de Sam saca a Dodger fuera de la casa. Dodger salta la cerca. Sigue a Sam a la escuela. Dodger hace daños en la clase. Dodger corre por el campo de juego cuando Sam juega béisbol. Agarra un bate y sale corriendo con él.

Ahora Sam se levanta temprano. Entrena a Dodger. Sam le enseña a buscar y traer cosas. Sam le enseña cómo quedarse quieto. Sam lleva a Dodger al juego de béisbol. Dodger agarra una pelota que se iba al *foul*. Dodger es un buen perro.

Multilingual Summaries

Chinese

壞狗狗，道奇！

山姆生日那天收到一隻小狗狗當生日禮物，山姆幫牠取了一個名字，叫道奇。道奇不乖，做了很多壞事：牠打翻垃圾桶，和莫利一起跳進澡盆裡，亂咬山姆的棒球帽，還把窗簾扯下來。

山姆的媽媽把道奇關在屋外，可是道奇卻跳過籬笆，跟著山姆到學校去，把教室弄得亂七八糟。道奇跑到山姆比賽棒球的運動場上，牠接到別人打出來的球，然後一溜煙地跑掉了。

終於，山姆決定要好好訓練道奇，他起了個大早，教道奇接東西，還教牠坐下。 山姆帶道奇一起去參加棒球比賽，比賽時道奇接到一個界外球。道奇真是好狗狗。

Vietnamese

Dodger, Chó Hư!

Sam được một chú chó con vào sinh nhật của mình. Nó đặt tên cho con chó là Dodger. Dodger làm nhiều điều hư xấu. Dodger làm ngả thùng rác. Dodger nhảy vào bồn tắm với Molly. Dodger cắn nón chơi bóng chày của Sam. Dodger kéo màn cửa xuống.

Mẹ của Sam đem Dodger ra ngoài. Dodger nhảy qua hàng rào. Nó theo Sam đi học. Dodger tiêu tiểu bừa bãi trong lớp học. Ở trận đấu bóng chày của Sam, Dodger chạy ra ngoài sân đấu. Nó gặm lấy cây gậy đánh bóng rồi bỏ chạy.

Bây giờ, Sam thức dậy sớm. Cậu quyết định phải huấn luyện Dodger. Sam dạy Dodger chạy đi lấy đồ. Sam dạy Dodger ngồi tại chỗ. Sam dẫn Dodger đến một trận đấu bóng chày. Dodger chụp được một quả bóng đánh trái luật. Dodger là một con chó ngoan.

Multilingual Summaries

Korean

도저는 나쁜 개!

샘은 생일 선물로 강아지 한 마리를 받아 도저라고 이름짓는다. 도저는 나쁜 일을 많이 저지른다. 쓰레기통을 뒤집어 놓고 몰리와 함께 목욕통으로 뛰어들며 샘의 야구 모자를 물어뜯고 또 커튼을 끌어내리도 한다.

샘의 어머니는 도저를 밖에 내보낸다. 도저는 울타리를 뛰어넘어 샘을 따라 학교에 가서 교실을 난장판으로 만들어버린다. 또한 샘의 야구 경기장으로 달려가 야구 방망이를 물고 도망친다.

이제 샘은 일찍 일어난다. 도저를 교육 좀 시켜야겠다고 결심한 것이다. 샘은 도저에게 물건을 가져오는 것과 가만히 있는 법을 가르친 후 도저를 데리고 야구장에 간다. 도저가 파울볼을 가지고 온다. 도저는 말을 잘 듣는다.

Hmong

Aub Phem, Dodger!

Thaum Sam hnub yug nws tau ib tug me nyuam aub. Nws hu tus aub hu ua Dodger. Dodger ua ntau yam phem. Dodger ncaws lub thoob khib nyiab vau. Dodger dhia mus rau hauv lub dab da dej nrog Molly. Dodger muab Sam lub kaus mom noj. Dodger rub tej ntaub thaiv qhov rais.

Sam niam cab Dodger mus nraum zoov. Dodger dhia mus saum daim laj kab. Nws raws Sam mus kawm ntawv. Dodger ua hoob kawm ntawv ntxhov tas. Dodger dhia mus nraum zoov mus nraum chav ua si. Nws cab tus pas ntaus npas thiab dhia khiav mus.

Nim no, Sam sawv ntxov ntxov. Nws txiav txim siab qhuab qhia Dodger. Sam qhia Dodger mus khawv khoom. Sam qhia Dodger nyob twb ywm. Sam coj Dodger mus saib lawv ntau npas. Dodger txhom tau lub npas uas lawv ntaus tawm qhov chaw ntau npas. Dodger yog ib tug aub zoo.

Horace and Morris but Mostly Dolores

Student Edition pages 238–255

Week at a Glance	Customize instruction every day for your English Language Learners.				
	Day 1	**Day 2**	**Day 3**	**Day 4**	**Day 5**
Teacher's Edition	Use the ELL Notes that appear throughout each day of the lesson to support instruction and reading.				
ELL Poster 24	• Assess Prior Knowledge • Develop Concepts and Vocabulary	• Preteach Tested Vocabulary	• Good Friend Commercial	• Friendly Stories	• Monitor Progress
ELL Teaching Guide	• Picture It! Lesson, pp. 162–163 • Multilingual Summaries, pp. 166–168	• ELL Reader Lesson, pp. 258–259	• Vocabulary Activities and Word Cards, pp. 164–165 • Multilingual Summaries, pp. 166–168		
ELL Readers	• Reread *Puppy Show*	• Teach *Hello, Friend!*	• Reread *Hello, Friend!* and other texts to build fluency		
ELL and Transition Handbook	Use the following as needed to support this week's instruction and to conduct alternative assessments: • Phonics Transition Lessons • Grammar Transition Lessons • Assessment				

Picture It! Comprehension Lesson

Author's Purpose

Use this lesson to supplement or replace the skill lesson on pages 234–235 of the Teacher's Edition.

Teach

Distribute copies of the Picture It! blackline master on page 163.

- Ask children to look at the pictures and describe what is happening.
- Read the story aloud. Ask: *What is the story about?* (a boy who can't go to the zoo and his friends) *What is the author trying to do?* (Answers will vary.)
- Share the Skill Points (at right) with children.
- Have children look at the pictures and sentences to find clues about the author's purpose.

Skill Points

✓ The **author's purpose** is his or her reason for writing.

✓ An author can write to share important information, to explain something, or to tell an interesting or funny story.

✓ Ask yourself questions before, during, and after you read to figure out the author's purpose.

Practice

Read aloud the directions on page 163. Have children answer the questions about the story.

Answers for page 163: 1. He could not go to the zoo. **2.** drew pictures **3.** Possible response: to tell a story about how friends help each other

Name ______________________________

Look at the pictures. **Read** the story.

A Field Trip

Marc's class was at the zoo, but Marc was in bed with a broken leg. He did not get to go on the field trip.

Marc's friends missed him. They knew he was sad about missing the trip. They wanted to do something to make him feel better.

Mai and Devon drew pictures of the animals. They took the pictures to Marc. It was like going to the zoo! Marc was happy to have such good friends.

Answer the questions below.

1. Why was Marc sad?
- O He could not go to the zoo.
- O He broke his arm.
- O He did not have friends.

2. What did Mai and Devon do?
- O got in trouble
- O stayed at home
- O drew pictures

3. Why do you think the author wrote the story?

____

Vocabulary Activities and Word Cards

Copy the Word Cards on page 165 as needed for the following activities.
Use the blank card for an additional word that you want to teach.
Also see suggestions for teaching vocabulary in the ELL and Transition Handbook.

Tell a Story	Bingo	Concentration
• Give two Word Cards to each child, and arrange the children in a circle. • Start a story with a sentence that uses one of the vocabulary words. For example: *We had an adventure today.* • The next child continues the story, finding a way to use one of his or her words in a sentence. Children can help each other make sentences. • Children take turns until all the Word Cards have been used and the group decides that the story is complete.	• Give each child a set of Word Cards. Have children paste six of their cards on a piece of paper in two columns with three rows. • Pass out coins, beans, or other counters to use as bingo chips. • Say the definition of or a phrase that describes one of the vocabulary words. For example: *This is the opposite of worst. (greatest); This is where a club meets. (clubhouse)* Have children look for the correct word and cover it with a chip. If necessary, announce the answer before moving on to the next word. • A child calls *bingo* and wins the game when he or she has placed bingo chips on three words in a row. • You may wish to have children trade bingo boards and play the game again.	• Give two sets of Word Cards to small groups of children, and ask them to spread out the cards face down. • Children take turns picking up a card, reading it aloud, and trying to find its matching card. • If a match is made, the child says a sentence using that word and keeps the match. If no match is made, the child returns both cards to their places. • The game ends when all the cards have been matched.

adventure	**climbed**
clubhouse	**exploring**
greatest	**truest**
wondered	

Multilingual Summaries

English

Horace and Morris but Mostly Dolores

Dolores, Horace, and Morris are friends. They like to explore. Then Horace and Morris join a club. Girls cannot join this club. Horace and Morris won't play with Dolores. Dolores is sad. She joins a club for girls. She soon becomes bored.

The girls in the club don't like to explore. Dolores quits the club. Chloris quits too. They find Horace and Morris and Boris. They all like to explore. Horace, Morris, Dolores, Chloris, and Boris build their own clubhouse.

Spanish

Horacio y Morris pero sobre todo Dolores

Dolores, Horacio y Morris son amigos. Les gusta explorar. Horacio y Morris se hacen miembros de un club. Las niñas no pueden pertenecer al club. Horacio y Morris no jugarán con Dolores. Dolores está triste. Ella se afilia al club de las niñas. Se aburre enseguida.

A las niñas del club no les gusta explorar. Dolores deja el club. Chloris también lo deja. Después se encuentran con Horacio, Morris y Boris. A todos les gusta explorar. Horacio, Morris, Dolores, Chloris y Boris forman su propio club.

Multilingual Summaries

Chinese

多洛蕾斯是大功臣

多洛蕾斯、哈瑞斯和莫利斯是朋友，他們都喜歡探險。哈瑞斯和莫利斯參加了一個社團，因為女生不能參加這個社團，所以哈瑞斯和莫利斯以後就不跟多洛蕾斯玩了。多洛蕾斯好難過。她去參加一個女生的社團，可是過沒多久，就開始覺得無聊。

社團裡的女生不喜歡探險，所以多洛蕾斯就不去那個社團了，有一隻叫做克蘿莉斯的老鼠也不去了，她們找到哈瑞斯、莫利斯和伯里斯。因為大家都喜歡探險，所以哈瑞斯、莫利斯、多洛蕾斯、克蘿莉斯和伯里斯就合力建了一個專屬他們的社團小屋。

Vietnamese

Horace và Morris nhưng phần nhiều là Dolores

Dolores, Horace, và Morris là bạn. Chúng thích thám hiểm. Rồi Horace và Morris gia nhập một câu lạc bộ. Con gái không được vào câu lạc bộ này. Horace và Morris không chơi với Dolores. Dolores buồn. Cô bé gia nhập một câu lạc bộ dành cho con gái. Chẳng bao lâu cô bé thấy chán.

Các cô gái trong câu lạc bộ không thích thám hiểm. Dolores bỏ câu lạc bộ. Chloris cũng bỏ nữa. Họ đi tìm Horace, Morris, và Boris. Ai trong chúng nó cũng thích thám hiểm. Horace, Morris, Dolores, Chloris, và Boris lập ra một câu lạc bộ riêng.

Multilingual Summaries

Korean

호레이스와 모리스 그리고 돌로레스

돌로레스와 호레이스, 그리고 모리스는 친구 사이로 모두 탐험을 좋아한다. 호레이스와 모리스가 한 클럽에 가입하는데 여자들은 이 클럽에 가입할 수 없어 돌로레스와는 어울리지 않는다. 돌로레스는 슬퍼하며 여자애들만을 위한 클럽에 가입을 하지만 곧 싫증이 난다.

클럽의 여자애들이 탐험을 싫어하기에 돌로레스는 클럽을 그만 두었고 클로리스라는 이름의 한 귀여운 여자 아이도 클럽을 그만둔다. 그들은 호레이스와 모리스 그리고 보리스를 찾는다. 모두들 탐험을 좋아한다. 호레이스, 모리스, 돌로레스, 클로리스, 그리고 보리스는 그들만의 클럽 회관을 만든다.

Hmong

Horace thiab Morris Tiam sis Feem Ntau Yog Dolores

Dolores, Horace, and Morris yog phooj ywg. Lawv nyiam mus saib xyuas ntau yam kawm. Ces Horace thiab Morris koom nrog ib lub koom haum. Cov me nyuam ntxhais koom nrog lub koom haum no tsis tau. Horace thiab Morris tsis kam ua si nrog Dolores. Dolores tu siab. Nws koom nrog ib lub koom haum rau cov me nyuam ntxhais. Tsis ntev nws laj laj koom nrog lub koom haum no.

Cov me nyuam ntxhais tsis nyiam mus saib xyuas ntau yam kawm. Dolores tau tso lub koom haum no tseg. Ib tug nas hu ua Chloris kuj tau tso lub koom haum no tseg thiab. Nkawd nrhiav tau Horace thiab Morris thiab Boris. Lawv sawv daws nyiam mus siab xyuas ntau yam kawm. Horace, Morris, Dolores, Chloris, and Boris tau tsim tsa ib lub koom haum rau lawv tus kheej.

The Signmaker's Assistant Student Edition pages 268–283

Week at a Glance	Customize instruction every day for your English Language Learners.				
	Day 1	**Day 2**	**Day 3**	**Day 4**	**Day 5**
Teacher's Edition	Use the ELL Notes that appear throughout each day of the lesson to support instruction and reading.				
ELL Poster 25	• Assess Prior Knowledge • Develop Concepts and Vocabulary	• Preteach Tested Vocabulary	• Taking Responsibility	• Kids Rule!	• Monitor Progress
ELL Teaching Guide	• Picture It! Lesson, pp. 169–170 • Multilingual Summaries, pp. 173–175	• ELL Reader Lesson, pp. 260–261	• Vocabulary Activities and Word Cards, pp. 171–172 • Multilingual Summaries, pp. 173–175		
ELL Readers	• Reread *Hello, Friend!*	• Teach *Three Little Kittens Learn A Lesson*	• Reread *Three Little Kittens Learn A Lesson* and other texts to build fluency		
ELL and Transition Handbook	Use the following as needed to support this week's instruction and to conduct alternative assessments: • Phonics Transition Lessons • Grammar Transition Lessons • Assessment				

Picture It! Comprehension Lesson

Realism and Fantasy

Use this lesson to supplement or replace the skill lesson on pages 264–265 of the Teacher's Edition.

Teach

Distribute copies of the Picture It! blackline master on page 170.

- Ask children to look at the pictures and describe what is happening.
- Read the sentences aloud. Ask: *Does anything happen in this story that could not really happen?* (Yes: The dog talks.)
- Share the Skill Points (at right) with children.
- Have children explain which parts of the story are realistic and which parts are fantasy. Discuss whether the story is a fantasy or a realistic story.

Skill Points

✓ A **realistic story** tells about things that could happen in real life.

✓ A **fantasy** is a story that tells about things that could never happen.

✓ A fantasy story can have realistic parts.

Practice

Read aloud the directions on page 170. Have children fill in the chart about realism and fantasy.

Answers for page 170: Possible answers: *Real:* Julia has a puppy named Paco. The puppy chews on papers. Julia has to do her work twice. *Not Real:* The dog talks. The dog asks for pizza.

Name ______________________________

Look at the pictures. **Read** the sentences.

- **Fill in** the chart. **Write** what is real in the story and what is not real.

The Dog Ate It!

Julia had a puppy named Paco. Paco liked to chew on things. He really liked to chew on Julia's homework.

Every day Julia told her teacher, "The dog ate my homework!" And every day, Julia had to do her work again.

Finally, Julia said to Paco, "Will you please stop eating my papers? I'm tired of doing my work twice." Paco smiled and said, "OK. Could I have some pizza instead?"

What Is Real	What Is Not Real

Vocabulary Activities and Word Cards

Copy the Word Cards on page 172 as needed for the following activities.
Use the blank cards for additional words that you want to teach.
Also see suggestions for teaching vocabulary in the ELL and Transition Handbook.

Word Toss	Making Rules	Guess the Word
• Tape one set of Word Cards onto an open space on the floor. Provide a mini beanbag or a small stuffed toy. • Have a child gently toss the beanbag onto one of the words on the floor. If the bag does not fall directly on a word, have the child use the word that is closest to the bag. • Ask the child to read the word and then use it in a sentence. • Play the game until each child has had at least one turn to throw the beanbag and create a sentence.	• Divide children into pairs, and give one set of Word Cards to each pair. • Ask children to write two or three rules for the classroom using at least one tested vocabulary word in each rule. • The rules can be silly or serious. For example: *We will take a nap every afternoon. No townspeople are allowed in class.* • Ask children to share their rules with the class.	• Give each child two or three Word Cards. • Ask children to use the back of the card to draw a picture, write a synonym, write a definition, or write a cloze sentence using the word from the front of the card. Assist children as necessary. • Collect the completed cards and stack them word side down. • Have each child draw a card (not the child's own), look at the clue, and name the vocabulary word on the front of the card. • Continue until all the cards have been used.

afternoon	**blame**
ideas	**important**
signmaker	**townspeople**

Multilingual Summaries

English

The Signmaker's Assistant

Norman works for the town signmaker. People love the beautiful signs they make. Norman wants to grow up to be a signmaker too.

One day Norman makes a new sign. He puts a sign on the school door that says, "No School Today." Teachers and students see the sign and go home. Then Norman puts silly new signs all over town.

People get angry about the new signs. They tear down all the signs. Norman is sorry. He stays up all night to make new signs. In the morning, he apologizes to everyone.

Spanish

El asistente del rotulista

Norman trabaja para el rotulista del pueblo. La gente adora los letreros que ellos hacen. Norman quiere hacerse rotulista cuando sea mayor también.

Un día, Norman hace un nuevo letrero. Pone el letrero que dice "Hoy no hay clases" en la puerta de la escuela. Los maestros y los estudiantes ven el letrero y se van a sus casas. Luego, Norman pone nuevos letreros tontos por todo el pueblo.

La gente se enoja con los nuevos letreros y los quitan todos. Norman está arrepentido. Se queda despierto toda la noche para hacer nuevos letreros. En la mañana se disculpa con todo el mundo.

Multilingual Summaries

Chinese

招牌師父的助手

諾曼在鎮上的招牌師父那兒工作。大家都喜歡他們做的漂亮招牌。諾曼長大以後也想當招牌師父。

有一天，諾曼做了一個新招牌。他把招牌掛在學校門口，上面寫著「今天停課」。老師和學生看見招牌後就回家了。然後，諾曼在整個鎮上都放滿了他新做的蠢招牌。

大家對這些新招牌很生氣，他們把招牌全部拆掉了。諾曼覺得很對不起大家，於是整夜不睡趕工做新招牌。第二天早上，他向大家道歉了。

Vietnamese

Phụ Tá của Ông Thợ Làm Bảng Hiệu

Norman làm việc cho ông thợ làm bảng hiệu của thành phố. Người ta yêu thích những bảng hiệu đẹp của họ làm. Norman muốn khi lớn lên sẽ trở thành thợ làm bảng hiệu.

Ngày nọ Norman làm một bảng mới. Cậu bé để một cái bảng trên cửa trường có ghi: “Hôm Nay Trường Đóng Cửa” Thầy cô và học sinh thấy bảng này và quay về nhà. Sau đó Norman để những bảng vớ vẩn khắp nơi trong thành phố.

Người ta tức giận vì những tấm bảng mới này. Họ phá hủy tất cả các bảng. Norman ân hận. Cậu thức suốt đêm để làm những tấm bảng mới. Đến sáng, cậu ta xin lỗi mọi người.

Multilingual Summaries

Korean

간판 제작자의 조수

노먼은 마을에 있는 간판 제작소에서 일하는데 사람들은 여기서 만드는 예쁜 간판을 좋아한다. 노먼도 커서 간판 제작자가 되고 싶어한다.

어느 날 노먼은 새로운 간판을 만드는데 "금일 휴교" 라고 써 있는 간판을 학교 문에 단다. 선생님과 학생들이 간판을 보고 집으로 돌아간다. 그 후 노먼은 마을 전체에 장난기 있는 새 간판을 단다.

사람들은 새로운 간판 때문에 화가 단단히 나서 모든 간판을 떼 버린다. 노먼은 미안하게 생각하며 새 간판을 만들면서 밤을 샌다. 아침이 되자 노먼은 모든 사람들에게 사과를 한다.

Hmong

Tus Neeg Tsim Tej Pib Tus Pab Cuam

Norman ua hauj lwm rau lub zos tus uas tsim tej pib. Tib neeg nyiam cov pib zoo nkauj uas nws ua. Norman xav hlob los ua ib tug neeg tsim tej pib thiab.

Muaj ib hnub Norman tau ua ib daim pib tshiab. Nws muab daim pib dai rau saum lub tsev kawm ntawv lub qhov rooj uas hais tias "Tsis Kawm Ntawv Hnub No." Cov nais khus thiab cov tub ntxhias kawm ntawv pom daim pib thiab mus tsev. Ces Norman muab tej pib tsis tseem ceeb tso thoob plaws lub zos.

Tib neeg npaw taws txog tej pib tshiab. Lawv dua tag nrho cov pib. Norman tau tu siab. Nws nyob ib hmo ua ib cov pib tshiab. Yav sawv ntxov, nws tau hais thov txim rau sawv daws.

Just Like Josh Gibson

Student Edition pages 300–313

Week at a Glance	Customize instruction every day for your English Language Learners.				
	Day 1	**Day 2**	**Day 3**	**Day 4**	**Day 5**
Teacher's Edition	Use the ELL Notes that appear throughout each day of the lesson to support instruction and reading.				
ELL Poster 26	• Assess Prior Knowledge • Develop Concepts and Vocabulary	• Preteach Tested Vocabulary	• Review Compare and Contrast	• Town Sports	• Monitor Progress
ELL Teaching Guide	• Picture It! Lesson, pp. 176–177 • Multilingual Summaries, pp. 180–182	• ELL Reader Lesson, pp. 262–263	• Vocabulary Activities and Word Cards, pp. 178–179 • Multilingual Summaries, pp. 180–182		
ELL Readers	• Reread *Three Little Kittens Learn a Lesson*	• Teach *Play Ball!*	• Reread *Play Ball!* and other texts to build fluency		
ELL and Transition Handbook	Use the following as needed to support this week's instruction and to conduct alternative assessments: • Phonics Transition Lessons • Grammar Transition Lessons • Assessment				

Picture It! Comprehension Lesson

Compare and Contrast

Use this lesson to supplement or replace the skill lesson on pages 296–297 of the Teacher's Edition.

Teach

Distribute copies of the Picture It! blackline master on page 177.

- Ask children to describe the pictures.
- Read the paragraph aloud. Ask: *How are baseball and basketball alike?*
- Share the Skill Points (at right) with children.
- Have children look at the pictures and sentences to find clues about comparing and contrasting.

Practice

Read aloud the directions on page 177. Have children fill in the compare and contrast chart.

Answers for page 177: Possible responses: *Alike:* Both sports use a ball. Players run and throw the ball. Players wear uniforms. *Different:* Baseball players also use bats and gloves. They hit the ball with the bat. Baseball is always played outside. Basketball can be played inside or outside.

Skill Points

✓ When you **compare** two things, you tell how they are alike.

✓ When you **contrast** two things, you tell how they are different.

✓ You can compare and contrast things you read about with things you already know.

Name ______________________________

Look at the pictures. **Read** the paragraph.

- **Fill in** the chart. **Write** how the two sports are alike. **Write** how the two sports are different.

The Best Sport

My friend Maya and I play different sports. I think baseball is more fun. I can throw the ball, hit the ball, and run fast. We use bats and gloves. Also, the games are always outside! Maya thinks that basketball is better. She likes to run fast and shoot the ball. She is glad she doesn't need any extra gear to play. She also likes to play inside. Which do you like better?

Baseball and Basketball

How They Are Alike	How They Are Different

Vocabulary Activities and Word Cards

Copy the Word Cards on page 179 as needed for the following activities.
Use the blank cards for additional words that you want to teach.
Also see suggestions for teaching vocabulary in the ELL and Transition Handbook.

Concentration	Tell a Story	Tick-Tack-Toe
• Give each pair of children a set of Word Cards and six blank cards (or more, if you include additional words you want to teach). • Ask the children to work together to draw simple pictures for each vocabulary word on each of the blank cards. Note: The picture for *plate* should show home plate for a baseball game, not a dish. • Children can then shuffle all of their cards together and lay them face down in a grid. They take turns choosing two cards. If the cards show a vocabulary word and its matching picture, the student keeps them. If not, the cards are put back and the other student takes a turn. • Play continues until all cards have been matched. The student holding the most cards wins.	• Give one or two Word Cards to each child, and arrange the children in a circle. • Start a story with a sentence that uses one of the vocabulary words. For example: *I ran onto the field.* • The next child continues the story, finding a way to use one of his or her words in a sentence. Allow children to help each other make up sentences. • Children take turns until all the Word Cards have been used and the group decides that the story is complete.	• Use one set of Word Cards plus several Word Cards from previous units. Divide children into teams of X and O. • Draw a tick-tack-toe grid on the board. Tape the Word Cards next to the grid. • Players take turns taking a Word Card off the board and using the word in a complete sentence. If a player uses the word correctly, he or she draws an X or O on the grid and gives you the Word Card. If the player uses the word incorrectly, the card is put back on the board and the other team takes a turn. • The game ends when a team has three Xs or Os in a row, or when all the grid spaces have been filled.

bases	**cheers**
field	**plate**
sailed	**threw**

Multilingual Summaries

English

Just Like Josh Gibson

Grandmama's favorite baseball player was Josh Gibson. He was an excellent hitter. Grandmama's father saw Gibson play on the day that she was born. He wanted his daughter to be a great baseball player too.

In Grandmama's childhood, girls did not play in baseball games. She watched her cousin Danny play. Danny's team let Grandmama play while they practiced. She was a very good player. They were sorry that she could not be on the team.

Danny hurt his arm. The team needed another player. They let Grandmama play. She played as well as Josh Gibson. Grandmama still has the ball.

Spanish

Igual que Josh Gibson

El jugador de béisbol favorito de mi abuela era Josh Gibson. Era un excelente bateador. El papá de mi abuela vio a Gibson jugar el día que ella nació. Él quería que su hija también fuera una gran jugadora de béisbol.

Cuando mi abuela era pequeña, las niñas no jugaban al béisbol. Ella siempre veía jugar a su primo Danny. El equipo de Danny dejaba jugar a mi abuela cuando ellos practicaban. Era muy buena jugadora. Ellos sentían mucho que ella no pudiera formar parte del equipo.

Un día Danny se lastimó el brazo. El equipo necesitaba otro jugador y por eso dejaron jugar a mi abuela. Ella jugó tan bien como Josh Gibson. Mi abuela todavía guarda la pelota.

Multilingual Summaries

Chinese

跟喬許・吉布森一樣出色

祖母最喜愛的棒球選手是喬許・吉布森，他是一個很出色的擊球手。祖母出生那天，她爸爸剛好看了吉布森的棒球比賽。他希望女兒也是一個偉大的棒球選手。

祖母的小時候，女孩子不能打棒球，她只能看她表哥丹尼玩。當丹尼的球隊練習時，也讓祖母跟他們一起打棒球。祖母的棒球打得很好，可是他們還是不能讓她加入球隊。

有一次，丹尼的手臂受了傷，他們棒球隊需要另一個選手來代替他。他們讓祖母參加比賽，結果她打得跟喬許・吉布森一樣好。直到現在，祖母仍保留著當時比賽用的球。

Vietnamese

Giống Như Josh Gibson

Cầu thủ chơi bóng chày mà Bà thích nhất là Josh Gibson. Ông ấy là một người đánh xuất sắc. Ba của Bà xem Gibson chơi bóng đúng vào ngày bà chào đời. Ông cũng muốn con gái của mình được trở thành một cầu thủ chơi bóng chày tuyệt hảo.

Thời niên thiếu của Bà, con gái không ai chơi đấu bóng chày. Bà xem anh họ của mình là Danny chơi. Đội của Danny để cho Bà chơi khi họ đang tập dợt. Bà là một người chơi giỏi. Họ tiếc là bà không được vào trong đội.

Danny bị đau cánh tay. Đội cần một người vào thay. Họ để cho Bà vào chơi. Bà chơi giỏi như Josh Gibson. Bà vẫn còn giữ quả bóng.

Multilingual Summaries

Korean

조쉬 깁슨처럼

할머니가 제일 좋아하는 야구 선수는 조쉬 깁슨으로 그는 훌륭한 타자였다. 할머니의 아버지는 할머니가 태어난 날에 깁슨의 야구 경기를 보았다. 아버지는 딸도 위대한 야구선수가 되길 원했다.

할머니가 어릴 적에 여자애들은 야구 경기를 하지 않았다. 할머니는 사촌인 대니가 경기하는 것을 지켜보았다. 대니의 팀은 연습 경기에선 할머니도 끼워 주었는데 할머니는 야구에 소질이 있었다. 대니의 팀원들은 할머니가 팀원이 될 수 없는 것을 아쉬워했다.

대니가 팔을 다치자 팀에서는 다른 선수가 필요했다. 그들은 할머니를 경기에서 뛰게 했고 할머니는 조쉬 깁슨처럼 훌륭히 경기를 했다. 할머니는 아직도 그 야구공을 갖고 있다.

Hmong

Zoo Ib Yam Li Josh Gibson

Tus neeg ntau pob uas pog nyiam tshaj yog Josh Gibson. Nws keeb ntau pob heev. Pog txiv tau pom Gibson ntau pob hnub uas pog tau yug. Nws xav kom nws tus ntxhais txhawj ntau pob thiab.

Thaum pog tseem yog me nyuam yaus, cov me nyuam ntxhais tsis ntau pob. Nws saib nws tus num Danny ntau pob. Danny pab ntau pob cia pog ntau pob thaum lawv xyaum. Nws yog ib tug txhawj ntau pob. Lawv tu siab nws nrog lawv ntau pob tsis tau.

Danny ua rau nws txhais caj npab mob. Nws pab ntau pob xav tau ib tug ntau pob ntxiv. Lawv cia pog ntau pob. Nws ntau pob keej ib yam li Josh Gibson. Pog tseem tau lub pob.

Red, White, and Blue

Student Edition pages 326–343

Week at a Glance	Customize instruction every day for your English Language Learners.				
	Day 1	**Day 2**	**Day 3**	**Day 4**	**Day 5**
Teacher's Edition	Use the ELL Notes that appear throughout each day of the lesson to support instruction and reading.				
ELL Poster 27	• Assess Prior Knowledge • Develop Concepts and Vocabulary	• Preteach Tested Vocabulary	• Make Flags	• Symbols of Freedom	• Monitor Progress
ELL Teaching Guide	• Picture It! Lesson, pp. 183–184 • Multilingual Summaries, pp. 187–189	• ELL Reader Lesson, pp. 264–265	• Vocabulary Activities and Word Cards, pp. 185–186 • Multilingual Summaries, pp. 187–189		
ELL Readers	• Reread *Play Ball!*	• Teach *The Stars and Stripes*	• Reread *The Stars and Stripes* and other texts to build fluency		
ELL and Transition Handbook	Use the following as needed to support this week's instruction and to conduct alternative assessments: • Phonics Transition Lessons • Grammar Transition Lessons • Assessment				

Picture It! Comprehension Lesson

Fact and Opinion

Use this lesson to supplement or replace the skill lesson on pages 322–323 of the Teacher's Edition.

Teach

Distribute copies of the Picture It! blackline master on page 184.

- Ask children to look at the picture and describe what they see.
- Read the paragraph aloud. Ask: *Can you find a fact in the paragraph?*
- Share the Skill Points (at right) with children.
- Have children look at the picture and paragraph to find facts and opinions.

Practice

Read aloud the directions on page 184. Have children fill in the chart.

Answers for page 184: Possible answers: *Facts:* The Fourth of July is a holiday. We have a party with the other families on our street. We hang the United States flag. The flag has thirteen stripes and fifty stars. There is a star for each state. At the end of the night, we watch fireworks. *Opinions:* It is the best holiday of the year. I think it is very pretty. Fireworks are great. I love the Fourth of July.

Skill Points

✓A **fact** can be proven true or false. You can check in a book, ask someone who knows, or see for yourself.

✓An **opinion** tells someone's beliefs or feelings. Clue words such as *I think* and *best* show statements of opinion.

✓If you are not sure if you are reading facts or opinions, go back and reread.

Name ______________________________

Look at the picture. **Read** the paragraph.

- **Fill in** the chart. **Write** two facts and two opinions from the paragraph.

What a Day!

The Fourth of July is a holiday. It is the best holiday of the year. We have a party with the other families on our street. We hang the United States flag. I think it is very pretty. The flag has thirteen stripes and fifty stars. There is a star for each state in the country. At the end of the night, we watch the fireworks. Fireworks are great! I love the Fourth of July.

Facts	**Opinions**

Vocabulary Activities and Word Cards

Copy the Word Cards on page 186 as needed for the following activities.
Use the blank card for an additional word that you want to teach.
Also see suggestions for teaching vocabulary in the ELL and Transition Handbook.

Go Fish	What's the Word?	Teacher's Chair
• Have small groups of children play Go Fish. Give each group four sets of Word Cards. • One child mixes the cards, gives five cards to each child, and places the remaining cards face down in a stack. • Before play begins, children look at their cards and lay down any matching pairs, saying the vocabulary words aloud. • Then the first player chooses a card in his or her hand and asks one other player for a matching card. For example: *Do you have the word* stripes? • If the other player has the card, he or she must give it up, and the first player then puts down the pair, saying the vocabulary word and using it in a sentence. If not, the other player says *Go Fish,* and the first player picks a card from the pile. • Play continues until all the pairs have been made.	• Give each child a set of Word Cards to look at during the activity. Keep another set at the front of the room. • Ask a volunteer to come to the front of the room and choose a Word Card without showing it to the group. • Have the child write the word on the board, leaving out two or three letters. The child should write an underscore for any missing letters, for example, f r _ _ d o _ *(freedom).* • Ask the other children to write down the word and fill in the missing letters. Have a volunteer use the word in a sentence. • Continue until each child has had at least one turn at the front of the room and all the Word Cards have been used.	• Use one set of Word Cards. Invite a child to sit in your chair and "teach" the other children. • Ask the child to choose a Word Card, show it to the group, and read the word. Then have the child use the word in a sentence or define the word. Have the other children repeat after the "teacher." • Allow each child at least one turn in the teacher's chair.

America	**birthday**
flag	**freedom**
nicknames	**stars**
stripes	

Multilingual Summaries

English

Red, White, and Blue

No one is sure who created the American flag. In the 1700s, America didn't have a flag. During the American Revolution, America needed a flag.

In 1777, Congress decided that the flag should have thirteen red and white stripes. It would have thirteen white stars on a blue background.

At first, another star and stripe were added whenever the United States added a new state. In 1818, Congress decided that the flag would have only thirteen stripes. A star would stand for each state.

Today our flag has fifty stars. We celebrate the flag every June 14, which is Flag Day.

Spanish

Rojo, blanco y azul

Nadie sabe quién creó la bandera norteamericana. En los años 1700, Estados Unidos no tenía una bandera. Durante la Guerra de Independencia, los norteamericanos necesitaban tener una bandera.

En 1777, el Congreso decidió que la bandera debería tener trece franjas rojas y trece franjas blancas. Además, colocadas sobre un fondo azul, debería tener trece estrellas blancas.

Al principio le añadían a la bandera una estrella y una franja por cada estado que se agregaba. En 1818, el Congreso decidió que la bandera tendría sólo trece franjas. Se le agregaría, sin embargo, una estrella por cada estado.

Hoy en día nuestra bandera tiene cincuenta estrellas. Cada 14 de junio se celebra el Día de la Bandera.

Multilingual Summaries

Chinese

紅、白、藍

沒有人可以確定美國國旗究竟是誰創的。十八世紀，美國還沒有國旗。獨立戰爭期間，美國人才覺得他們需要一面國旗。

1777 年，美國國會決定，國旗要有 13 條紅白相間的條紋，以及 13 顆白色襯著藍底的星星。

剛開始的時候，美國每增加一州，就會在國旗加上一顆星星和一條條紋。1818 年，美國國會決定，國旗以後都只有 13 條條紋，而每一顆星星則代表著一州。

如今，美國國旗上總共有 50 顆星星。每年 6 月 14 日是美國的國旗紀念日，美國人會為國旗慶祝一番。

Vietnamese

Đỏ, Trắng, và Xanh

Không ai biết rõ ai là người đã tạo ra lá cờ Hoa Kỳ. Trong những năm 1700, Hoa Kỳ không có cờ. Vào thời kỳ Cách Mạng Hoa Kỳ, nước này mới cần có một lá cờ.

Vào năm 1777, Quốc Hội quyết định lá cờ phải có mười ba sọc đỏ và trắng. Cờ sẽ có mười ba ngôi sao trên một nền xanh.

Thoạt đầu, một ngôi sao và một sọc được thêm vào mỗi khi Hiệp Chủng Quốc Hoa Kỳ có thêm một tiểu bang. Vào năm 1818, Quốc Hội quyết định rằng lá cờ sẽ chỉ có mười ba sọc. Một ngôi sao tiêu biểu cho mỗi tiểu bang.

Ngày nay lá cờ của chúng ta có năm mươi ngôi sao. Chúng ta mừng lễ kỷ niệm lá cờ vào ngày 14 Tháng Sáu mỗi năm, đó là Ngày Kỷ Niệm Lá Cờ.

Multilingual Summaries

Korean

빨강, 하양, 파랑

성조기를 만든 사람이 누구인지 아무도 정확히 알지 못한다. 1700년대에 미국은 국기가 없었다. 미국 독립 혁명 시기에 미국은 국기가 필요했다.

1777년 의회는 국기가 13 개의 빨간색과 흰색 줄로 구성되어야 한다고 결정했고 파란색 배경에 13개의 흰 별을 그려 넣었다.

처음에 미국은 새로운 주가 하나씩 생길 때마다 별과 줄을 추가했다. 1818년에 의회는 국기에 13개의 줄과 각 주를 상징하는 별이 포함되도록 결정했다.

오늘날 성조기에는 50개의 별이 있고 미국인들은 국기제정기념일인 6월 14일마다 이 날을 기념한다.

Hmong

Liab, Dawb, thiab Xiav

Tsis muaj leej twg paub tseeb tseeb leej twg yog tus tsim Mikas tus Chij. Hauv xyoo 1700, lub chaws Mikas tsis muaj ib tug chij. Thaum lub sij hawm Mikas Sawv Tua A-kis, Mikas yuav tsum muaj ib tug chij.

Hauv xyoo 1777, Tsoom Fwv txiav txim tias tus chij yuav tsum muaj kaum peb txoj kab liab thiab dawb. Nws muaj kawm peb lub hnub qub dawb nyob ntawm qhov chaw xiav.

Ua ntej, ib lub hnub qub thiab ib txoj kab raug muab ntxiv rau tus chij thaum muaj ib lub xeev tshiab. Hauv xyoo 1818, Tsoom Fwv txiav txim tias tus chij yuav tsum muaj kaum peb txoj kab xwb. Ib lub hnub qub yuav sawv cev rau ib lub xeev.

Hnub no peb tus chij muaj tsib caug lub hnub qub. Peb ua kev zoo siab rau tus chij hauv lub Rau Hlis Ntuj Hnub Tim 14, uas hu ua Hnub Chij.

A Birthday Basket for Tía

Student Edition pages 354–367

Week at a Glance	Customize instruction every day for your English Language Learners.				
	Day 1	**Day 2**	**Day 3**	**Day 4**	**Day 5**
Teacher's Edition	Use the ELL Notes that appear throughout each day of the lesson to support instruction and reading.				
ELL Poster 28	• Assess Prior Knowledge • Develop Concepts and Vocabulary	• Preteach Tested Vocabulary	• More Celebrations	• Let's Plan a Rescue	• Monitor Progress
ELL Teaching Guide	• Picture It! Lesson, pp. 190–191 • Multilingual Summaries, pp. 194–196	• ELL Reader Lesson, pp. 266–267	• Vocabulary Activities and Word Cards, pp. 192–193 • Multilingual Summaries, pp. 194–196		
ELL Readers	• Reread *The Stars and Stripes*	• Teach *Twelve Grapes for the New Year*	• Reread *Twelve Grapes for the New Year* and other texts to build fluency		
ELL and Transition Handbook	Use the following as needed to support this week's instruction and to conduct alternative assessments: • Phonics Transition Lessons • Grammar Transition Lessons • Assessment				

Picture It! Comprehension Lesson

Draw Conclusions

Use this lesson to supplement or replace the skill lesson on pages 350–351 of the Teacher's Edition.

Teach

Distribute copies of the Picture It! blackline master on page 191.

- Read the paragraph aloud and tell children to look at the picture. Ask: *What are the children doing?* If necessary, explain what a piñata is in greater detail.
- Share the Skill Points (at right) with children.
- Have children look at the picture and paragraph to draw conclusions about the characters and what happens in the story.

Practice

Read aloud the directions on page 191. Have children answer the questions about drawing conclusions.

Answers for page 191: 1. It is a birthday party. There are presents and balloons. **2.** No, the girls each had a piñata last year. Sam says breaking it is his favorite part.

Skill Points

✓ When you **draw a conclusion**, you figure out more about the characters and what happens in a story.

✓ You can put together what you know about real life and what you have read to draw conclusions.

Name ______________________________

Look at the picture. **Read** the paragraph.

The Piñata

Clara asked Sam and Sarah to help fill the piñata for her party. "This is a great piñata! Last year I had one that looked like a fish," Sarah said. "Mine was a flower!" said Clara. "I love all the pretty colors." "I love breaking the piñata and getting treats!" said Sam. They all agreed.

Answer the questions below.

1. What kind of party is Clara having? How do you know?

____

____

2. Is this the first time the children have seen a piñata? How do you know?

____

____

Vocabulary Activities and Word Cards

Copy the Word Cards on page 193 as needed for the following activities.
Use the blank cards for additional words that you want to teach.
Also see suggestions for teaching vocabulary in the ELL and Transition Handbook.

Word Card Jar	Guess the Word	Another Way to Say It
• Put one set of Word Cards in a jar. Add more cards for other words you would like children to practice. • Ask a volunteer to pick a word out of the jar, read it, and chant the spelling. For example, if the word *basket* is selected, the child will say *basket, b-a-s-k-e-t*. The other children repeat the word and the spelling. • The child with the card says a sentence using the word. The other children then repeat the sentence. • Continue with children taking turns drawing cards from the jar until all of the Word Cards have been used.	• Give each child two or three Word Cards. • Ask children to use the back of the card to draw a picture, write a synonym, write a definition, or write a cloze sentence using the word from the front of the card. Assist children as necessary. • Collect the completed cards and stack them word side down. • Have each child draw a card (not the child's own), look at the clue, and name the vocabulary word on the front of the card. • Continue until all the cards have been used.	• Give one set of Word Cards to each child. • Write context sentences on the board, but substitute other words for the vocabulary words. Underline the substituted words. For example: *She is my <u>mom's sister</u>. (aunt); I opened my <u>container for money</u>. (bank)* • Invite volunteers to read each sentence aloud, substituting a vocabulary word for the underlined word or words.

aunt	bank
basket	collects
favorite	present

Multilingual Summaries

English

A Birthday Basket for Tía

It is Tía's ninetieth birthday. Tía is Cecilia's great-aunt. Cecilia's mother gets ready for the surprise party. Cecilia puts presents in a basket for Tía.

Cecilia puts in a book that Tía reads to her. Cecilia puts in a mixing bowl that they use to make cookies. Cecilia puts in a flowerpot. She puts in a teacup. She puts in the ball they play with. Cecilia decorates the basket with flowers.

Cecilia helps her mother get ready for the party. Family and friends and musicians come. Tía is surprised when she gets to the party. She likes her presents. Tía and Cecilia dance together.

Spanish

Una cesta de cumpleaños para Tía

Hoy se celebran los noventa años de Tía. Ella es la tía abuela de Cecilia. La mamá de Cecilia se prepara para hacerle la fiesta sorpresa. Cecilia pone en una cesta los regalos para Tía.

Cecilia pone un libro que Tía siempre le lee. Pone un tazón de mezclar que usan cuando hacen galletas. Pone un florero. Pone una taza de té. Pone la pelota con la que ellas juegan. Cecilia decora la cesta con flores.

Cecilia ayuda a su mamá a prepararlo todo para la fiesta. Más tarde llegan la familia, los amigos y los músicos. Tía se sorprende cuando llega a la fiesta. A ella le gustan mucho los regalos. Tía y Cecilia bailan juntas.

Multilingual Summaries

Chinese

蒂亞的生日禮物籃

今天是蒂亞的 90 歲生日，蒂亞是賽西莉亞的姑婆。賽西莉亞的媽媽準備為蒂亞辦一個驚喜的生日會。賽西莉亞將禮物放進籃子裡送給蒂亞。

賽西莉亞把蒂亞讀給她聽的書放進去，把她們做餅乾用的攪拌碗放進去，把花盆放進去，把茶杯放進去，把她們玩的球放進去，最後，賽西莉亞還用鮮花裝飾籃子。

賽西莉亞幫媽媽準備生日會。家人、朋友和樂手都來了。蒂亞看到大家為她開的生日會時，非常驚訝。她喜歡她的禮物，而且還跟賽西莉亞一起跳舞。

Vietnamese

Một Giỏ Quà Sinh Nhật cho Tia

Đây là lễ Sinh Nhật lần thứ chín mươi của Tia. Tia là Bà Cô của Cecilia. Mẹ của Cecilia chuẩn bị một bữa tiệc bất ngờ. Cecilia đặt các món quà vào một cái giỏ cho Bà Cô Tia.

Cecilia đặt vào một quyển sách mà Bà Cô Tia đọc cho cô bé. Cecilia đặt vào một cái thau để pha trộn mà họ dùng để làm bánh. Cecilia đặt vào một chậu để trồng hoa. Cô bé đặt vào một tách để dùng trà. Cô bé đặt một quả bóng để họ cùng chơi. Cecilia trang trí cái giỏ với những cành hoa.

Cecilia giúp mẹ chuẩn bị bữa tiệc. Bạn bè, gia đình và các nhạc sĩ đến. Bà Cô Tia ngạc nhiên khi bà đến nơi. Bà thích những món quà. Cecilia và Bà Cô Tia cùng nhau nhảy múa.

Multilingual Summaries

Korean

티아 할머니의 생일 바구니

오늘은 세실리아의 대고모인 티아 할머니의 90번째 생일이다. 세실리아의 어머니는 깜짝 파티를 준비하고 있고 세실리아는 티아 할머니를 위해 바구니에 선물들을 넣는다.

세실리아는 티아 할머니가 그녀에게 읽어준 책 한 권과 과자를 구울 때 쓰던 대접, 화분, 찻잔과 함께 가지고 놀던 공을 넣고 꽃으로 바구니를 장식한다.

세실리아는 어머니가 파티 준비하는 것을 돕고 가족들과 친구들과 음악가들이 집에 도착한다. 티아 할머니는 파티장에 도착해서 깜짝 놀란다. 선물을 마음에 들어 하는 티아 할머니와 세실리아가 함께 춤을 춘다.

Hmong

Ib Lub Kawm Rau Tia Hnub Yug

Yog Tia lub kaum cuaj xyoo hnub yug. Tia yog Cecilia tus phauj koob. Cecilia niam npaj rau pluag mov noj zoo siab rau hnub yug. Cecilia tso tej khoom plig rau hauv lub kawm rau Tia.

Cecilia tso ib phau ntawv uas Tia nyeem rau nws. Cecilia tso ib lub tais uas lawv siv ci khaub noom. Cecilia tso ib tsob paj rau hauv. Nws tso ib lub khob hauv dej kub rau hauv. Nws tso ib lub npas uas nkawd tau ua siv nrog rau hauv. Cecilia muab tej paj ntoos los ua kom lub kawm zoo nkauj.

Cecilia pab nws niam npaj rau pluag mov noj zoo siab. Tsev neeg thiab cov phooj ywg thiab cov neeg ntau nkauj tau tuaj. Tia zoo siab kawg thaum nws tuaj txog. Nws nyiam nws cov khoom plig. Tia thiab Cecilia seev cev ua ke.

Cowboys Student Edition pages 380–401

Week at a Glance	Customize instruction every day for your English Language Learners.				
	Day 1	**Day 2**	**Day 3**	**Day 4**	**Day 5**
Teacher's Edition	Use the ELL Notes that appear throughout each day of the lesson to support instruction and reading.				
ELL Poster 29	• Assess Prior Knowledge • Develop Concepts and Vocabulary	• Preteach Tested Vocabulary	• Review Cause and Effect	• Cowboy Riddles	• Monitor Progress
ELL Teaching Guide	• Picture It! Lesson, pp. 197–198 • Multilingual Summaries, pp. 201–203	• ELL Reader Lesson, pp. 268–269	• Vocabulary Activities and Word Cards, pp. 199–200 • Multilingual Summaries, pp. 201–203		
ELL Readers	• Reread *Twelve Grapes for the New Year*	• Teach *What Does a Cowboy Do?*	• Reread *What Does a Cowboy Do?* and other texts to build fluency		
ELL and Transition Handbook	Use the following as needed to support this week's instruction to conduct alternative assessments: • Phonics Transition Lessons • Grammar Transition Lessons • Assessment				

Picture It! Comprehension Lesson

Cause and Effect

Use this lesson to supplement or replace the skill lesson on pages 376–377 of the Teacher's Edition.

Teach

Distribute copies of the Picture It! blackline master on page 198.

- Ask children to look at the pictures and describe what is happening in them.
- Read the sentences aloud. Ask: *What happens in the story? Why does it happen?*
- Share the Skill Points (at right) with children.
- Have children look at the pictures and sentences to explain cause and effect in the story.

Practice

Read aloud the directions on page 198. Have children fill in the graphic organizer.

Answers for page 198: Possible answers: *Cause:* A storm was coming. *Effect:* The cowboys watched the sky. *Cause:* The thunder boomed and scared the cattle. *Effect:* The cattle started to run. *Cause:* The storm ended and the cattle were quiet again. *Effect:* The cowboys ate their dinner.

Skill Points

✓ Look for what happens in a story. Think about why it happens.

✓ An **effect** is what happens. A **cause** is why it happens.

✓ Clue words such as *because, so,* and *since* help you figure out what happens and why.

Name ______________________________

Cause and Effect

Look at the pictures. **Read** the sentences.

- **Fill in** the chart. **Write** two causes and two effects from the story.

A Storm

The weather is changing. A storm is coming. The cowboys watch the sky and their cattle.

Because the thunder booms, the cattle get scared. They start to run. But the cowboys know what to do.

The storm is over. The cattle are quiet again, so the cowboys eat their dinner.

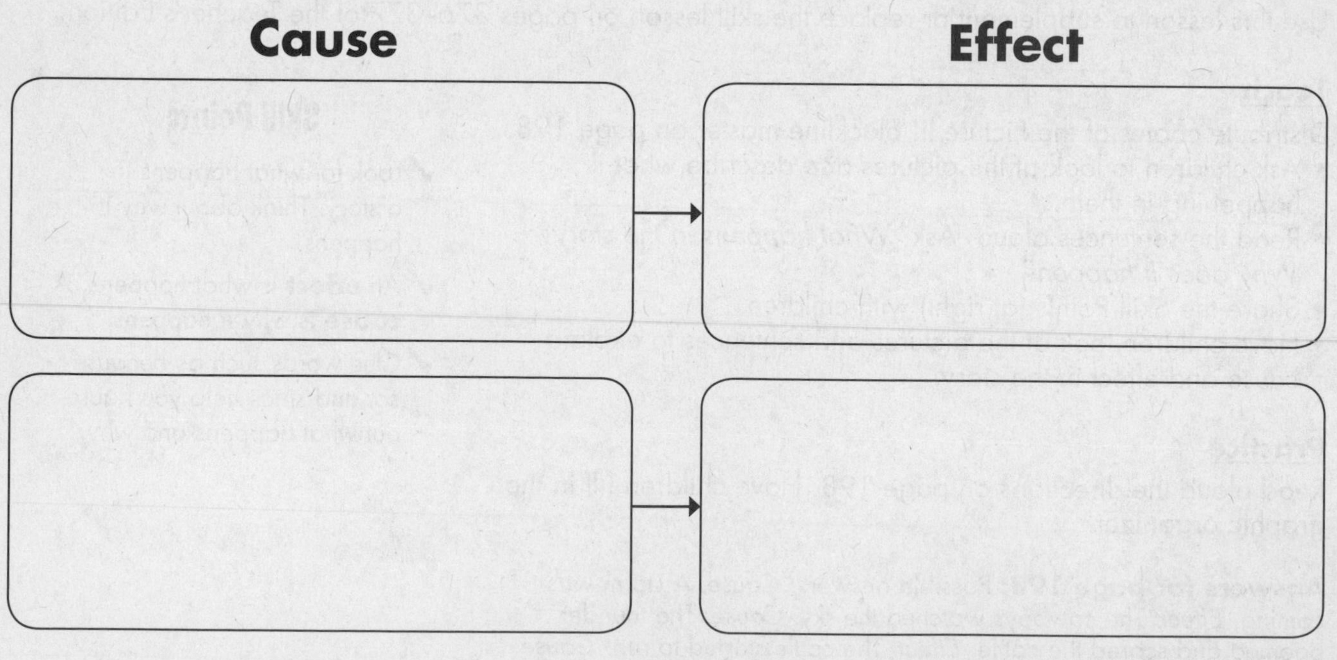

Vocabulary Activities and Word Cards

Copy the Word Cards on page 200 as needed for the following activities.
Use the blank card for an additional word that you want to teach.
Also see suggestions for teaching vocabulary in the ELL and Transition Handbook.

Poster Game	Cowboy Bingo	Mind Reader
• Use one set of Word Cards. Display this week's ELL Poster. • Have children take turns choosing a card without showing it to the others, and pointing to a scene or detail on the Poster that illustrates the word on the card. The child should talk about the scene and give clues about the vocabulary word without saying the word. • The first child to correctly guess the word takes the next turn.	• Give each child a set of Word Cards. Have children paste six of their cards on a piece of paper in two columns with three rows. • Pass out coins, beans, or other counters to use as bingo chips. • Provide children with the definition of or a phrase that describes one of the vocabulary words. For example: *This burns and is warm. (campfire); The horse ran fast—it _____. (galloped)* If necessary, announce the answer before moving on to the next word. • A child calls *bingo* and wins the game when he or she has placed bingo chips on three words in a row. • You may wish to have children trade bingo boards and play the game again.	• Give each child a set of Word Cards. Have children spread out their cards face up so they can see them. • Write these sentence frames on the board: *This word starts with the letter _____. This word means _____. This word ends with the letter _____.* • Pick up a Word Card and give children clues about the word by reading and completing the sentence frames. • Children hold up the correct Word Card when they believe they have the answer. • The child who correctly guesses the word may choose another card and provide the group with the next riddle. Allow children to use the sentence frames or make up their own clues.

campfire

cattle

cowboy

galloped

herd

railroad

trails

Multilingual Summaries

English

Cowboys

In the 1800s in the western United States cowboys lived on cattle ranches. Twice a year, cowboys rounded up the cattle. They herded cattle to a market town to be sold. The cows and cowboys walked on a long trail to get to a market town. This trail drive might take months.

At night, the cook made a meal for the cowboys. Cowboys went to sleep early. They slept on the ground.

Sometimes a cowboy's job was dangerous. Many dangerous things could happen. Frightened cattle could stampede. Rustlers could steal cattle. At the end of the trail, cowboys were paid. Then they took baths!

Spanish

Vaqueros

En los años 1800, en el oeste de Estados Unidos los vaqueros vivían en ranchos ganaderos. Dos veces al año, reunían el ganado. Llevaban la manada a un pueblo con un mercado para venderlo. Las vacas y los vaqueros recorrían largas sendas para llegar al mercado. A veces ese viaje duraba meses.

Por las noches, el cocinero preparaba la comida para los vaqueros. Los vaqueros se acostaban temprano. Ellos dormían en el piso.

Algunas veces, el trabajo de los vaqueros era difícil. Podían pasar cosas muy peligrosas. El ganado asustado podía salir en estampida. Los ladrones podían robarse al ganado. Al final de la jornada, los vaqueros recibían su paga. ¡Entonces se bañaban!

Multilingual Summaries

Chinese

牛仔

十九世紀時，美國西部的牛仔住在大牧場裡。牛仔每年都要把牛集合起來兩次，將整群牛趕到鎮上市場賣。牛仔和牛要沿著長長的小路走到鎮上去，這可能會花上好幾個月的時間。

晚上，廚師會煮飯給牛仔吃。牛仔吃完以後很早就睡了。他們沒有床，只能睡在地上。

牛仔的工作有時會很危險，什麼驚險的事情也可能發生，像是受驚嚇的牛會到處亂跑，偷牛賊會前來偷牛。到達目的地以後，牛仔就可以拿到薪金，然後他們會去洗個香噴噴的好澡。

Vietnamese

Những Người Chăn Bò

Vào những năm 1800 ở miền tây Hoa Kỳ, những người chăn bò sống ở những trang trại nuôi bò. Mỗi năm hai lần, những người chăn bò đi gom đàn bò về. Họ lùa đàn bò đi đến phố chợ để bán. Những con bò và người chăn đi trên một chặng đường dài để đi đến phố chợ. Chặng đường này có thể đi mất mấy tháng.

Đêm đến, đầu bếp nấu ăn cho những người chăn bò. Những người chăn bò đi ngủ sớm. Họ ngủ trên đất.

Thỉnh thoảng công việc của một người chăn bò trở nên nguy hiểm. Nhiều điều nguy hiểm có thể xảy ra. Đàn bò hoảng sợ có thể chạy tán loạn. Những tên trộm bò có thể ăn cắp đàn bò. Ở cuối chặng đường, những người chăn bò được trả tiền. Lúc đó họ đi tắm!

Multilingual Summaries

Korean

카우보이

1800년대 미국 서부에서는 카우보이들이 소 방목장에서 살았다. 일년에 두 번 카우보이들은 소 떼를 몰아들였다. 그들은 소를 몰아서 장에 내다 팔았는데 장에 도착하기 위해서는 소들도 카우보이들도 몇 달이 걸리는 기나긴 산길을 걸어야만 했다.

밤에는 요리사가 카우보이를 위해 음식을 만들었다. 카우보이들은 일찍 잠을 청했는데 땅바닥에서 잠을 잤다.

때때로 카우보이의 일은 위험했다. 놀란 소들이 일제히 우르르 달아나버리거나 가축 도둑들이 소를 훔쳐가는 그런 많은 위험한 일들이 벌어질 수도 있었다. 여정이 끝날 때 카우보이들은 돈을 받고는 목욕을 즐겼다.

Hmong

Cowboys

Thaum 1800 yuav kawg nyob hauv sab hnub poob ntawm lub Teb Chaws Mikas cov cowboys tau nyob hauv tej teb yug tsiaj txhua. Ob zaug ib xyoos, cov cowboys tau tav cov nyuj. Lawv tav cov nyuj mus rau qhov chaw muag nyuj thiab muab cov nyuj muag. Cov nyuj thiab cov cowboys mus kev ua ke kom mus txog qhov chaw muag nyuj. Tej zaum yuav siv li ntau lub hlis thiaj mus txog.

Thaum tsaus ntuj, tus uas mov noj ua mov rau cov cowboys noj. Cov cowboys mus pw ntxov ntxov. Lawv pw hauv pem teb.

Txhia zaus cov cowboy txoj hauj lwm txaus ntshai heev. Yeej muaj tau ntau yam txaus ntxhais uas tshwm sim. Cov nyuj uas ntshai yeej ceeb thiab dhia. Cov tub sab yeej nyiag tau cov nyuj. Thaum kawg, cov cowboy khwv tau nyiaj. Ces lawv da dej.

Jingle Dancer

Student Edition pages 412–425

Week at a Glance	Customize instruction every day for your English Language Learners.				
	Day 1	**Day 2**	**Day 3**	**Day 4**	**Day 5**
Teacher's Edition	Use the ELL Notes that appear throughout each day of the lesson to support instruction and reading.				
ELL Poster 30	• Assess Prior Knowledge • Develop Concepts and Vocabulary	• Preteach Tested Vocabulary	• Review Character, Setting, Plot	• Ways to Celebrate	• Monitor Progress
ELL Teaching Guide	• Picture It! Lesson, pp. 204–205 • Multilingual Summaries, pp. 208–210	• ELL Reader Lesson, pp. 270–271	• Vocabulary Activities and Word Cards, pp. 206–207 • Multilingual Summaries, pp. 208–210		
ELL Readers	• Reread *What Does a Cowboy Do?*	• Teach *A Wild Onion Dinner*	• Reread *A Wild Onion Dinner* and other texts to build fluency		
ELL and Transition Handbook	Use the following as needed to support this week's instruction and to conduct alternative assessments: • Phonics Transition Lessons • Grammar Transition Lessons • Assessment				

Picture It! Comprehension Lesson

Character, Setting, Plot

Use this lesson to supplement or replace the skill lesson on pages 408–409 of the Teacher's Edition.

Teach

Distribute copies of the Picture It! blackline master on page 205.

- Ask children to look at the pictures and describe what happens.
- Read the sentences aloud. Ask: *Who is the story about? What happens in the story?*
- Share the Skill Points (at right) with children.
- Have children give you examples from the pictures that helped them determine the setting and plot of the story.

Practice

Read aloud the directions on page 205. Have children answer the questions about character, setting, and plot.

Answers for page 205: 1. Carmen **2.** at a party **3.** Sample response: Carmen's family has a birthday party for her. Everyone dances. Carmen cuts her cake.

Skill Points

✓ A **character** is a person or an animal in a story.

✓ Authors tell the reader what the characters look like and what they say and do.

✓ The **setting** is where and when a story takes place.

✓ The **plot** is what happens at the beginning, middle, and end of a story.

Name ______________________________

Look at the pictures. **Read** the sentences.

Sweet Fifteen

Carmen is very happy. Today is her fifteenth birthday. Her family is having a special party for her.

Carmen dances with her father. Her friends and family dance too. Everyone is having a good time.

Finally, Carmen cuts her beautiful birthday cake. What a happy day it has been!

Answer the questions below.

1. Who is the story mainly about?
O Carmen O Carmen's father O Carmen's mother

2. Where does the story take place?
O at school O at a party O at a park

3. Write what happens in the story.

____

____

Vocabulary Activities and Word Cards

Copy the Word Cards on page 207 as needed for the following activities.
Use the blank cards for additional words that you want to teach.
Also see suggestions for teaching vocabulary in the ELL and Transition Handbook.

Guess the Word	Definition Match	Word Toss
• Give each child two or three Word Cards. • Ask children to use the back of the card to draw a picture, write a synonym, write a definition, or write a cloze sentence using the word from the front of the card. Assist children as necessary. • Collect the completed cards and stack them word side down. • Have each child draw a card (not the child's own), look at the clue, and name the vocabulary word on the front of the card. • Continue until all the cards have been used.	• Before play begins, write a brief definition for each of the vocabulary words on your own set of Word Cards. • Give each child a set of Word Cards. Have them arrange their cards face up in front of them. • Say the definition of a word. Do not say the word. • Children hold up the word that matches the definition. Have the first child to hold up the word read it aloud. • Continue until all the cards have been held up.	• Use one set of Word Cards. You will also need a mini beanbag or a small stuffed toy. • Tape the Word Cards onto an open space on the floor. • Have a child gently toss the beanbag onto one of the words on the floor. If the bag does not fall directly on a word, have the child use the word that is closest to the bag. • Ask the child to read the word and then use it in a sentence. • Play the game until each child has had at least one turn to throw the beanbag and create a sentence.

borrow	**clattering**
drum	**jingles**
silver	**voice**

Multilingual Summaries

English

Jingle Dancer

Grandma Wolfe once danced with jingles on her dress. Jenna wants to jingle dance at the powwow. But she needs four rows of jingles for her dress.

The next day, Jenna goes to see Great-Aunt Sis. Jenna borrows a row of jingles from her. She visits Mrs. Scott. Jenna borrows another row of jingles from her. She visits Cousin Elizabeth. Jenna borrows another row of jingles from her. Then she borrows a row of jingles from Grandma Wolfe.

Grandma Wolfe and Jenna sew the jingles onto Jenna's dress. The next weekend, Jenna jingle dances at the powwow.

Spanish

Danza con tintineo

Hace tiempo la señora Wolfe, la abuela de Jenna, danzaba con su tintineante vestido de cascabeles. Jenna quiere hacer una danza con un vestido así en el powwow, pero necesita cuatro hileras de cascabeles para ponerle a su vestido.

Al día siguiente, Jenna va a ver a su tía abuela Sis. Jenna le pide prestada una hilera de cascabeles. Luego, va a visitar a la Sra. Scott y le pide prestada otra hilera de cascabeles. Después visita a su prima Elizabeth y le pide prestada otra hilera de cascabeles. Por último, le pide prestada otra hilera de cascabeles a la abuela Wolfe.

La abuela Wolfe y Jenna cosen los cascabeles en el vestido de Jenna. Ese fin de semana se escucha el tintineo del vestido de Jenna cuando danza en el powwow.

Multilingual Summaries

Chinese

鈴鐺舞衣

吳爾芙奶奶曾經穿著鈴鐺舞衣跳舞。珍娜想要在族裡的傳統聚會上跳鈴鐺舞，但是她的舞衣需要四排鈴鐺。

第二天，珍娜去看姑婆西西，跟她借了一排鈴鐺。珍娜又去拜訪史考特太太，也跟她借了一排鈴鐺。珍娜還拜訪了表姐伊莉莎白，跟她借了第三排鈴鐺。最後，珍娜跟吳爾芙奶奶借了最後一排鈴鐺。

吳爾芙奶奶和珍娜一起把鈴鐺縫到舞衣上。下週末，珍娜就要穿著有鈴鐺的舞衣，在族裡的傳統聚會上表演跳舞。

Vietnamese

Người Múa Vũ Điệu Rung Chuông

Bà Nội Wolfe đã từng nhảy múa với những chiếc chuông nhỏ trên áo của bà. Jenna muốn được vũ điệu rung chuông ở buổi lễ hội. Nhưng cô bé cần phải có bốn dây chuông để may lên áo của mình.

Hôm sau, Jenna đi đến gặp Bà Dì. Jenna mượn một dây chuông của bà. Cô bé đến thăm Bà Scott. Jenna mượn một dây chuông nữa từ bà ấy. Cô đến thăm chị họ Elizabeth. Jenna mượn một dây chuông nữa từ chị này. Rồi cô mượn một dây chuông từ Bà Nội Wolfe.

Bà Nội Wolfe và Jenna may những chiếc chuông lên áo của Jenna. Tuần sau, Jenna sẽ múa vũ điệu rung chuông ở buổi lễ hội.

Multilingual Summaries

Korean

딸랑딸랑 무용수

울페 할머니는 한때 딸랑이 옷을 입고 춤을 추었다. 제나는 사교 모임에서 딸랑이 춤을 추고 싶어하지만 옷에 네 줄짜리 딸랑이가 필요하다.

이튿날 제나는 시스 대고모를 만나러 가서 딸랑이 한 줄을 빌리고 스캇 여사 집을 방문해서 또 딸랑이 한 줄을 빌린다. 그리고 사촌인 엘리자베스 집에 방문해서 다른 한 줄의 딸랑이를 빌린 다음 울페 할머니한테서 나머지 딸랑이 한 줄을 빌린다.

제나는 울페 할머니와 옷에 딸랑이를 꿰매 달고 다음 주말에 사교 모임에서 딸랑이 춤을 춘다.

Hmong

Seev Cev Nrov Nrov

Pog Wolfe tau hnav nws daim tiab uas muaj tej nyiaj nrov nrov seev cev. Jenna xav hnav daim tiab muaj nyiaj nrov nrov seev cev rau hauv lub powwow. Tiam sis nws yuav tsum muaj plaub txoj nyiaj kom nrov tso rau saum daim tiab.

Hnub tom ntej, Jenna mus saib nws tus Phauj Koob Sis. Jenna nqiv ib kab nyiaj nrov nrov ntawm tus phauj no. Nws mus saib Niam Scott. Jenna nqiv ib kab nyiaj nrov nrov ntawm nws. Nws mus saib nws tus viv ncaus Elizabeth. Jenna nqiv ib kab nyiaj nrov nrov ntawm nws. Ces nws nqiv ib kab nyiaj nrov nrov ntawm Pog Wolfe.

Pog Wolfe thiab Jenna xaws cov nyiaj nrov nrov rau saum daim tiab. Lub lim tim tom ntej, Jenna seev cev nrog daim tiab hauv lub powwow.

ELL Reader Lessons and Study Guides

Off to School We Go!

by Laura Vey

ELL Reader 2.1.1 Fiction

INTRODUCE THE BOOK

Activate Prior Knowledge/Build Background Read the title. Discuss with children all the different ways that they go to school. Ask children to describe what they see around them on their way to school.

Preview/Use Text Features Preview the reader by talking about the illustrations together and naming the labeled items.

Preteach Vocabulary Review the high-frequency words that appear in this book: **friend** and **country**. Introduce these key words from the book: **city** (p. 2), **street** (p. 4), **road** (p. 5), and **field** (p. 7). Discuss these words and add them to a Word Wall.

READ THE BOOK

Choose among these options for reading to support children at all English proficiency levels.

Read Aloud Read the book aloud as children follow along. Pause to verify comprehension and to explain unfamiliar concepts.

Monitored Reading Have children silently read a few pages at a time. Use the following questions to support comprehension:

- **Pages 2–5** How is walking to school in the city the same as walking to school in the country? (Children wear coats outside when it is cold. Children walk to school with an adult. They cross streets or roads.)
- **Pages 6–8** How is walking to school in the city different from walking to school in the country? (Children in the city see stores, buildings, street signs, and busy streets. Children in the country see fields, trees, and plants.)

Reread Have children reread the book with a partner, in small groups, or independently. Have them complete the Study Guide on page 213.

RESPOND

Answers to the Reader's Inside Back Cover:

Talk About It
1. The child in the city sees buildings, stores, and busy streets. The child in the country sees fields, a truck, trees, and plants. (Character and Setting)
2. The season is fall. I know because the leaves are falling off the trees and pumpkins are growing. (Draw Conclusions)

Write About It
3. Remind children of the discussion you had at the beginning of the lesson. Help children decide which things they will write about. (Setting) Support writers at various English proficiency levels.

Beginning Display a sentence frame such as: *On my way to school, I see* ___. Have children dictate their endings.
Intermediate Provide the same sentence frame, but have children copy it and write their own endings.
Advanced Have children describe three or four things that they see on their way to school.

Extend Language Drivers should stop their cars and look to see if it is safe to go when they see a stop sign. Drivers should stop their cars at a red light and wait for a green light before they go again. Invite children to talk about other street signs and what they mean.

Answers to page 213:
Responses will vary. Labels could include: *field, tree, bush, house, road, snow, stop sign, building, store, car, street, red light, people.*

Family Link Read aloud the Family Link activity on page 213 before sending copies of the Study Guide home with children. Later, have children share what family members said about what they see on their way to school or work.

Name ______________________________ **Off to School We Go!**

- **Read** *Off to School We Go!* again.
- **Label** the things the boy and his mother see as they walk to school.
- **Label** the things the girl and her father see as they walk to school.

Family Link

Have family members describe what they see as they go to school or work in the morning.

The First Trip to the Moon

by Stephanie True Peters

ELL Reader 2.1.2 Narrative Nonfiction

INTRODUCE THE BOOK

Activate Prior Knowledge/Build Background Read the title, and look at the photograph on the cover. Discuss with children what the person in the photograph is wearing and why he is wearing it.

Preview/Use Text Features Preview the reader by talking about the photographs together and naming the labeled items.

Preteach Vocabulary Review the high-frequency words that appear in this book: **live**, **work**, and **move**. Introduce these key words from the book: **Moon** (p. 1), **spacecraft** (p. 2), and **astronauts** (p. 2). Discuss these words and add them to a Word Wall.

READ THE BOOK

Choose among these options for reading to support children at all English proficiency levels.

Read Aloud Read the book aloud as children follow along. Pause to verify comprehension and to explain unfamiliar concepts.

Monitored Reading Have children silently read a few pages at a time. Use the following questions to support comprehension:

- **Pages 2–3** How many astronauts were on the *Apollo 11* spacecraft? (three) Where did they go? (They went to the Moon.)
- **Pages 4–5** How did the astronauts get down to the Moon from the *Apollo 11* space ship? (They flew down in the part of the spacecraft called the *Eagle*.)
- **Pages 6–7** What was the first thing the astronauts did when they landed on the Moon? (They sent a message to Earth.)
- **Page 8** Where did the astronauts land when they came back to Earth? (in the ocean)

Reread Have children reread the book with a partner, in small groups, or independently. Have them complete the Study Guide on page 215.

RESPOND

Answers to the Reader's Inside Back Cover:

Talk About It

1. They flew to the Moon in a spacecraft. (Main Idea and Details)

2. They walked on the Moon, put up an American flag, took pictures, and collected rocks and dust. (Main Idea and Details)

Write About It

3. Children should write about their favorite part of the *Apollo 11* trip. Answers will vary. Support writers at various English proficiency levels.

Beginning Display a sentence frame such as: *My favorite part of the trip is* ___. Have children dictate their endings.

Intermediate Provide the same sentence frame, but have children copy it and write their own endings.

Advanced Have children also write *why* they chose that part of the trip.

Extend Language *Everyone* is made up of the words *every* and *one*. *Everyone* does mean the same as "every person." Invite children to give other examples of compound words.

Answers to page 215:

Pictures should show astronauts flying to or walking on the Moon. Pictures should include a spacecraft with three astronauts inside or a spacecraft landed on the Moon with two astronauts on the surface of the Moon. Possible sentence: My picture shows the first trip to the Moon.

Family Link Read aloud the Family Link activity on page 215 before sending copies of the Study Guide home with children. Later, have children share what family members said about the first Moon landing.

Name ______________________________

The First Trip to the Moon

- **Read** *The First Trip to the Moon* again.
- **Draw** a picture that shows what the book is about.
- **Write** a sentence that goes with your picture.

____

____

Family Link

Ask family members to tell you what they know about the first time astronauts walked on the Moon.

I Spy Fun

by Janet Kovalcik

ELL Reader 2.1.3 Fiction

INTRODUCE THE BOOK

Activate Prior Knowledge/Build Background Read the title, and look at the illustration on the cover. Ask children to tell what they know about camping.

Preview/Use Text Features Preview the reader by talking about the illustrations together and naming the labeled items.

Preteach Vocabulary Review the high-frequency words that appear in this book: **mother** and **father**. Introduce these key words from the book: **spy** (p. 1), **campsite** (p. 2), and **leaves** (p. 4). Discuss these words and add them to a Word Wall.

READ THE BOOK

Choose among these options for reading to support children at all English proficiency levels.

Read Aloud Read the book aloud as children follow along. Pause to verify comprehension and to explain unfamiliar concepts.

Monitored Reading Have children read aloud a few pages at a time. Use the following questions to support comprehension:

- **Pages 2–5** What are the first three colors the family spies during the game? (brown, green, and blue)
- **Pages 6–7** What two things does the family spy in the sky? (a cloud and the Sun)
- **Page 8** What does Lida want to do tomorrow? (She wants to go to the beach and play I Spy again.)

Reread Have children reread the book with a partner, in small groups, or independently. Have them complete the Study Guide on page 217.

RESPOND

Answers to the Reader's Inside Back Cover:

Talk About It

1. The family was camping in the woods. (Character and Setting)

2. Possible response: Yes, I think the family had fun playing the game. The children want to play the game again. (Draw Conclusions)

Write About It

3. Children should choose items that are visible in the room to use for a game of I Spy.

Support writers at various English proficiency levels.

Beginning Let children draw pictures of the items and then write or dictate labels and colors.

Intermediate Have children brainstorm lists of colors and then find and list items of each color in the room.

Advanced Have children help less proficient speakers generate lists of items and colors.

Extend Language Accept all reasonable responses. Possible responses: The sky is blue. Grass is green. Grapes are purple. Carrots are orange. Invite children to name other colors and things that are those colors.

Answers to page 217:

1. It is brown and has fur.

2. a blueberry

3. It is getting dark.

4. They think camping is fun.

Family Link Read aloud the Family Link activity on page 217 before sending copies of the Study Guide home with children. Later, have children share what family members said about their camping trips.

Name ______________________________

- **Read** *I Spy Fun* again.
- Use the information in the book to **answer** the questions.

Pages	Question	Answer
2–3	**1.** What two things does Mother tell about the squirrel?	
4–5	**2.** Father sees something blue you can eat. What is it?	
6–7	**3.** Why does the family stop playing the game?	
8	**4.** How does the family feel about camping?	

Family Link

Has anyone in your family ever gone camping? Ask family members to tell you about a time they went camping.

The Saguaro Cactus

by J. Hernandez

ELL Reader 2.1.4 Expository Nonfiction

INTRODUCE THE BOOK

Activate Prior Knowledge/Build Background Read the title, and look at the photograph on the cover. Talk with children about characteristics of a cactus and where you would find one.

Preview/Use Text Features Preview the reader by talking about the photographs together, naming the labeled items, and reading the captions.

Preteach Vocabulary Review the high-frequency words that appear in this book: **water**, **animals**, and **full**. Introduce these key words from the book: **cactus** (p.1), **desert** (p. 2), and **spines** (p. 6). Discuss these words and add them to a Word Wall.

READ THE BOOK

Choose among these options for reading to support children at all English proficiency levels.

Read Aloud Read the book aloud as children follow along. Pause to verify comprehension and to explain unfamiliar concepts.

Monitored Reading Have children silently read a few pages at a time. Use the following questions to support comprehension:

- **Pages 2–5** How is a saguaro cactus the same as a plant you might find in your home? How is it different? (Possible answers: It is the same because it starts as a seed, it grows, and it has flowers and branches. It is different because it can live in the desert, and it can grow as big as a house.)
- **Pages 6–7** What two things help the saguaro get water? (Spines help rain go down to the roots. The roots are spread out near the top of the ground so they can get a lot of water.)
- **Page 8** What do bats get from the saguaro cactus? (They get food from the flowers.)

Reread Have children reread the book with a partner, in small groups, or independently. Have them complete the Study Guide on page 219.

RESPOND

Answers to the Reader's Inside Back Cover:

Talk About It

1. Birds build nests in holes in the cactus. Bugs eat the seeds. Bats get food from the flowers. (Main Idea and Details)

2. The sharp spines protect it from some animals. (Main Idea and Details)

Write About It

3. Children should create reasonable drawings of saguaros and write about what they draw. (Main Idea and Details)

Support writers at various English proficiency levels.

Beginning Using the book as a reference, have children add labels to their drawings.

Intermediate Have children look through the book to find words and details that they can use in their writing.

Advanced Have children write at least four details about the cactus.

Extend Language The opposite of *fat* is *thin*. It is on page 3.

Answers to page 219:

1. A saguaro is a plant (or cactus).

2. It looks fat when it is full of water.

3. They grow into new saguaros. Another possible answer: They are eaten.

4. Spines have sharp points.

5. Saguaros help birds, bugs, and bats.

Family Link Read aloud the Family Link activity on page 219 before sending copies of the Study Guide home with children. Later, have children share what family members said about the desert.

Name ______________________________ **The Saguaro Cactus**

- **Read** *The Saguaro Cactus* again.
- **Answer** the questions.

Pages	Question	Answer
2–3	**1.** What is a saguaro?	
2–3	**2.** When does a saguaro look fat?	
4–5	**3.** What happens to some saguaro seeds?	
6–7	**4.** What do spines have?	
8	**5.** What do saguaros help?	

Family Link

Has anyone in your family ever been to a desert? Ask family members to tell you what they know about the desert.

Rabbit and Coyote

by Gustavo Juana

ELL Reader 2.1.5 Fiction

INTRODUCE THE BOOK

Activate Prior Knowledge/Build Background Read the title, and ask children to look at the illustration on the cover. Ask them what game they think Rabbit and Coyote are playing.

Preview/Use Text Features Preview the reader by talking about the illustrations together and naming the labeled items.

Preteach Vocabulary Review the high-frequency words that appear in this book: **together** and **very**. Introduce these key words from the book: **chase** (p. 2), **tricks** (p. 2), and **canyon** (p. 3). Discuss these words and add them to a Word Wall.

READ THE BOOK

Choose among these options for reading to support children at all English proficiency levels.

Read Aloud Read the book aloud as children follow along. Pause to verify comprehension and to explain unfamiliar concepts.

Monitored Reading Have children read aloud a few pages at a time. Use the following questions to support comprehension:

- **Pages 2–3** What do Rabbit and Coyote like to do? (Coyote likes to chase Rabbit, and Rabbit likes to trick Coyote.)
- **Pages 4–5** What does Rabbit ask Coyote to do? (He asks Coyote to help him hold up the canyon wall so it won't fall on them.)
- **Page 6–8** What two things does Coyote believe are true? (The wall will fall if he doesn't hold it. There is cheese in the pond.) How does Coyote learn he has been tricked? (The wall doesn't fall when he runs away.)

Reread Have children reread the book with a partner, in small groups, or independently. Have them complete the Study Guide on page 221.

RESPOND

Answers to the Reader's Inside Back Cover:

Talk About It

1. He wanted to play a trick on Coyote. He wanted Coyote to stop chasing him. (Cause and Effect)

2. They continued to play the chasing game because it was fun.

Write About It

3. Children should describe any kind of game that they like to play with their friends.

Support writers at various English proficiency levels.

Beginning Let children dictate their ideas as someone else records the words. Have children practice reading aloud and writing the recorded words.

Intermediate Have children tell partners about their ideas before writing.

Advanced Invite children to write about their games in both English and the home language.

Extend Language *Chase* and *-ing* make the word *chasing* (p. 3). Point out the spelling change. Invite children to find other story words that end in *-ing* (playing, leaning).

Answers to page 221:

1. Coyote was chasing him.
2. Coyote helped Rabbit hold the wall.
3. Coyote drank all the water in the pond.
4. He was full of water.

Family Link Read aloud the Family Link activity on page 221 before sending copies of the Study Guide home with children. Later, have children share what they learned about family members' favorite games.

Name ______________________________

Rabbit and Coyote

- **Read** *Rabbit and Coyote* again.
- **Complete** the *What and Why* chart.

What and Why

Page	What happened?	Why did it happen?
4	**1.** Rabbit hid in the canyon.	**1.**
5	**2.**	**2.** Rabbit said the wall would fall.
8	**3.**	**3.** Rabbit said there was cheese in the pond.
8	**4.** Coyote could not chase Rabbit.	**4.**

Family Link

Ask family members to tell you about games they like to play.

Sandy to the Rescue!

by Rose Lin

ELL Reader 2.2.1 Fiction

INTRODUCE THE BOOK

Activate Prior Knowledge/Build Background Read the title. Discuss with children what it means to rescue someone. Ask children to talk about stories they have heard about people being rescued.

Preview/Use Text Features Preview the reader by talking about the illustrations together and naming the labeled items.

Preteach Vocabulary Review the high-frequency words that appear in this book: **pull** and **family**. Introduce these key words from the book: **rescue** (p. 1), **lost** (p. 2), **trainer** (p. 3), and **smells** (p. 5). Discuss these words and add them to a Word Wall.

READ THE BOOK

Choose among these options for reading to support children at all English proficiency levels.

Read Aloud Read the book aloud as children follow along. Pause to verify comprehension and to explain unfamiliar concepts.

Monitored Reading Have children silently read a few pages at a time. Use the following questions to support comprehension:

- **Pages 2–3** Why does Kim bring her dog Sandy to a trainer? (The trainer is teaching Sandy how to be a rescue dog.)
- **Pages 4–6** How does Sandy find the hidden trainer? (Sandy smells the trainer's cap and then sniffs the air to find the same smell and the trainer.)
- **Pages 7–8** Why is Kim proud of Sandy at the end of the story? (She is proud because Sandy finds the trainer and is doing a good job learning to be a rescue dog.)

Reread Have children reread the book with a partner, in small groups, or independently. Have them complete the Study Guide on page 223.

RESPOND

Answers to the Reader's Inside Back Cover:

Talk About It

1. Sandy learned how to find someone who is lost. First, she smelled the trainer's cap. Next, she sniffed the air. Then, she found the trainer because she knew what he smelled like. (Sequence)

2. No. The trainer was pretending to be lost to help teach Sandy how to find someone who is really lost.

Write About It

3. Ask children to look at the illustrations in the book. Have children look carefully at the pictures of the dog as they write their descriptions. Support writers at various English proficiency levels.

Beginning Pair children with more-proficient speakers to complete their descriptions of Sandy.

Intermediate Have children brainstorm lists of words they can use to describe Sandy.

Advanced Have children help less-proficient speakers generate lists of words they can use when writing about Sandy.

Extend Language Sandy used her nose to find the trainer. She smelled his cap to learn what he smelled like and sniffed around the park until she found him. Invite children to discuss what they do with all their senses.

Answers to page 223:

Illustrations will vary. Possible sentence: The book is about training a dog to find someone who is lost.

Family Link Read aloud the Family Link activity on page 223 before sending copies of the Study Guide home with children. Later, have children share what family members said about rescues.

Name ______________________ **Sandy to the Rescue!**

- **Read** *Sandy to the Rescue!* again.
- **Draw** a picture that shows what the book is about.
- **Write** a sentence that goes with your picture.

____

____

____

Family Link

Has anyone in your family ever rescued a person or an animal or read about a rescue? Ask them to tell what happened.

The Soccer Picnic

by Artis Gilroy

ELL Reader 2.2.2 Realistic Fiction

INTRODUCE THE BOOK

Activate Prior Knowledge/Build Background Read the title and look at the picture on the cover. Discuss with children what a picnic is. Ask children to describe a time that they went on a picnic and how they contributed to it.

Preview/Use Text Features Preview the reader by talking about the illustrations together and naming the labeled items.

Preteach Vocabulary Review the high-frequency words that appear in this book: **great** and **you're**. Introduce these key words from the book: **picnic** (p. 1), **team** (p. 2), **help** (p. 3), and **together** (p. 8). Discuss these words and add them to a Word Wall.

READ THE BOOK

Choose among these options for reading to support children at all English proficiency levels.

Read Aloud Read the book aloud as children follow along. Pause to verify comprehension and to explain unfamiliar concepts.

Monitored Reading Have children read aloud a few pages at a time. Use the following questions to support comprehension:

- **Page 2** Why does Pablo's soccer team decide to have a picnic? (The team won the last game of the season.)
- **Pages 3–6** How did the children on the team help get ready for the picnic? (Each child helped a parent make a special food.)
- **Pages 7–8** How did the children act like a team at the picnic? (The children helped set up the benches and tables at the playground. They also worked together to help clean up when the picnic was over.)

Reread Have children reread the book with a partner, in small groups, or independently. Have them complete the Study Guide on page 225.

RESPOND

Answers to the Reader's Inside Back Cover:

Talk About It

1. Responses will vary. Possible response: My family gets dinner ready together. My mom and dad cook. My sister and I set the table.

2. Working with a team makes a job easier because everybody does part of the work. (Cause and Effect)

Write About It

3. Help children think of jobs that could best be done by a group of people. (Cause and Effect) Support writers at various English proficiency levels.

Beginning Let children dictate their answers as someone else records their words. Have them practice reading aloud and writing the recorded words.

Intermediate Have children tell partners what they want to say before writing it down.

Advanced Have children describe at least three good jobs for a team.

Extend Language A food that has lots of spice in it can be called *spicy*. Ask children what they would call a food with lots of salt in it *(salty)*.

Answers to page 225:

Illustrations and sentences will vary. Possible response: The children worked as a team when they cleaned up after the picnic together.

Family Link Read aloud the Family Link activity on page 225 before sending copies of the Study Guide home with children. Later, have children share what family members said about being part of a team.

Name ________________________________

- **Read** *The Soccer Picnic* again.
- **Draw** an example of working together from the story.
- **Write** a sentence that goes with your picture.

____

____

____

Family Link

Has anyone in your family ever been on a team? Have family members describe a time when they were part of a team.

Summer Returns to the Pond

by Fiona Killorin

ELL Reader 2.2.3 Nonfiction

INTRODUCE THE BOOK

Activate Prior Knowledge/Build Background Read the title, and look at the illustration on the cover. Discuss with children what the animals are building in the picture.

Preview/Use Text Features Preview the reader by talking about the illustrations together and naming the labeled items.

Preteach Vocabulary Review the high-frequency words that appear in this book: **enough**, **whole**, and **above**. Introduce these key words from the book: **summer** (p. 1), **builds** (p. 2), **lodge** (p. 2), and **nest** (p. 4). Discuss these words and add them to a Word Wall.

READ THE BOOK

Choose among these options for reading to support children at all English proficiency levels.

Read Aloud Read the book aloud as children follow along. Pause to verify comprehension and to explain unfamiliar concepts.

Monitored Reading Have children silently read a few pages at a time. Use the following questions to support comprehension:

- **Pages 2–3** What does the beaver build in the pond? (a lodge)
- **Pages 4–5** Where does the robin build a nest? (on a branch above the pond)
- **Pages 6–7** Who shares the log with the turtle? (some birds)
- **Page 8** What do all the animals of the pond do? (They work, share, and rest.)

Reread Have children reread the book with a partner, in small groups, or independently. Have them complete the Study Guide on page 227.

RESPOND

Answers to the Reader's Inside Back Cover:

Talk About It

1. The robin brings food to the nest to feed its babies. (Cause and Effect)

2. The beaver builds the lodge as a safe home to share with its babies. (Cause and Effect)

Write About It

3. Help children think of places where they have seen animals. Allow children to write about pets as well as wild animals.

Support writers at various English proficiency levels.

Beginning Pair children with more proficient speakers to complete the assignment.

Intermediate Have children look through the book to find words and details that they can use in their writing.

Advanced Have children write three or four sentences about animals they have seen.

Extend Language The robins and birds can fly. Invite children to give examples of animals that run and swim.

Answers to page 227:

Children should draw a picture of a nest in a tree. The mother robin is giving food to her babies. Possible sentence: The robin builds a nest and brings food to her babies.

Family Link Read aloud the Family Link activity on page 227 before sending copies of the Study Guide home with children. Later, have children share what family members taught them about their favorite animals.

Name ______________________________

Summer Returns to the Pond

- **Read** *Summer Returns to the Pond* again.
- **Draw** a picture that shows how a robin and her babies live.
- **Write** a sentence that goes with your picture.

____

____

____

Family Link

Ask family members about their favorite animals. What kind of home does each animal have?

Big News in the Barn

by Michelle Kerner

ELL Reader 2.2.4 Fiction

INTRODUCE THE BOOK

Activate Prior Knowledge/Build Background Read the title, and discuss with children what animals and things they might find in a barn.

Preview/Use Text Features Preview the reader by talking about the illustrations together and naming the labeled items. Point out the sign on the barn door.

Preteach Vocabulary Review the high-frequency words that appear in this book: **shall** and **scared**. Introduce these key words from the book: **barn** (p. 1), **piglet** (p. 3), **clean** (p. 4), and **messy** (p. 5). Discuss these words and add them to a Word Wall.

READ THE BOOK

Choose among these options for reading to support children at all English proficiency levels.

Read Aloud Read the book aloud as children follow along. Pause to verify comprehension and to explain unfamiliar concepts.

Monitored Reading Have children read aloud a few pages at a time. Use the following questions to support comprehension:

- **Pages 2–3** What big news does Dog have? (A baby pig is coming to live in the barn.)
- **Pages 4–5** How do the animals decide to get ready for the piglet? (They agree to clean the barn.)
- **Pages 6–8** What do the animals need to do in order to clean the barn well? (They need to work together.)

Reread Have children reread the book with a partner, in small groups, or independently. Have them complete the Study Guide on page 229.

RESPOND

<u>Answers to the Reader's Inside Back Cover:</u>

Talk About It

1. They worked together to clean the barn for the piglet. (Character, Setting, Plot)

2. Working together is a good way to get things done. (Author's Purpose)

Write About It

3. Children should write about two or more people working together.

Support writers at various English proficiency levels.

Beginning Allow children to dictate their ideas. Have them practice reading aloud and writing the recorded words.

Intermediate Before writing, have children talk about their ideas with partners.

Advanced Have each child also write about a time when it is better to work alone.

Extend Language A puppy will be a dog; a kitten will be a cat; a chick will be a chicken; a calf will be a cow.

<u>Answers to page 229:</u>

Before: Children should draw a picture of a messy barn. *After*: Children should draw a picture of a barn where the hay is neat, the sticks are in a pile, and there are no seeds on the floor.

Family Link Read aloud the Family Link activity on page 229 before sending copies of the Study Guide home with children. Later, have children share what family members said about working with other people.

Name ______________________ **Big News in the Barn**

- **Read** *Big News in the Barn* again.
- **Draw** a picture of the barn before it was cleaned.
- Then **draw** a picture of the barn after the animals cleaned it.

Barn (Before)

Barn (After)

Family Link

Have family members tell you about a time when they worked with other people to get something done.

A Thanksgiving Party

by Rosa García

ELL Reader 2.2.5 Fiction

INTRODUCE THE BOOK

Activate Prior Knowledge/Build Background Read the title and look at the cover. Discuss with children what Thanksgiving is all about.

Preview/Use Text Features Preview the reader by talking about the illustrations together and naming the labeled items. Point out the signs on pages 2 and 3.

Preteach Vocabulary Review the high-frequency words that appear in this book: **promise** and **everybody**. Introduce these key words from the book: **party** (p. 1), **turkeys** (p. 3), **table** (p. 4), and **feast** (p. 7). Discuss these words and add them to a Word Wall.

READ THE BOOK

Choose among these options for reading to support children at all English proficiency levels.

Read Aloud Read the book aloud as children follow along. Pause to verify comprehension and to explain unfamiliar concepts.

Monitored Reading Have children silently read a few pages at a time. Use the following questions to support comprehension:

- **Page 2** What kind of a party do the people of Alameda Apartments plan to have? (They plan to have a Thanksgiving party.)
- **Pages 3–6** What are some things that people bring to the party? (Sula brings tablecloths, paper cups, and paper plates. Kamal's family and Rebecca's family bring the turkey. Ibrahim and his parents bring juice and salad. Manuel and Martha bring sweet potatoes and apple pies.)
- **Pages 7–8** What do the people do at the Thanksgiving party? (They all eat. After dinner, the adults dance and sing. The children run around and have a good time.)

Reread Have children reread the book with a partner, in small groups, or independently. Have them complete the Study Guide on page 231.

RESPOND

Answers to the Reader's Inside Back Cover:

Talk About It

1. The Thanksgiving party at Alameda Apartments looks very fun. There are many people and lots of food. Everyone is having a good time.

2. The people at the party had fun together eating, dancing, singing, and playing. (Draw Conclusions)

Write About It

3. Encourage children to picture in their minds a big dinner with friends and family. Then have them list the foods they see on the table. Support writers at various English proficiency levels.

Beginning Allow children to dictate their lists in English or write them in the home language.

Intermediate Have children look through the book to find words that they can use on their lists of favorite foods.

Advanced Invite children to write their lists of favorite foods in English and the home language.

Extend Language People from Mexico can be called *Mexicans*. People from Russia can be called *Russians*. Invite children to discuss where their families are from.

Answers to page 231:

Items that may be labeled: *turkey, corn, fruit, plate, cup, table, pie, tablecloth, salad, sweet potatoes*. Possible response: It is Thanksgiving. I know because there are lots of people sitting at a table. The people are eating turkey. There is a sign that says *Happy Thanksgiving*.

Family Link Read aloud the Family Link activity on page 231 before sending copies of the Study Guide home with children. Later, have children share what family members said about their favorite holidays and foods.

Name ____________________ **A Thanksgiving Party**

- **Read** *A Thanksgiving Party* again.
- **Label** as many items in the picture as you can.
- **Write** what holiday you see in the picture. Explain how you know.

____

____

____

Family Link

Have family members tell you about their favorite holidays. Then, ask family members what they like to eat on those holidays.

Ada's Castle

by Lilly Meador

ELL Reader 2.3.1 Fiction

INTRODUCE THE BOOK

Activate Prior Knowledge/Build Background Read the title, and look at the art on the cover of the book. Ask children to guess what the characters are trying to build. Then ask if they have ever built anything.

Preview/Use Text Features Preview the reader by talking about the illustrations together and naming the labeled items.

Preteach Vocabulary Review the high-frequency words that appear in this book: **pretty** and **watch**. Introduce these key words from the book: **castle** (p. 1), **build** (p. 2), and **finish** (p. 5). Discuss these words and add them to a Word Wall.

READ THE BOOK

Choose among these options for reading to support children at all English proficiency levels.

Read Aloud Read the book aloud as children follow along. Pause to verify comprehension and to explain unfamiliar concepts.

Monitored Reading Have children read aloud a few pages at a time. Use the following questions to support comprehension:

- **Pages 2–3** What do Ada, Emma, and their mother decide to build? (a swing set with three swings and a castle)
- **Pages 4–6** What do they need to build their project? When will they finish? (They need wood, chains, nails, and screws. They will finish in about a week.)
- **Pages 7–8** Who helps Ada and Emma? How do Ada and Emma thank their helpers? (Their mother and friends help. They give their mother a thank-you card and plan to have a party for their friends.)

Reread Have children reread the book with a partner, in small groups, or independently. Have them complete the Study Guide on page 233.

RESPOND

Answers to the Reader's Inside Back Cover:

Talk About It

1. Possible response: My favorite playground is big and has swings, slides, and many places to climb.

2. Possible response: Children would like a swing set that has many swings and that looks fun. (Draw Conclusions)

Write About It

3. Children should think of something that would be fun to use with the entire family.

Support writers at various English proficiency levels.

Beginning Display a sentence frame such as *I would like to build a ____ because ____.* Have children dictate ideas to complete the sentence.

Intermediate Provide the same sentence frame, but have children copy it and write their own ideas.

Advanced Have children write two or three sentences about what they would like to build.

Extend Language The word *playground* means "an area or *ground* where children can *play*." Invite children to give other examples of compound words.

Answers to page 233:

Labels for the picture: *hammer, plan, nails, friends/people, wood, chain, swing*

Family Link Read aloud the Family Link activity on page 233 before sending copies of the Study Guide home with children. Later, have children share what family members have built for fun.

Name ______________________________

- **Read** *Ada's Castle* again.
- **Label** everything that is needed to build a swing set.

Family Link

Has anyone in your family ever built something for fun? Ask family members to describe what they built.

Letters from Here to There

by Alfred M. Evans

ELL Reader 2.3.2 Expository Nonfiction

INTRODUCE THE BOOK

Activate Prior Knowledge/Build Background Read the title, and discuss with children what they know about sending and receiving mail.

Preview/Use Text Features Preview the reader by talking about the illustrations together and naming the labeled items. Point out the letter on page 3 and the flow chart on page 8.

Preteach Vocabulary Review the high-frequency words that appear in this book: **school** and **answer**. Introduce these key words from the book: **letter** (p. 1), **mail** (p. 2), and **sort** (p. 6). Discuss these words and add them to a Word Wall.

READ THE BOOK

Choose among these options for reading to support children at all English proficiency levels.

Read Aloud Read the book aloud as children follow along. Pause to verify comprehension and to explain unfamiliar concepts.

Monitored Reading Have children silently read a few pages at a time. Use the following questions to support comprehension:

- **Pages 2–4** How do you write a letter? (I write my friend's name on a piece of paper, I write a message, and I sign my name.) How do you prepare the envelope? (I put that letter in an envelope. I write my friend's address and my address, and I put on a stamp.)
- **Pages 5–8** What happens after you put your letter in the mailbox? (The letter is taken to the post office, it is sorted into a bin, a mail carrier delivers the letter, and the letter reaches my friend.)

Reread Have children reread the book with a partner, in small groups, or independently. Have them complete the Study Guide on page 235.

RESPOND

Answers to the Reader's Inside Back Cover:

Talk About It

1. I can make sure I have the person's name, the correct address, and a stamp on the envelope so that it will go to the right address. (Cause and Effect)

2. Possible response: I helped my parents to send holiday cards. I put stamps on the envelopes and put them in the mailbox. I like to receive mail.

Write About It

3. Help children decide who will receive their letters and what they will write about.

Support writers at various English proficiency levels.

Beginning Allow children to dictate their letters in English or write them in the home language.

Intermediate Have children use the letter on page 3 as a model for their own writing.

Advanced Invite children to write their letters in both English and the home language.

Extend Language In this book, the word *letter* means a note to someone. Discuss other examples of words with multiple meanings.

Answers to page 235:

First: The girl puts her letter in the mailbox.

Next: The mail carrier delivers the letter.

Last: The boy receives the letter.

Family Link Read aloud the Family Link activity on page 235 before sending copies of the Study Guide home with children. Later, have children share what family members said about mailing a package.

Name ________________________________

Letters from Here to There

- **Read** *Letters from Here to There* again.
- **Look** at the pictures. **Write** what happens *first*, *next*, and *last*.

First, ______________________________

____

____

Next, ______________________________

____

____

Last, ______________________________

____

____

Family Link

Ask a family member to explain how mailing a big package is different from mailing a letter.

Webs and Other Catchers

by Hope Ting

ELL Reader 2.3.3 Expository Nonfiction

INTRODUCE THE BOOK

Activate Prior Knowledge/Build Background Read the title, and look at the picture on the cover. Discuss with children what a web is and why a spider makes one.

Preview/Use Text Features Preview the reader by talking about the illustrations and photographs, naming the labeled items, and reading the captions.

Preteach Vocabulary Review the high-frequency words that appear in this book: **believe** and **caught**. Introduce these key words from the book: **webs** (p. 1), **spin** (p. 2), **nets** (p. 3), and **holes** (p. 7). Discuss these words and add them to a Word Wall.

READ THE BOOK

Choose among these options for reading to support children at all English proficiency levels.

Read Aloud Read the book aloud as children follow along. Pause to verify comprehension and to explain unfamiliar concepts.

Monitored Reading Have children silently read a few pages at a time. Use the following questions to support comprehension:

- **Pages 2–3** What do spiders and people have in common? (People use nets and spiders use webs to catch food.)
- **Pages 4–5** How does a baseball player use a web? (Part of a baseball glove has a web.)
- **Pages 6–8** What happens when the holes in a net or a web are too big? (They do not catch anything because objects go right through them.)

Reread Have children reread the book with a partner, in small groups, or independently. Have them complete the Study Guide on page 237.

RESPOND

Answers to the Reader's Inside Back Cover:

Talk About It

1. The web in a baseball glove makes it easier for a baseball player to catch a ball. (Cause and Effect)

2. A spider web is sticky, and insects are caught when they fly into the web. (Cause and Effect)

Write About It

3. Help children think of times when they might have seen a net or a web.

Support writers at various English proficiency levels.

Beginning Have children dictate sentences about their pictures.

Intermediate Have children brainstorm lists of words that they can use to write about nets and webs.

Advanced Have children write three or four sentences about their pictures.

Extend Language It is called a butterfly net. Invite children to think of other types of nets.

Answers to page 237:

1. Insects fly into sticky spider webs.

2. Baseball players catch balls.

3. The net's holes are too big.

Family Link Read aloud the Family Link activity on page 237 before sending copies of the Study Guide home with children. Later, have children share what family members said about catching things with nets and webs.

Name ______________________________

- **Read** *Webs and Other Catchers* again.
- **Write** to fill in the *What and Why* chart.

What and Why

What happens?	Why does it happen?
1. Insects are caught.	1.
2.	2. Baseball gloves have webs.
3. Fish swim through the holes in a net.	3.

Family Link

Have family members describe nets or webs that they have used to catch things. What did they catch?

American Hero Day

by Alice Cary

ELL Reader 2.3.4 Fiction

INTRODUCE THE BOOK

Activate Prior Knowledge/Build Background Read the title, and discuss with children what it means to be a hero. Ask children to name some heroes that they know about.

Preview/Use Text Features Preview the reader by paging through the book and talking about the illustrations together.

Preteach Vocabulary Review the high-frequency words that appear in this book: **their** and **many**. Introduce these key words from the book: **hero** (p. 1), **mask** (p. 2), **save** (p. 3), and **borrow** (p. 4). Discuss these words and add them to a Word Wall.

READ THE BOOK

Choose among these options for reading to support children at all English proficiency levels.

Read Aloud Read the book aloud as children follow along. Pause to verify comprehension and to explain unfamiliar concepts.

Monitored Reading Have children read aloud a few pages at a time. Use the following questions to support comprehension:

- **Pages 2–3** What problem do the second graders have? (A cat has ruined many of their masks of famous Americans. They do not have time to make new ones.)
- **Pages 4–5** How does the class solve the problem? (A child in the class remembers that another school had Hero Day. The class is able to borrow the other school's masks.)
- **Pages 6–8** Why does the class need the masks? (They need the masks to play the parts of famous American heroes. The children's parents would come to see.)

Reread Have children reread the book with a partner, in small groups, or independently. Have them complete the Study Guide on page 239.

RESPOND

Answers to the Reader's Inside Back Cover:

Talk About It

1. The class borrowed masks from another school. (Plot)
2. Possible response: Helping someone makes a person a hero. I think my mother is a hero. (Theme)

Write About It

3. Children should draw a picture or mask of a famous person they admire. They should write about why they think that person is a hero. (Theme)
Support writers at various English proficiency levels.

Beginning Ask children to dictate or write an ending to this sentence frame: *I think this person is a hero because* ___.
Intermediate Have children write two or three reasons why they think that person is a hero.
Advanced Have children help less-proficient speakers with their writing assignment.

Extend Language The words *our masks* mean "masks that belong to *us*." If a girl owned a mask, she would call it "*my* mask."

Answers to page 239:

1. The cat stepped in paint and then on the masks.
2. They could try to borrow the masks from Baker School.
3. Mrs. Clay
4. to see the art and hear about American heroes
5. Ben Franklin and Sally Ride

Family Link Read aloud the Family Link activity on page 239 before sending copies of the Study Guide home with children. Later, have children share what family members said about their favorite American heroes.

Name ______________________________

American Hero Day

- **Read** *American Hero Day* again.
- **Write** the answers to the questions.

Pages	Question	Answer
2–3	**1.** What did the cat do?	
4–5	**2.** What good idea does Carlos have?	
4–5	**3.** Who lends some hero masks to the class?	
6–7	**4.** Why do parents come to the classroom?	
7–8	**5.** Name two American heroes the children talked about.	

Family Link

Ask family members to tell you about their favorite American heroes.

Inventions Help People

by Stanley Brown

ELL Reader 2.3.5 Nonfiction

INTRODUCE THE BOOK

Activate Prior Knowledge/Build Background Read the title, and look at the photograph on the cover. Have children tell what they think the invention is and how it helps people.

Preview/Use Text Features Preview the reader by talking about the photographs together and naming the labeled items.

Preteach Vocabulary Review the high-frequency words that appear in this book: **hours**, **clothes**, and **only**. Introduce these key words from the book: **inventions** (p. 1), **idea** (p. 2), and **easier** (p. 2). Discuss these words and add them to a Word Wall.

READ THE BOOK

Choose among these options for reading to support children at all English proficiency levels.

Read Aloud Read the book aloud as children follow along. Pause to verify comprehension and to explain unfamiliar concepts.

Monitored Reading Have children silently read a few pages at a time. Use the following questions to support comprehension:

- **Page 2** How do inventors think of ideas? (They watch people do things and think of ways to make those things easier.)
- **Pages 3–7** What do washing machines, typewriters, and cars have in common? (They make people's lives easier by helping them get things done faster.)
- **Page 8** Why were kites and basketball invented? (They were invented for fun.)

Reread Have children reread the book with a partner, in small groups, or independently. Have them complete the Study Guide on page 241.

RESPOND

Answers to the Reader's Inside Back Cover:

Talk About It

1. Inventions help people by making their lives easier. For example, if people did not have washing machines, they would have to wash clothes by hand. (Cause and Effect)

2. Possible response: I think people would ride everywhere on bicycles.

Write About It

3. Children should draw a picture of an original invention. They should describe their invention and tell whether it is for fun or to help people. Support writers at various English proficiency levels.

Beginning After children draw and label their inventions, have each child write or dictate a sentence to tell what the invention does.

Intermediate Have children brainstorm lists of words they can use to write about their inventions.

Advanced Have children include at least three or four details about their inventions.

Extend Language *Washboard* is made up of the words *wash* and *board.* Invite children to give other examples of compound words.

Answers to page 239:

1. It would be easier to wash clothes.
2. the typewriter
3. People could go from place to place faster.
4. the game of basketball

Family Link Read aloud the Family Link activity on page 241 before sending copies of the Study Guide home with children. Later, have children share what family members said about what they would like to invent.

Name ________________________________

- **Read** *Inventions Help People* again.
- **Write** to fill in the *What and Why* chart.

What and Why

What was invented?	Why was it invented?
1. the washing machine	**1.**
2.	**2.** Writing would be easier.
3. cars	**3.**
4.	**4.** People could play a sport in the winter.

Family Link

Ask family members to describe an invention that they would like to create.

For Good Luck!

by Katrina Gold

ELL Reader 2.4.1 Realistic Fiction

INTRODUCE THE BOOK

Activate Prior Knowledge/Build Background Read the title. Discuss with children what they think it means to have good luck. Ask children if they have any treasures that they believe bring them good luck.

Preview/Use Text Features Preview the reader by talking about the illustrations together and naming the labeled items. Point out the highlighted words and definitions on pages 2, 4, and 8.

Preteach Vocabulary Review the tested vocabulary words that appear in this book: **unpacked** and **wrapped**. Introduce these key words from the book: **luck** (p. 1), **memory** (p. 2), and **treasures** (p. 2). Discuss these words and add them to a Word Wall.

READ THE BOOK

Choose among these options for reading to support children at all English proficiency levels.

Read Aloud Read the book aloud as children follow along. Pause to verify comprehension and to explain unfamiliar concepts.

Monitored Reading Have children read aloud a few pages at a time. Use the following questions to support comprehension:

- **Pages 2–3** What do Lyn, David, and their mother decide to do on a rainy day? (They decide to look into the memory box.)
- **Pages 4–7** Why are the earrings special to Lyn and David's mother? (The earrings were a gift from her father to her mother. The earrings gave her mother good luck.)
- **Page 8** Where did the piece of jade come from? (Lyn and David's grandfather found it by the mountains in China and carried it in his pocket every day.)

Reread Have children reread the book with a partner, in small groups, or independently. Have them complete the Study Guide on page 243.

RESPOND

Answers to the Reader's Inside Back Cover:

Talk About It

1. The mother will give her mother's earrings to Lyn and her father's jade to David. (Main Idea and Details)

2. Possible response: I think their mom has a memory box so she can keep special things in one place. (Draw Conclusions)

Write About It

3. Help children think of items in their homes that are special to their families. (Main Idea)

Support writers at various English proficiency levels.

Beginning Pair children with more-proficient speakers to complete their lists.

Intermediate Have children brainstorm lists of words that they can use when writing their lists for the memory box.

Advanced Have children help less-proficient speakers complete their lists.

Extend Language *Shoelace* is a compound word made of the words *shoe* and *lace*. A shoelace is what you use to tie your shoes. Invite the children to give other examples of compound words.

Answers to page 243:

Pictures and sentences will vary. Possible items in the memory box could include old photos, a pair of baby shoes, a tooth, a cloth bag, a piece of jade, and a small case.

Family Link Read aloud the Family Link activity on page 243 before sending copies of the Study Guide home with children. Later, have children share what family members said about their treasures.

Name ______________________________

- **Read** *For Good Luck!* again.
- **Draw** a picture that shows three things that were in the memory box in the story.
- **Write** a sentence that goes with your picture.

____

____

____

____

Family Link

Does anyone in your family have a special treasure that brings good luck? Ask family members to tell you about a favorite treasure.

The Tomato Times

by Albert Hinton

ELL Reader 2.4.2 Nonfiction

INTRODUCE THE BOOK

Activate Prior Knowledge/Build Background Read the title, and look at the picture on the cover. Ask children to brainstorm words that describe a tomato.

Preview/Use Text Features Preview the reader by talking about the photographs together and naming the labeled items.

Preteach Vocabulary Review the tested vocabulary words that appear in this book: **fruit**, **soil**, and **root**. Introduce these key words from the book: **tomato** (p. 1), **vegetables** (p. 2), **healthy** (p. 3), and **garden** (p. 5). Discuss these words and add them to a Word Wall.

READ THE BOOK

Choose among these options for reading to support children at all English proficiency levels.

Read Aloud Read the book aloud as children follow along. Pause to verify comprehension and to explain unfamiliar concepts.

Monitored Reading Have children silently read a few pages at a time. Use the following questions to support comprehension:

- **Pages 2–3** Why do some people love tomatoes? (Because they are healthy and tasty and can be put in many foods.)
- **Page 4** What do tomatoes look like? (They can be red, green, yellow, or orange, and big or small.)
- **Pages 5–8** What is good to know if you want to grow your own tomatoes? (The plants need sunlight and water; cold weather can hurt them; you should plant tomato seeds in the spring; flowers on the tomato plants turn into tomatoes.) How do people eat tomatoes? (sliced or cooked)

Reread Have children reread the book with a partner, in small groups, or independently. Have them complete the Study Guide on page 245.

RESPOND

Answers to the Reader's Inside Back Cover:

Talk About It

1. Responses will vary. Reasons may concern how tomatoes taste. (Fact and Opinion)

2. Possible response: I learned that the flowers on tomato plants turn into tomatoes. (Main Idea and Details)

Write About It

3. Children should draw pictures of plants they would like to grow and then write about the plants.

Support writers at various English proficiency levels.

Beginning Let children dictate short sentences about their pictures.

Intermediate Have children brainstorm lists of words they can use when writing about plants.

Advanced Have children write three or four sentences about their pictures.

Extend Language Leaves get more sunlight than roots because leaves grow above the ground.

Answers to page 245:

Possible responses: *Facts:* Tomatoes are the fruit of the tomato plant. They have vitamins. They can be many colors. They need sunlight and water. *My Opinion:* I think tomatoes are good to eat.

Family Link Read aloud the Family Link activity on page 245 before sending copies of the Study Guide home with children. Later, have children share what family members said about eating tomatoes.

Name ______________________________

The Tomato Times

- **Read** *The Tomato Times* again.
- Fill in the web. **Write** four facts from the book.
- At the bottom, **write** your own opinion about tomatoes.

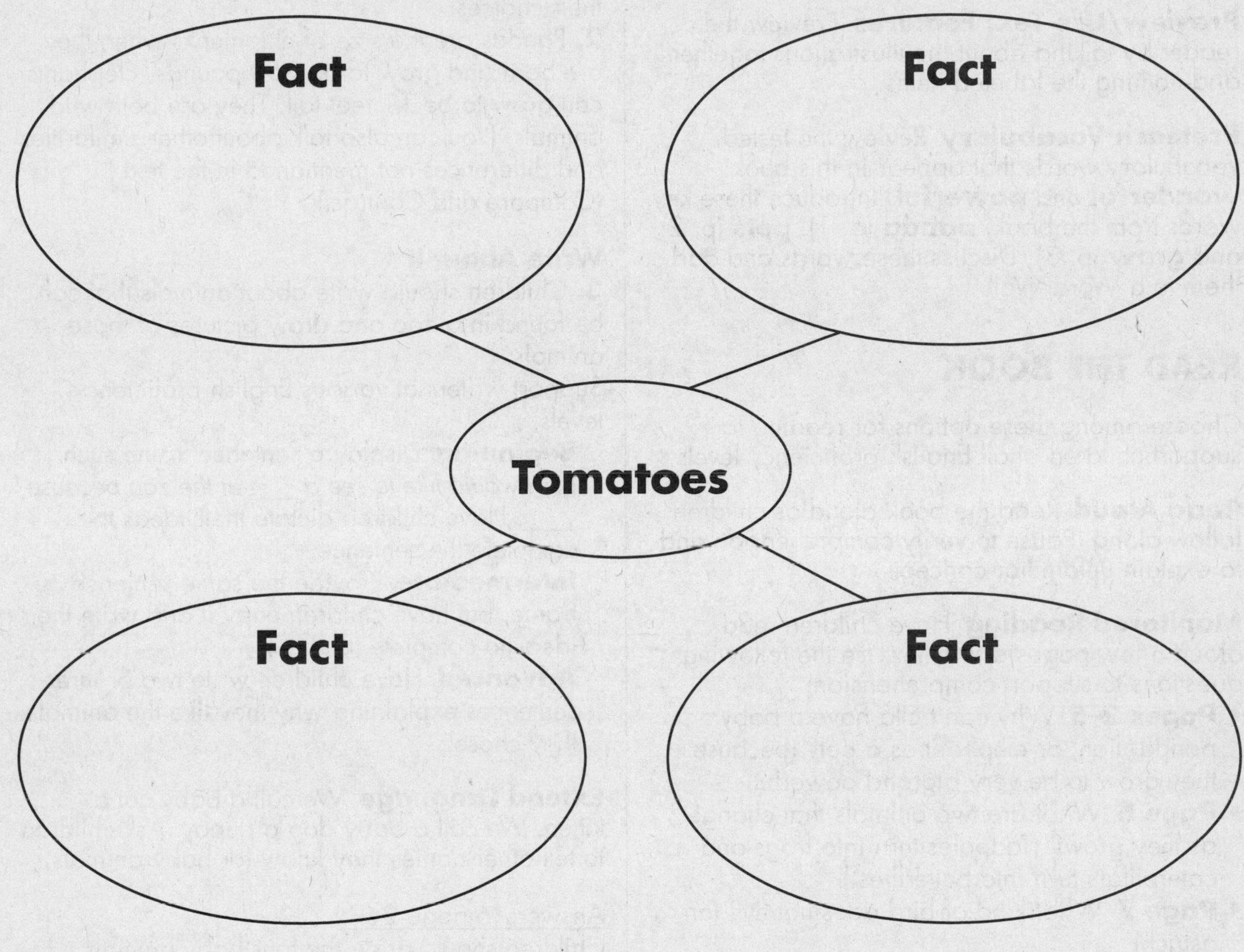

My Opinion: I think tomatoes are ________________.

Family Link

Ask family members whether they like tomatoes. If they do, how do they like to eat them? If they do not, why not?

The Panda Gift

by Pedro Damon

ELL Reader 2.4.3 Fiction

INTRODUCE THE BOOK

Activate Prior Knowledge/Build Background Read the title, and look at the picture on the cover. Ask children to name animals they might see at a zoo.

Preview/Use Text Features Preview the reader by talking about the illustrations together and naming the labeled items.

Preteach Vocabulary Review the tested vocabulary words that appear in this book: **wonderful** and **powerful**. Introduce these key words from the book: **panda** (p. 1), **pets** (p. 2), and **grow** (p. 3). Discuss these words and add them to a Word Wall.

READ THE BOOK

Choose among these options for reading to support children at all English proficiency levels.

Read Aloud Read the book aloud as children follow along. Pause to verify comprehension and to explain unfamiliar concepts.

Monitored Reading Have children read aloud a few pages at a time. Use the following questions to support comprehension:

- **Pages 2–5** Why can't Ella have a baby panda, lion, or elephant as a pet? (because they grow to be very big and powerful)
- **Page 6** What are two animals that change as they grow? (Tadpoles turn into frogs and caterpillars turn into butterflies.)
- **Page 7** What kind of bird does not fly? (an ostrich)
- **Page 8** What makes Ella feel better about not getting a baby panda? (Mama gives her a toy panda as a gift.)

Reread Have children reread the book with a partner, in small groups, or independently. Have them complete the Study Guide on page 247.

RESPOND

Answers to the Reader's Inside Back Cover:

Talk About It

1. Responses will vary. Ask children to explain their choices.

2. Pandas are the size of chipmunks when they are born and grow to be 250 pounds. Elephants can grow to be 11 feet tall. They are both wild animals. (You can also talk about other similarities and differences not mentioned in the text.) (Compare and Contrast)

Write About It

3. Children should write about animals that can be found in a zoo and draw pictures of those animals.

Support writers at various English proficiency levels.

Beginning Display a sentence frame such as: *I would like to see a ____ at the zoo because ____*. Have children dictate their ideas to complete the sentence.

Intermediate Provide the same sentence frame, but have children copy it and write their ideas to complete it.

Advanced Have children write two or three sentences explaining why they like the animals they chose.

Extend Language We call a baby cat a kitten. We call a baby dog a puppy. Ask children to tell other names they know for baby animals.

Answers to page 247:

Children should draw the four baby animals and provide one fact from the book about each animal. Possible responses: Pandas grow to be 250 pounds. Lions grow to be more than 500 pounds. Elephants can be 11 feet tall. Ostriches cannot fly.

Family Link Read aloud the Family Link activity on page 247 before sending copies of the Study Guide home with children. Later, have children share what family members told them about favorite wild animals.

Name ____________________________________

- **Read** *The Panda Gift* again.
- **Draw** each baby animal that Ella saw at the zoo.
- **Write** one thing you learned about each animal.

Baby Panda (pages 2–3)	Baby Lion (page 4)
______________________________ ______________________________	______________________________ ______________________________
Baby Elephant (page 5)	Baby Ostrich (page 7)
______________________________ ______________________________	______________________________ ______________________________

Family Link

Ask family members to tell you about their favorite wild animals.

Adam's New Soccer Team

by Will Lee

ELL Reader 2.4.4 Fiction

INTRODUCE THE BOOK

Activate Prior Knowledge/Build Background Read the title, and look at the picture on the cover. Ask children to tell how the boy is feeling. Why might he feel that way?

Preview/Use Text Features Preview the reader by talking about the illustrations together and naming labeled items.

Preteach Vocabulary Review the tested vocabulary words that appear in this book: **fair** and **trouble**. Introduce these key words from the book: **team** (p. 1), **practice** (p. 2), **pass** (p. 4), and **kicking** (p. 4). Discuss these words and add them to a Word Wall.

READ THE BOOK

Choose among these options for reading to support children at all English proficiency levels.

Read Aloud Read the book aloud as children follow along. Pause to verify comprehension and to explain unfamiliar concepts.

Monitored Reading Have children read aloud a few pages at a time. Use the following questions to support comprehension:

- **Page 2** Why is Adam sad on his first day of practice? (He does not know anyone. He misses his old team.)
- **Pages 3–4** How do the Strikers get ready for their first game? (They work hard. They practice kicking the ball, passing the ball, and talking to each other on the field.)
- **Pages 5–8** How do the Strikers win the soccer game? (They work as a team together. They pass the ball and score four goals.)

Reread Have children reread the book with a partner, in small groups, or independently. Have them complete the Study Guide on page 249.

RESPOND

Answers to the Reader's Inside Back Cover:

Talk About It

1. Adam has new friends on his new team. (Plot)
2. Friends make you feel comfortable and help you have fun. (Theme)

Write About It

3. Help children decide which teacher or coach they will write about. Have children think about why that person is important to them.
Support writers at various English proficiency levels.

Beginning Allow children to write or dictate their description in the home language. If feasible, have children translate their work with the help of a partner.
Intermediate Have children tell partners about their favorite coach or teacher before writing.
Advanced Have children help less-proficient speakers complete their descriptions.

Extend Language Some other soccer words in the story are *team, practice, ball, field, score* (noun), *teammates, net,* and *whistle.* Invite children to think of words associated with another sport. Point out words that are the same for both sports.

Answers to page 249:

1. He wants to be on his old soccer team.
2. He works with Chuck and Lara. He kicks and passes the ball.
3. He thinks it is not fair that he can't be on their team.
4. He has to think about his new team, not his old team.
5. He feels proud and happy.

Family Link Read aloud the Family Link activity on page 249 before sending copies of the Study Guide home with children. Later, have children share what family members told them about making new friends.

Name ______________________________

Adam's New Soccer Team

- **Read** *Adam's New Soccer Team* again.
- **Write** answers to the questions.

Pages	Question	Answer
2	**1.** At the beginning of the story, what does Adam want?	
3–4	**2.** What does Adam do at practice?	
5	**3.** What does Adam think when he sees Sonny and Liam?	
6–7	**4.** What does Adam have to think about during the game?	
8	**5.** How does Adam feel at the end of the story?	

Family Link

Have family members tell you about a time when they had to make new friends.

How Is the Weather?

by Jim Collins

ELL Reader 2.4.5 Nonfiction

INTRODUCE THE BOOK

Activate Prior Knowledge/Build Background Read the title, and look at the picture on the cover. Have children compare the weather in the photo to the weather today.

Preview/Use Text Features Preview the reader by talking about the photographs together, naming the labeled items, and reading the captions.

Preteach Vocabulary Review the tested vocabulary words that appear in this book: **special** and **picnic**. Introduce these key words from the book: **weather** (p. 1), **plans** (p. 2), **thermometer** (p. 3), and **report** (p. 5). Discuss these words and add them to a Word Wall.

READ THE BOOK

Choose among these options for reading to support children at all English proficiency levels.

Read Aloud Read the book aloud as children follow along. Pause to verify comprehension and to explain unfamiliar concepts.

Monitored Reading Have children silently read a few pages at a time. Use the following questions to support comprehension:

- **Pages 2–5** What are some ways you can find out about the weather? (You can look at a thermometer, listen to a weather report on the radio, or watch a weather report on television.)
- **Pages 6–7** How does the weather spoil one family's plans? (It is too windy to go for a balloon ride.) How does the weather help the two girls? (Lots of snow means they can keep their plans to go sledding and build a snowman.)
- **Page 8** How can we stay comfortable in all kinds of weather? (We can heat our homes and wear warm clothing when we are cold. We can use fans and swimming pools to cool off when we are hot.)

Reread Have children reread the book with a partner, in small groups, or independently. Have them complete the Study Guide on page 251.

RESPOND

Answers to the Reader's Inside Back Cover:

Talk About It

1. Responses will vary. Ask children to explain their choices.

2. Responses will vary. Supply English words such as *storm, lightning, flood,* or *degrees* if necessary. (Cause and Effect)

Write About It

3. Discuss with children ways in which weather can be bad. Then have them think and write about the worst weather they have ever seen. Support writers at various English proficiency levels.

Beginning Display a sentence frame such as: *The worst weather I ever saw was* ___. Have children dictate an ending.

Intermediate Provide the same sentence frame, but have children copy it and write their own endings.

Advanced Have children include at least four details about the worst weather they have ever seen.

Extend Language Other words that can describe the weather are *cold, hot, perfect, bad, windy, sunny, rainy, stormy, snowy,* and *cloudy*. Have children help write and display a list of weather words.

Answers to page 251:

Pictures and labels will vary. Help children with words such as *sun, cloud,* or *rain* to clarify meanings.

Family Link Read aloud the Family Link activity on page 251 before sending copies of the Study Guide home with children. Later, have children share what family members said about their favorite and least favorite weather.

Name ______________________________ **How Is the Weather?**

- **Read** *How Is the Weather?* again.
- **Draw** a picture that shows your favorite weather. **Draw** yourself enjoying the weather.
- **Label** as many things in your picture as you can. Look at the book if you need help.

My Favorite Weather

Family Link

Have family members tell you about their favorite weather. Then, have them describe their least favorite weather.

At the Fire Station

by Victor Violi

ELL Reader 2.5.1 Nonfiction

INTRODUCE THE BOOK

Activate Prior Knowledge/Build Background Read the title, and look at the picture on the cover. Discuss with children some of the things that firefighters do.

Preview/Use Text Features Preview the reader by talking about the photographs together, naming the labeled items, and reading the captions.

Preteach Vocabulary Review the tested vocabulary words that appear in this book: **station**, **burning**, **building**, and **masks**. Introduce these key words from the book: **truck** (p. 2), **hose** (p. 3), **smoke** (p. 3), and **safety** (p. 5). Discuss these words and add them to a Word Wall.

READ THE BOOK

Choose among these options for reading to support children at all English proficiency levels.

Read Aloud Read the book aloud as children follow along. Pause to verify comprehension and to explain unfamiliar concepts.

Monitored Reading Have children silently read a few pages at a time. Use the following questions to support comprehension:

- **Pages 2–3** Why is it important for firefighters to work as a team during a fire? (because there are many different things that need to be done)
- **Pages 4–7** What do firefighters do when they are not fighting a fire? (They take classes. They visit schools to teach fire safety. They do chores at the fire station.)
- **Page 8** What happens when the fire alarm goes off? (Firefighters stop what they are doing and rush off to fight the fire.)

Reread Have children reread the book with a partner, in small groups, or independently. Have them complete the Study Guide on page 253.

RESPOND

Answers to the Reader's Inside Back Cover:

Talk About It

1. Some firefighters drive the truck. Some spray water on the fire with a hose. Some put on masks and go into the burning building. Firefighters also learn to use new equipment, teach fire safety, and do chores at the fire station. (Main Idea and Details)

2. Responses will vary. Possible response: I would like to be a firefighter because I could help people.

Write About It

3. Have children create a schedule that allows time for chores, training, eating, and sleeping. Support writers at various English proficiency levels.

Beginning Provide copies of a blank schedule for children to fill in.

Intermediate Display a copy of the blank schedule for children to copy and complete.

Advanced Have children create their own schedules.

Extend Language The word *teamwork* is made from *team* and *work*. Invite children to give other examples of compound words.

Answers to page 253:

Pictures and sentences will vary but should reflect the contents of the book.

Family Link Read aloud the Family Link activity on page 253 before sending copies of the Study Guide home with children. Later, have children share what family members said about firefighters and fire safety.

Name ______________________________ **At the Fire Station**

- **Read** *At the Fire Station* again.
- **Draw** a picture that shows what the book is about.
- **Write** a sentence that goes with your picture.

____

____

Family Link

Ask family members to share what they know about firefighters and fire safety.

Save the Ducks!

by Norma Morales

ELL Reader 2.5.2 Realistic Fiction

INTRODUCE THE BOOK

Activate Prior Knowledge/Build Background Read the title and look at the cover of the book. Discuss with children why they think the ducks in the picture need to be saved.

Preview/Use Text Features Preview the reader by talking about the illustrations together, naming the labeled items, and reading the captions.

Preteach Vocabulary Review the tested vocabulary words that appear in this book: **pounds** and **rolling**. Introduce these key words from the book: **save** (p. 1), **oil** (p. 2), **volunteers** (p. 3), and **healthy** (p. 6). Discuss these words and add them to a Word Wall.

READ THE BOOK

Choose among these options for reading to support children at all English proficiency levels.

Read Aloud Read the book aloud as children follow along. Pause to verify comprehension and to explain unfamiliar concepts.

Monitored Reading Have children silently read a few pages at a time. Use the following questions to support comprehension:

- **Pages 2–3** What has happened to the ducks at the beginning of the story? (They are stuck in water where oil has spilled.)
- **Pages 4–7** Why do the ducks need to be cleaned and given medicine? (They need to be cleaned because the oil on their feathers could cause them to drown. They need medicine because they drank water with oil in it.)
- **Page 8** Where do the volunteers bring the ducks when they are healthy? (The volunteers set the ducks free in clean water.)

Reread Have children reread the book with a partner, in small groups, or independently. Have them complete the Study Guide on page 255.

RESPOND

Answers to the Reader's Inside Back Cover:

Talk About It

1. The people in the story save the ducks from the dirty water. They clean the ducks, give them medicine, and take them to clean water. (Main Idea and Details)

2. Responses will vary. Possible response: I would like to be a volunteer and help animals. I like to be around animals.

Write About It

3. Remind children to write the steps for cleaning a duck in the correct order. (Sequence)

Support writers at various English proficiency levels.

Beginning Let children draw and label pictures that show the steps for cleaning a duck and returning it to the water.

Intermediate Have children look through the book to find words they can use when writing the steps for cleaning a duck.

Advanced Have children use dictionaries or thesauruses to find words to use in their writing.

Extend Language Ducks can also fly, eat, drink, waddle, and walk. Invite children to discuss what some other animals can do.

Answers to page 255:

Pictures and sentences will vary but should show the story in correct sequence. Possible sentences: Ducks have oil on them. Volunteers clean them and give them medicine. The ducks go to a new, clean home.

Family Link Read aloud the Family Link activity on page 255 before sending copies of the Study Guide home with children. Later, children may share what family members said about taking care of animals.

Name ______________________________

- **Read** *Save the Ducks!* again.
- **Draw** pictures to show what happens at the beginning, middle, and end of the story. **Write** words or sentences to go with your pictures.

Beginning (pages 2–3)

Middle (pages 4–7)

End (page 8)

Family Link

Has anyone in your family ever taken care of an animal? Ask family members to describe how they have helped or cared for an animal.

Puppy Show

by Sallie Carson

ELL Reader 2.5.3 Realistic Fiction

INTRODUCE THE BOOK

Activate Prior Knowledge/Build Background Read the title. Discuss with children how they think a puppy must behave in order to win a puppy show.

Preview/Use Text Features Preview the reader by talking about the illustrations together and naming the labeled items. Point out the *Extend Language* features on pages 5 and 7.

Preteach Vocabulary Review the tested vocabulary words that appear in this book: **chewing** and **wagged**. Introduce these key words from the book: **puppy** (p. 1), **behave** (p. 2), **leashes** (p. 4), and **command** (p. 5). Discuss these words and add them to a Word Wall.

READ THE BOOK

Choose among these options for reading to support children at all English proficiency levels.

Read Aloud Read the book aloud as children follow along. Pause to verify comprehension and to explain unfamiliar concepts.

Monitored Reading Have children read aloud a few pages at a time. Use the following questions to support comprehension:

- **Pages 2–3** What do Abby and Caleb need to do for their puppies? (They need to give their puppies food and water, take them on walks, give them baths, and teach them to behave.)
- **Pages 4–7** How do Abby and Caleb train their puppies? (Abby and Caleb put the puppies on leashes, teach the puppies one command at a time, practice with the puppies every day, and play with them after training time.)
- **Page 8** How did the puppies behave at the puppy show? (The puppies behaved well. They heeled, sat, stayed, and came when they were called.)

Reread Have children reread the book with a partner, in small groups, or independently. Have them complete the Study Guide on page 257.

RESPOND

<u>Answers to the Reader's Inside Back Cover:</u>

Talk About It

1. Abby and Caleb trained their puppies because it was their 4-H project. They also wanted to enter the puppies in a puppy show. (Cause and Effect)

2. Possible response: I think the children trained the puppies very well. The puppies did everything they were supposed to do at the puppy show.

Write About It

3. Help children decide what animals would be fun to have and play with. Discuss with children what kinds of things animals can be taught to do. Support writers at various English proficiency levels.

Beginning Display these sentence frames: *I would like to have a _____ for a pet. I would teach my pet to _____.* Have children dictate their ideas to complete the sentences.

Intermediate Provide the same sentence frames. Have children copy and complete the sentences.

Advanced Have children name at least three things that they would like to teach their pets.

Extend Language The puppy barked. Invite children to put the following actions in the past: *learn, train, behave, play,* and *heel.*

<u>Answers to page 257:</u>

1. because puppy training is their 4-H project

2. The children called *Come!* and pulled their leashes.

3. because they liked learning

4. Every puppy won a prize at the puppy show.

Family Link Read aloud the Family Link activity on page 257 before sending copies of the Study Guide home with children. Later, have children share what family members said about training pets.

Name ______________________________

- **Read** *Puppy Show* again.
- **Complete** the *What and Why* chart.

What and Why

What happened in the story?	Why did this happen?
1. Abby and Caleb plan to train their puppies. (pages 2–3)	**1.**
2.	**2.** because the puppies tried to run away (page 4)
3. The puppies wagged their tails. (page 7)	**3.**
4.	**4.** because the puppies heeled, sat, stayed, and came when they were called (page 8)

Family Link
Has anyone in your family ever trained an animal? Have family members describe what they did to train the animal.

Hello, Friend!

by Katy Black

ELL Reader 2.5.4 Nonfiction

INTRODUCE THE BOOK

Activate Prior Knowledge/Build Background Read the title and look at the photograph on the cover. Discuss with children what it means to be a friend to someone.

Preview/Use Text Features Preview the reader by talking about the photographs together. Point out the chart on page 7.

Preteach Vocabulary Review the tested vocabulary words that appear in this book: **wondered** and **greatest**. Introduce these key words from the book: **friend** (p. 1), **nice** (p. 2), **play** (p. 3), and **share** (p. 4). Discuss these words and add them to a Word Wall.

READ THE BOOK

Choose among these options for reading to support children at all English proficiency levels.

Read Aloud Read the book aloud as children follow along. Pause to verify comprehension and to explain unfamiliar concepts.

Monitored Reading Have children silently read a few pages at a time. Use the following questions to support comprehension:

- **Pages 2–3** Why would someone want to make a new friend? (because having a friend is a great part of life)
- **Pages 4–5** What are some things that good friends do? (Good friends help you, share with you, talk with you, and play with you.)
- **Pages 6–7** Why do friends sometimes not get along? (Sometimes friends forget to share or be nice.) How can friends solve a problem? (Friends can say they are sorry or try to share.)
- **Page 8** How can a good friend make you feel? (A good friend can make you feel happy.)

Reread Have children reread the book with a partner, in small groups, or independently. Have them complete the Study Guide on page 259.

RESPOND

Answers to the Reader's Inside Back Cover:

Talk About It

1. If you want to make a new friend, you should smile and say hello. You can also make a friend when you ask someone who is standing alone to play with you. (Author's Purpose)

2. When you don't get along with your friends you can take some time away, work together to solve a problem, or say that you are sorry. (Author's Purpose)

Write About It

3. Help children think of times when they have been good friends to someone.

Support writers at various English proficiency levels.

Beginning Let children dictate what makes them good friends as someone else records their words. Have children practice reading aloud and writing the recorded words.

Intermediate Have children tell partners what they want to say about being good friends before writing it down.

Advanced Have children also write about how they could be an even better friend.

Extend Language The word *friendly* means behaving as a friend to someone. *Friendship* is the feeling of liking between people who are friends.

Answers to page 259:

Illustrations will vary. Possible sentences:

1. One way to make a new friend is to say hello and shake hands.

2. A good friend shares.

Family Link Read aloud the Family Link activity on page 259 before sending copies of the Study Guide home with children. Later, have children share what family members said about being a good friend.

Name ______________________________________

Hello, Friend!

- **Read** *Hello, Friend!* again.
- In Box 1, **draw** a picture that shows one way to make a new friend. **Write** a sentence that goes with your picture.
- In Box 2, **draw** a picture that shows one way to be a good friend. **Write** a sentence that goes with your picture.

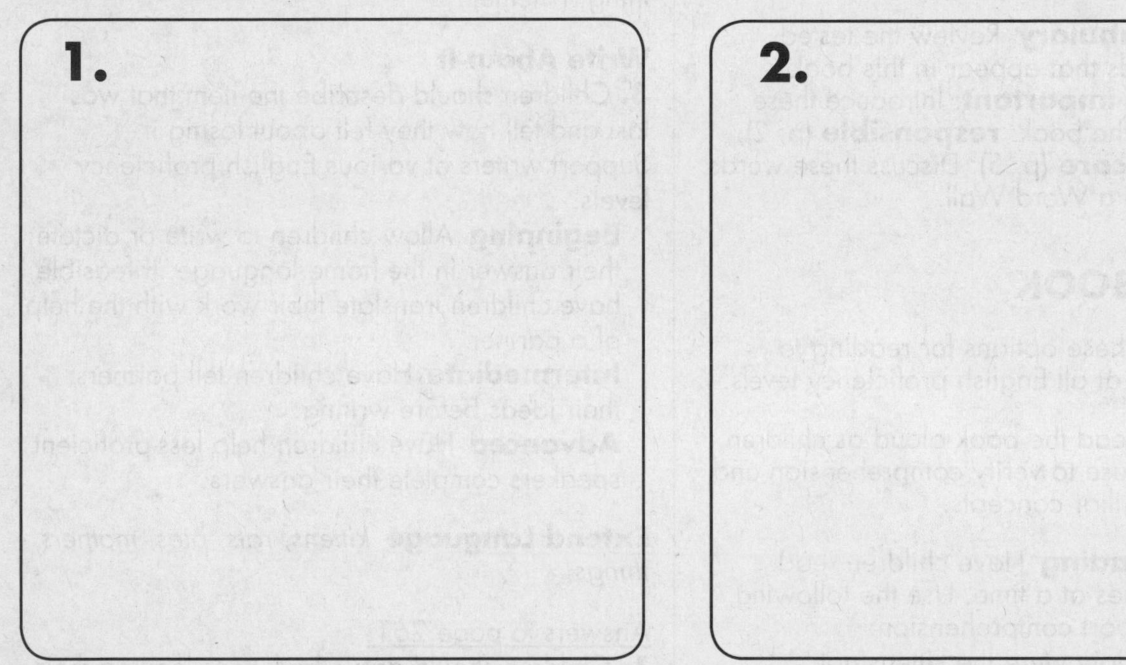

______________________________________ ______________________________________

______________________________________ ______________________________________

______________________________________ ______________________________________

Family Link

Have family members tell you how they are good friends to other people.

Three Little Kittens Learn a Lesson

by Bethany Lions

ELL Reader 2.5.5 Fiction

INTRODUCE THE BOOK

Activate Prior Knowledge/Build Background Read the title, and discuss with children what it means to be responsible. Have children give you an example of a time when they were responsible.

Preview/Use Text Features Preview the reader by talking about the illustrations together and naming the labeled items.

Preteach Vocabulary Review the tested vocabulary words that appear in this book: **afternoon** and **important**. Introduce these key words from the book: **responsible** (p. 2), **lost** (p. 3), and **care** (p. 5). Discuss these words and add them to a Word Wall.

READ THE BOOK

Choose among these options for reading to support children at all English proficiency levels.

Read Aloud Read the book aloud as children follow along. Pause to verify comprehension and to explain unfamiliar concepts.

Monitored Reading Have children read aloud a few pages at a time. Use the following questions to support comprehension:

- **Pages 2–4** How were the kittens not responsible? (They took off their mittens and left them on the playground.)
- **Page 5** What happened when the kittens got home? (They did not have their mittens, so their mother would not let them have any pie.)
- **Pages 6–8** How did the kittens solve their problem? (They went back to the playground, found their mittens, and washed them.)

Reread Have children reread the book with a partner, in small groups, or independently. Have them complete the Study Guide on page 261.

RESPOND

Answers to the Reader's Inside Back Cover:

Talk About It

1. The kittens got pie because they went back to the playground to find their mittens and then washed the mittens. (Plot)

2. The kittens learned to take care of their things, to solve problems themselves, and to do the right thing. (Theme)

Write About It

3. Children should describe the item that was lost and tell how they felt about losing it. Support writers at various English proficiency levels.

Beginning Allow children to write or dictate their answer in the home language. If feasible, have children translate their work with the help of a partner.

Intermediate Have children tell partners their ideas before writing.

Advanced Have children help less-proficient speakers complete their answers.

Extend Language *kittens, rats, pies, mothers, things*

Answers to page 261:

1. Children should draw the kittens leaving their mittens at the playground. Possible sentence: The kittens left their mittens.

2. Children should draw the kittens finding their mittens, washing their mittens, or showing their mittens to their mother. Possible sentence: The kittens looked for their mittens.

Family Link Read aloud the Family Link activity on page 261 before sending copies of the Study Guide home with children. Later, have children share what family members said about learning lessons.

Name ___________________________

Three Little Kittens Learn a Lesson

- **Read** *Three Little Kittens Learn a Lesson* again.
- In Box 1, **draw** a picture of the kittens doing the wrong thing.
- In Box 2, **draw** a picture of the kittens doing the right thing.
- **Write** two sentences that go with your pictures.

1.	2.

___________________________ ___________________________

___________________________ ___________________________

___________________________ ___________________________

Family Link

Have family members tell you about a time when they learned a lesson.

Play Ball!

by Bruce Blackwell

ELL Reader 2.6.1 Poetry

INTRODUCE THE BOOK

Activate Prior Knowledge/Build Background Read the title, and discuss baseball and softball with the class. Encourage children to describe the games to you.

Preview/Use Text Features Preview the reader by talking about the photos together and naming the labeled items.

Preteach Vocabulary Review the tested vocabulary words that appear in this book: **field** and **bases**. Introduce these key words from the book: **ball** (p. 1), **friends** (p. 2), and **team** (p. 5). Discuss these words and add them to a Word Wall.

READ THE BOOK

Choose among these options for reading to support children at all English proficiency levels.

Read Aloud Read the book aloud as children follow along. Pause to verify comprehension and to explain unfamiliar concepts.

Monitored Reading Have children read aloud a few pages at a time. Use the following questions to support comprehension:

- **Pages 2–5** What do you need to play ball? (You need friends to play with, bases, a bat, a ball, and two teams.)
- **Pages 6–7** How do you play ball? (You hit the ball and run from base to base.)
- **Page 8** What is "the best sound that a player hears"? (cheers)

Reread Have children reread the book with a partner, in small groups, or independently. Have them complete the Study Guide on page 263.

RESPOND

<u>Answers to the Reader's Inside Back Cover:</u>

Talk About It

1. To play baseball you need a bat, a ball, bases, teams, and mitts. (Fact and Opinion)

2. Possible response: You play baseball in a big space outside. (Draw Conclusions)

Write About It

3. Children should tell whether they like playing on a team and what they like most about sports or games. (Fact and Opinion)

Support writers at various English proficiency levels.

Beginning Display a sentence frame such as: *Playing on a team is fun because ___.* Have children write their endings.

Intermediate Have children tell partners what they want to say before writing down their ideas.

Advanced Using the poem in the book as an example, have children try to write their answers in rhyme.

Extend Language The player at home plate holds a bat. Invite children to discuss other positions in baseball.

<u>Answers to page 263:</u>

Accept any reasonable answers. Possible response: *Baseball:* mitt, bat, base, small ball; *Both*: run, field, ball; *Soccer:* net, kick, large ball

Family Link Read aloud the Family Link activity on page 263 before sending copies of the Study Guide home with children. Later, have children share what family members said about playing on a team.

Name ____________________________

- **Read** *Play Ball!* again.
- Pick a sport other than baseball that you like. **Write** the name of that sport on the blank line below.
- Use the Venn diagram to show how the two sports are alike and how they are different. You can **write** things you need to play the sport and actions that happen when you play.

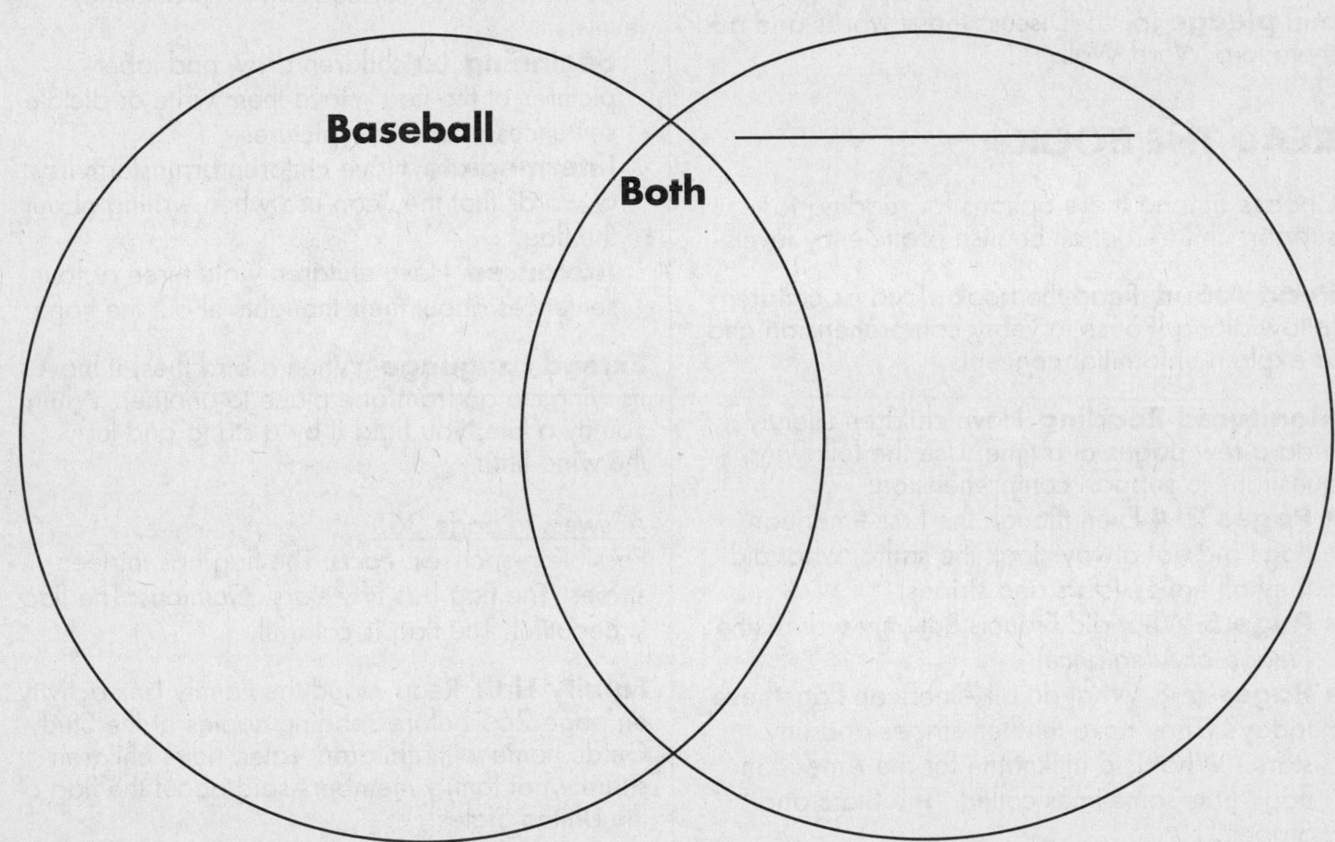

Family Link

Has anyone in your family ever played on a team? Ask family members to tell what they like about playing on a team.

The Stars and Stripes

by Melissa Valdez

ELL Reader 2.6.2 Nonfiction

INTRODUCE THE BOOK

Activate Prior Knowledge/Build Background Read the title, and look at the picture on the cover of the book. Discuss with children what they know about the American flag.

Preview/Use Text Features Preview the reader by talking about the illustrations and photographs together, naming the labeled items, and reading the captions.

Preteach Vocabulary Review the tested vocabulary words that appear in this book: **flag**, **stars**, and **stripes**. Introduce these key words from the book: **honor** (p. 2), **country** (p. 3), and **pledge** (p. 5). Discuss these words and add them to a Word Wall.

READ THE BOOK

Choose among these options for reading to support children at all English proficiency levels.

Read Aloud Read the book aloud as children follow along. Pause to verify comprehension and to explain unfamiliar concepts.

Monitored Reading Have children silently read a few pages at a time. Use the following questions to support comprehension:

- **Pages 2–4** Even though the first American flags did not always look the same, what did they all have? (stars and stripes)
- **Page 5** What did Francis Bellamy write? (the *Pledge of Allegiance*)
- **Pages 6–8** What do all American flags have today? (They have thirteen stripes and fifty stars.) What is a nickname for the American flag? (It is sometimes called "The Stars and Stripes.")

Reread Have children reread the book with a partner, in small groups, or independently. Have them complete the Study Guide on page 265.

RESPOND

Answers to the Reader's Inside Back Cover:

Talk About It

1. The first flag had thirteen stars and thirteen stripes. Later, flags did not always look the same. Now all flags have thirteen stripes and fifty stars, and they all look alike. (Compare and Contrast)

2. They take off their hats, stand, and place their hands over their hearts.

Write About It

3. Children should write their thoughts about the flag of the United States.

Support writers at various English proficiency levels.

Beginning Let children draw and label pictures of the flag. Have them write or dictate sentences about their pictures.

Intermediate Have children brainstorm lists of words that they can use when writing about the flag.

Advanced Have children write three or four sentences about their thoughts about the flag.

Extend Language When a bird flies, it moves its wings to go from one place to another. When you fly a kite, you hold it by a string and let the wind lift it.

Answers to page 265:

Possible responses: *Facts:* The flag has thirteen stripes. The flag has fifty stars. *Opinions:* The flag is beautiful. The flag is colorful.

Family Link Read aloud the Family Link activity on page 265 before sending copies of the Study Guide home with children. Later, have children share what family members said about the flag of the United States.

Name ______________________________ **The Stars and Stripes**

- **Read** *The Stars and Stripes* again.
- Fill in the chart. **Write** two facts you know and two opinions you have about the flag of the United States.

Fact: Can Be Proven
1. ______________________________
____
2. ______________________________
____

Opinion: How I Think and Feel
1. ______________________________
____
2. ______________________________
____

Family Link

Ask family members to explain what the flag of the United States means to them.

Twelve Grapes for the New Year

by Miguel Quintero

ELL Reader 2.6.3 Fiction

INTRODUCE THE BOOK

Activate Prior Knowledge/Build Background Read the title and look at the illustration on the cover. Discuss what a tradition is. Ask children if they follow any traditions to celebrate the New Year.

Preview/Use Text Features Preview the reader by talking about the illustrations together and naming the labeled items.

Preteach Vocabulary Review the tested vocabulary words that appear in this book: **collect** and **favorite**. Introduce these key words from the book: **year** (p. 1), **celebrate** (p. 2), **midnight** (p. 2), **sweet** (p. 5), and **traditions** (p. 7). Discuss these words and add them to a Word Wall.

READ THE BOOK

Choose among these options for reading to support children at all English proficiency levels.

Read Aloud Read the book aloud as children follow along. Pause to verify comprehension and to explain unfamiliar concepts.

Monitored Reading Have children read aloud a few pages at a time. Use the following questions to support comprehension:

- **Pages 2–3** What does Benito do just before midnight? (Benito puts twelve grapes in a cup for his grandfather and twelve grapes in a cup for himself.)
- **Pages 4–8** What will Benito, his grandfather, and the rest of the family do with the grapes? (They will eat twelve grapes at midnight, one grape for each month of the year.) What kind of a tradition is this? (It is a Spanish tradition.)

Reread Have children reread the book with a partner, in small groups, or independently. Have them complete the Study Guide on page 267.

RESPOND

Answers to the Reader's Inside Back Cover:

Talk About It

1. Benito's grandfather says that they eat grapes to wish that each month of the New Year will be sweet. (Main Idea and Details)

2. Possible response: I think Benito likes eating grapes at the New Year because he seems happy. I think he will eat grapes next year because it is a tradition that is important to his family. (Draw Conclusions)

Write About It

3. Ask children to think of times when their families celebrate. What traditions do their families follow during the celebrations? Support writers at various English proficiency levels.

Beginning Display a sentence frame such as: *When my family celebrates___, we always ___.* Have children dictate their ideas to complete the sentence.

Intermediate Provide the same sentence frame. Have children copy the sentence and write their own ideas to complete it.

Advanced Have children write at least three sentences about traditions that their families follow.

Extend Language Answers will vary.

Answers to page 267:

Pictures should show Benito and family members eating grapes. Sentences should explain that the family eats twelve grapes as a tradition to celebrate the coming of the New Year.

Family Link Read aloud the Family Link activity on page 267 before sending copies of the Study Guide home with children. Later, have children share what family members said about their favorite family traditions.

Name ______________________________

Twelve Grapes for the New Year

- **Read** *Twelve Grapes for the New Year* again.
- **Draw** a picture that shows what Benito and his family do in the story. **Label** the things in your picture.
- **Write** a sentence that tells what Benito is doing. **Write** a sentence that tells why he is doing it.

____

____

____

____

Family Link

Have family members describe their favorite family traditions. Ask why those traditions are their favorites.

What Does a Cowboy Do?

by Jesse Blackwell

ELL Reader 2.6.4 Nonfiction

INTRODUCE THE BOOK

Activate Prior Knowledge/Build Background Read the title, and look at the picture on the cover of the book. Ask children to name some things that a cowboy does.

Preview/Use Text Features Preview the reader by talking about the photographs together, naming the labeled items, and reading the captions.

Preteach Vocabulary Review the tested vocabulary words that appear in this book: **cattle**, **trails**, and **cowboy**. Introduce these key words from the book: **market** (p. 3), **saddle** (p. 6), and **rodeo** (p. 8). Discuss these words and add them to a Word Wall.

READ THE BOOK

Choose among these options for reading to support children at all English proficiency levels.

Read Aloud Read the book aloud as children follow along. Pause to verify comprehension and to explain unfamiliar concepts.

Monitored Reading Have children silently read a few pages at a time. Use the following questions to support comprehension:

- **Pages 2–4** What does a cowboy mostly do? (take care of the cattle)
- **Pages 5–6** Name some things that a cowboy needs. (boots, hats, chaps, bandannas, gloves, saddle, rope)
- **Pages 7–8** Is cowboy gear used only for work? (No, many kinds of people wear cowboy hats. Also, cowboys and cowgirls can wear their gear in a rodeo.)

Reread Have children reread the book with a partner, in small groups, or independently. Have them complete the Study Guide on page 269.

RESPOND

Answers to the Reader's Inside Back Cover:

Talk About It

1. Possible response: I know it is hard work because cowboys and cowgirls need lots of gear to protect them. (Cause and Effect)

2. Possible response: What do you like best about being a cowboy or cowgirl?

Write About It

3. As they describe a cowboy or cowgirl, encourage children to use what they already know as well as what they learned in the book. Support writers at various English proficiency levels.

Beginning Let children dictate their descriptions. Have them practice reading aloud and writing the recorded words.

Intermediate Have children look through the book to find words and details that they can use in their writing.

Advanced Have children help less-proficient speakers to complete their descriptions.

Extend Language A cowboy can ride his horse. Invite children to give other examples of words that sometimes tell actions and sometimes name things.

Answers to page 269:

Possible labels: chaps, jeans, bandanna, horse, hat, boots, spurs, rope, cattle, saddle

Family Link Read aloud the Family Link activity on page 269 before sending copies of the Study Guide home with children. Later, have children share what family members said about being a cowboy or cowgirl.

Name ______________________________

- **Read** *What Does a Cowboy Do?* again.
- **Label** everything that the cowgirl is wearing and everything that is around her.

Family Link

Ask family members to tell what they think it would be like to be a cowboy or cowgirl.

A Wild Onion Dinner

by Celeste Keys

ELL Reader 2.6.5 Fiction

INTRODUCE THE BOOK

Activate Prior Knowledge/Build Background Read the title and look at the illustration on the cover. Ask children what they think a Wild Onion Dinner might be.

Preview/Use Text Features Preview the reader by talking about the illustrations together and naming the labeled items. Point out the *Did You Know?* box on page 5.

Preteach Vocabulary Review the tested vocabulary words that appear in this book: **borrow** and **voice**. Introduce these key words from the book: **dinner** (p. 1), **dig** (p. 2), **bank** (p. 3), and **ready** (p. 5). Discuss these words and add them to a Word Wall.

READ THE BOOK

Choose among these options for reading to support children at all English proficiency levels.

Read Aloud Read the book aloud as children follow along. Pause to verify comprehension and to explain unfamiliar concepts.

Monitored Reading Have children read aloud a few pages at a time. Use the following questions to support comprehension:

- **Pages 2–3** What do David, Marco, and their mothers do after school? (They look for wild onions.)
- **Pages 4–5** Why do David and his mother need to collect wild onions? (They need to collect onions for their Wild Onion Dinner.)
- **Pages 6–8** Why does Marco want to go to the Wild Onion Dinner? (He wants to go because he has never been to one. Also, he wants to get ready for the summer.)

Reread Have children reread the book with a partner, in small groups, or independently. Have them complete the Study Guide on page 271.

RESPOND

Answers to the Reader's Inside Back Cover:

Talk About It

1. The story happens before summer. The Muscogee people have a Wild Onion Dinner in the spring so they will be ready for the summer. (Character, Setting, Plot)

2. Possible response: I think that David has been to a Wild Onion Dinner before. It is a tradition for his people and he knows all about it. (Draw Conclusions)

Write About It

3. Help children think of foods that are special to their families. Ask children to explain when they usually eat those foods.

Support writers at various English proficiency levels.

Beginning Allow children to talk about their special foods in English or to write about them in the home language.

Intermediate Have children brainstorm lists of words that they can use when writing about their special foods.

Advanced Invite children to write about their special foods in both English and their home language.

Extend Language The meaning of the word *bank* in the story is *the land at the side of a river or creek*. Invite children to give other examples of words with multiple meanings.

Answers to page 271:

1. David and Marco and their mothers dig wild onions.

2. The Muscogee are a group of Native Americans.

3. They celebrate the coming of summer with a Wild Onion Dinner.

4. Marco and his mother go to the dinner.

5. Marco thinks the food at the dinner must be good because there are so many people there.

Family Link Read aloud the Family Link activity on page 271 before sending copies of the Study Guide home with children. Later, have children share what family members said about their favorite holiday foods.

Name ______________________________ **A Wild Onion Dinner**

- **Read** *A Wild Onion Dinner* again.
- Use the information in the book to **answer** the questions.

Pages	Question	Answer
2–3	**1.** What happens at the beginning of the story?	
4–5	**2.** Who are the Muscogee?	
4–5	**3.** What is the Muscogee tradition in the story?	
6–7	**4.** Who goes to the dinner with David and his mom?	
8	**5.** Why does Marco think that the food at the dinner must be especially good?	

Family Link

Have family members describe their favorite holiday foods. Ask them to explain on which holiday they eat those foods.

Multilingual Lesson Vocabulary Unit 1

English	Spanish	Chinese	Vietnamese	Korean	Hmong
Week 1: Iris and Walter					
amazing	increíble	驚人	kinh ngạc	놀라운	ua rau yus ceeb
roller-skate	patinar	滑溜冰鞋	giày trượt	롤러 스케이트	khau muaj log
ladder	escalera	梯子	thang	사다리	ntaiv
meadow	prado	草地	đồng cỏ	초원	tiaj nyom
Week 2: Exploring Space with an Astronaut					
astronaut	astronauta	太空人	phi hành gia	우주비행사	tus neeg tsam dav hlau mus saum qaum ntuj
shuttle	transbordador	太空梭	phi thuyền con thoi	왕복선	dav hlau mus saum qaum ntuj
telescope	telescopio	望遠鏡	kính viễn vọng	망원경	koob xoom
gravity	gravedad	重力	trọng lực	중력	luj sib luag
experiment	experimento	實驗	thí nghiệm	실험	sim ua
Week 3: Henry and Mudge and the Starry Night					
shivered	tiritaba	顫抖	rùng mình	벌벌 떠는	tshee
lanterns	linternas	燈籠	lồng đèn	랜턴	teeb
snuggled	se acurrucaron	舒適地蜷伏	ôm quấn quít	다가붙다	sib puag sib qawg
drooled	babeó	流口水	chảy nước miếng	침을 흘리다	los qaub ncaug, siv qaub ncaug

English	Spanish	Chinese	Vietnamese	Korean	Hmong
Week 4: A Walk in the Desert					
cactus	cactus	仙人掌	cây xương rồng	선인장	ntoo tuaj pos nyob rau av suab puam
climate	clima	氣候	khí hậu	기후	huab cua
coyote	coyote	土狼	sói nhỏ ở sa mạc	코요테	hma
harsh	duro	惡劣	khắc nghiệt	가혹한, 모진	nyaum
desert	desierto	沙漠	sa mạc	사막	av suab puam
Week 5: The Strongest One					
narrator	narrador	敘事人	người kể chuyện	이야기하는 사람 내레이터	tus phiav zaj dab neeg
relatives	parientes	親戚	thân nhân họ hàng	친척	txheeb ze
dangerous	peligroso	危險	nguy hiểm	위험한	phom sij
gnaws	roe	咬	gặm nhấm	갉아먹다	tom, xo

Unit 2

English	Spanish	Chinese	Vietnamese	Korean	Hmong
Week 1: Tara and Tiree: Fearless Friends					
slipped	se resbalaron	滑倒	bị trượt	미끄러진	nplua
collar	collar	衣領	cổ áo	칼라,깃	tsho ntsej
brave	valiente	勇敢	can đảm	용감한	tsis ntshai
Week 2: Ronald Morgan Goes to Bat					
terrific	estupendo	妙極	tuyệt, xuất sắc	대단한	zoo heev
spirit	espíritu	精神	tinh thần	정신	ntsuj plig
clutched	agarré	抓住	nắm chặt	꽉 쥔, 꽉 잡다	tuav ruaj ruaj
Week 3: Turtle's Race with Beaver					
challenge	desafío	挑戰	thách đố	도전	sib tw
lodge	madriguera	小屋	hang để ở	오두막집	chaw so
embarrassed	avergonzado	窘迫	xấu hổ	난처한, 당황한	txaj muag
buried	enterró	埋沒	bị chôn vùi	가라앉은, 묻힌	faus
dam	presa	水壩	cái đập chắn nước	댐, 둑	paj dej tauv
halfway	a mitad de	半路	nửa đường	중도의	ib nrab kev
Week 4: The Bremen Town Musicians					
mill	molino	磨坊	cối xay	방앗간	tshuab zom txhu
excitement	emoción	興奮	sự hứng thú	흥분	zoo siab
musician	músico	音樂家	nhạc sĩ	음악가	cov neeg ntau nkauj
robbers	ladrones	強盜	tên trộm cướp	강도	tub sab
monsters	monstruos	妖怪	quái vật	괴물	pab laib

English	Spanish	Chinese	Vietnamese	Korean	Hmong
Week 5: A Turkey for Thanksgiving					
Thanksgiving	Día de Acción de Gracias	感恩節	Lễ Tạ Ơn	추수감사절	Caij noj qaib ntxhw
lumbered	caminó pesadamente	動作遲緩	bị kẹt, bề bộn	베어내다	ntoo
riverbank	orilla del río	河岸	bờ sông	강기슭	ntug dej
hooves	pezuñas	蹄	móng chân (nai, trâu, bò, ngựa, v.v)	발굽	rau taw tsiaj

Unit 3

English	Spanish	Chinese	Vietnamese	Korean	Hmong
Week 1: Pearl and Wagner: Two Good Friends					
electricity	electricidad	電力	điện	전기	hluav taws xob, faim fab
robot	robot	機械人	người máy	로봇	robot
trash	basura	垃圾	rác rưởi	쓰레기	khib nyiab
wad	bolita	一團	cuộn vải hoặc cuộn giấy để chèn	작은 뭉치	lub hau ntsaws
Week 2: Dear Juno					
persimmons	caquis	柿子	trái hồng	감	txiv qab nplaig
photograph	fotografía	照片	tấm ảnh chụp	사진	duab
envelope	sobre	信封	bao thư	봉투	hnab ntawv
smudged	emborronada	弄髒	bị bẩn, bị lem	더러워진	ua kom plooj
Week 3: Anansi Goes Fishing					
lazy	perezoso	懶惰	lười biếng	게으른	tub nkeeg
justice	justicia	正義	công lý	공정, 공평	caj ncees
weave	tejer	織	dệt	짜다, 엮다	ua ntos
delicious	delicioso	美味	ngon	맛있는	qab heev
Week 4: Rosa and Blanca					
tortillas	tortillas	未經發酵的玉米餅	bánh tráng mỏng bằng bột mì hoặc bột bắp	토티야(멕시코 지방의 빵)	ncuav pob kws
chiles	chiles	番椒	ớt	칠리	kua txob (hmoov)
luckiest	más afortunada	最幸運的	may mắn nhất	운이 좋은	muaj hmoo tshaj

English	Spanish	Chinese	Vietnamese	Korean	Hmong
Week 5: A Weed Is a Flower					
laboratory	laboratorio	實驗室	phòng thí nghiệm	연구실	chav tsev sim khoom los yog ua tshuaj
greenhouse	invernadero	溫室	nhà kính để trồng cây	온실	tsev yug paj ntoos
agriculture	agricultura	農業	nông nghiệp	농업	ua liaj ua teb
college	universidad	大學	đại học	대학	tsev kawm ntawv qib siab

Unit 4

English	Spanish	Chinese	Vietnamese	Korean	Hmong
Week 1: The Quilt Story					
blankets	mantas	假裝	chăn mền	담요	pam
pretended	imaginó	被子	đã giả vờ	인 체 하는	dag
quilt	edredón	填塞	tấm chăn bông	퀼트	pam
stuffing	relleno	樹幹	dồn bông	채우기	ntsaws
trunks	baúles	打開	rương	여행용 가방	thawv
unpacked	desempacaron	包裹	lấy đồ ra	풀어놓은	thaum khoom
wrapped	envolvió	毛毯	được gói lại	포장한	qhwv
Week 2: Life Cycle of a Pumpkin					
bumpy	desiguales	果實	dằn xốc	울퉁불퉁한	thawv thawv
fruit	fruta	收穫	trái cây	과일	txiv
harvest	cosecha	根	thu hoạch	수확	caij sau noob loos
root	raíz	平滑	gốc rễ	뿌리	cag (ntoo)
smooth	lisas	泥土	bằng phẳng, êm ái	부드러운	du du
soil	tierra	藤蔓	đất	토양	hmoov av
vine	enredadera	高低不平	dây leo	포도나무	hmab
Week 3: Frogs					
crawls	gatea	昆蟲	bò	기다	nkag
insects	insectos	池塘	côn trùng	곤충	kab thiab yoov uas muaj 6 txais tes taw
pond	estanque	強大	ao	연못	pas dej
powerful	fuertes	棚	mạnh mẽ	힘센	muaj zog heev
shed	mudado	皮膚	lột bỏ	오두막집	tsev rau khoom

English	Spanish	Chinese	Vietnamese	Korean	Hmong
skin	piel	奇妙	da	피부	tawv nqaij
wonderful	maravilloso	爬行	tuyệt vời	훌륭한	zoo nkawg nkaus li
Week 4: I Like Where I Am					
block	cuadra	巨大	dãy phố	블록	block
chuckle	echan risitas	強	cười khẽ	낄낄 웃다	luag
fair	justo	眼淚	công bằng	공평한	caj ncees
giant	enorme	麻煩	khổng lồ	거인	loj loj, nyav
strong	fuertes	塊	mạnh mẽ	강한, 힘센	muaj zog
tears	lágrimas	暗笑	những giọt nước mắt	눈물, 슬픔	kua muag
trouble	problemas	定期集市	việc rắc rối	걱정(거리), 고민	teeb meem
Week 5: Helen Keller and the Big Storm					
angry	enojada	分枝	giận dữ	화난	npau ntaws
branches	ramas	緊貼	các cành cây	나뭇가지	ceg
clung	se aferró	手指	đã bám chặt	달라붙다	tuav ruaj ruaj
fingers	dedos	野餐	các ngón tay	손가락	ntiv tes
picnic	comida campestre	按	buổi pic-nic	소풍	noj mov tom tshav puam
pressing	presionando	專門的	đè ép	누르는	thawb thawb
special	especial	發怒	đặc biệt	특별한	tseem ceeb, muaj nuj nqis

Unit 5

English	Spanish	Chinese	Vietnamese	Korean	Hmong
Week 1: Firefighter!					
building	edificio	燃燒	tòa nhà	건물	tsev
burning	ardiente	面罩	đang cháy	불타는	kub nyhiab
masks	máscaras	迅速	khẩu trang, dụng cụ che mặt	가면	daim looj ntsej muag
quickly	rápidamente	呼叫	mau lẹ	빨리	tsuag tsuag
roar	rugido	站	gầm thét	고함치다	qw nrov nrov
station	estación	緊緊	trạm	역, 정거장	tshooj
tightly	bien	建築物	một cách chặt chẽ	단단히	nruaj nruaj
Week 2: One Dark Night					
lightning	relámpago	閃電	tia sét	번개	xob
flashes	destella	閃光	rọi sáng	번쩍이는	laim
pounds	golpea	磅	đập vào	세게 치다	pounds
pours	llueve a cántaros	傾注	đổ	(비가) 내리퍼붓다	nchuav
rolling	retumbando	滾動	cuồn cuộn	구르는	dov
storm	tormenta	暴風雨	cơn bão	폭풍	los nag hlob hlob cua tshuab thuab heev
thunder	truenos	打雷	cơn sấm	천둥	xob quaj

English	Spanish	Chinese	Vietnamese	Korean	Hmong
Week 3: Bad Dog, Dodger!					
chased	persiguieron	咀嚼	rượt đuổi	뒤쫓다	caum
chewing	mordiendo	滴下	nhai	씹다, 깨물다	xo
dripping	goteando	抓取	chảy nhỏ giọt	(젖어서) 물방울이 떨어지는	(dej) los ib teem ib teem
grabbed	agarró	訓練	chộp lấy	잡다, 잡아채다	tuav
practice	entrenamiento	款待	tập dợt	연습	xyaum
treat	galleta (de perro)	搖擺	món ăn đặc biệt ưa thích	다루다	qhaub noom
wagged	meneó	追逐	vẫy đuôi	흔들다	co tw
Week 4: Horace and Morris but mostly Dolores					
adventure	aventura	爬	cuộc phiêu lưu	모험	mus loj leeb
climbed	subieron	社團小屋	đã leo	기어오르다	nce
clubhouse	casa del club	探險	nhà ở câu lạc bộ	클럽 회관	tsev koos haum
exploring	explorando	最偉大	thám hiểm	탐험하는	soj ntsuam
greatest	mejores	最真實	vĩ đại nhất	최고의	zoo tshaj
truest	más verdaderos	驚異	thật nhất	진실의	ntseeg tau
wondered	se preguntaba	冒險	tự hỏi	놀라운	xav txog
Week 5: The Signmaker's Assistant					
afternoon	tarde	下午	buổi chiều	오후	tav su
blame	culpen	責備	đổ tội	비난하다	liam
ideas	ideas	主意	ý kiến	아이디어, 생각	tsw yim
important	importante	重要	quan trọng	중요한	tseem ceeb
signmaker	rotulista	招牌師父	thợ làm bảng hiệu	간판 제작자	tu ua daim sign
townspeople	ciudadanos	市民	dân ở phố	마을 사람	neeg zos

Unit 6

English	Spanish	Chinese	Vietnamese	Korean	Hmong
Week 1: Just Like Josh Gibson					
bases	bases	方法	vị trí để bắt được quả bóng (trong bóng chày/dã cầu)	베이스	cov base
cheers	gritos de entusiasmo	歡呼	lời reo mừng cổ võ	격려하다, 응원하다	qw quas
field	campo	場地	sân	필드	teb
plate	base meta	板	vị trí đứng đánh quả bóng	홈 플레이트, 마운드	daim plate
sailed	volaban	航行	lướt	날리다	ya puag saum ntuj
threw	tiró	投擲	ném liệng	던지다	txawb
Week 2: Red, White, and Blue: The Story of the American Flag					
America	Estados Unidos	美國	Hoa Kỳ	미국	teb chaws mis kas
birthday	cumpleaños	生日	sinh nhật	생일	hnub yug
flag	bandera	國旗	lá cờ	깃발	chij
freedom	libertad	自由	tự do	자유	kev ywj pheej, kev ywj siab
nicknames	apodos	綽號	biệt danh	별명	sis npe
stars	estrellas	星星	những ngôi sao	별	hnub qub
stripes	franjas	條紋	các đường sọc	줄무늬	kab txaij
Week 3: A Birthday Basket for Tía					
aunt	tía	姑母	cô, dì	이모, 고모	ntsaum
bank	alcancía	堤	ngân hàng	은행	tsev rau nyiaj
basket	cesta	籃子	cái rổ	바구니	pob tawb
collects	recoge	收集	thu thập	수집하다	khaws cia
favorite	favorito	特別喜愛	thích nhất	좋아하는	nyiam tshaj
present	regalo	禮物	món quà	선물	khoom plig

English	Spanish	Chinese	Vietnamese	Korean	Hmong
Week 4: Cowboys					
campfire	fuego (de campamento)	營火	lửa trại	모닥불	cub ntawg
cattle	ganado	牛	trâu bò	소	ib pab nyuj
cowboy	vaquero	牛仔	người chăn bò	카우보이	neeg yug nees thiab nyuj
galloped	galoparon	疾馳	phi nước đại	질주하다, 서두르다	dhia (nees dhia ya)
herd	manada	群	đàn, bầy	무리	ib pab tsiaj
railroad	ferrocarril	鐵路	đường rầy xe lửa	철로	kev luv train
trails	sendas	足迹	đường mòn	끌고 가다	kab kev
Week 5: Jingle Dancer					
borrow	pedir prestado	借	mượn	빌리다	txais, qiv
clattering	ruidosos	喧嚷	kêu loảng xoảng	덜커덕거리다	nrov nrov
drum	tambor	鼓	trống	북	nruas
jingles	cascabeles	鈴鐺	những chiếc chuông	딸랑딸랑 소리 나다	co co
silver	plata	銀	bạc	은	nyiaj
voice	voz	聲音	giọng	목소리	lub suab